UNDERSTANDING FOREIGN POLICY DECISION MAKING

Understanding Foreign Policy Decision Making presents a decision making approach to foreign policy analysis. The benefits of such an approach are its ability to explain not only outcomes of decisions but also the processes that lead to decisions and the decision dynamics. The book includes a wealth of extended real-world case studies and examples of decisions made by leaders of the United States, Israel, New Zealand, Cuba, Iceland, United Kingdom, and others. In addition to coverage of the rational actor model of decision making, levels of analysis, and types of decisions, the book covers alternatives to the rational choice model, the marketing and framing of decisions, cognitive biases and errors, and domestic, cultural, and international influences on decision making in international affairs. If we are to understand decision making, we need to understand how information processing and various biases affect decision making. Existing textbooks do not present such an explicit approach to foreign policy decision making, American foreign policy, and comparative foreign policy.

Alex Mintz is Dean of the Lauder School of Government, Diplomacy and Strategy at IDC-Herzliya, Israel. He is editor-in-chief of the journal *Political Psychology*, former co-editor of *Foreign Policy Analysis*, and former associate editor of the *Journal of Conflict Resolution*. Mintz is the 2005 recipient of the Distinguished Scholar Award for distinguished contribution to the field from the Foreign Policy Analysis section of the International Studies Association (ISA). He has published, edited, or co-edited nine books and is the author of multiple articles in top journals, such as *American Political Science Review* and *American Journal of Political Science*.

Karl DeRouen Jr. is Professor of Political Science, Director of the International Studies Program, and a College of Arts and Science Leadership Board Faculty Fellow (2008–2011) at the University of Alabama. His work has appeared in the *Journal of Politics, International Organization, Journal of Peace Research, Journal of Conflict Resolution, British Journal of Political Science*, and a number of other journals. He is currently working on Civil War related projects funded by the Folke Bernadotte Academy of Sweden and the Marsden Fund of New Zealand (with Jacob Bercovitch and several others) and a National Science Foundation funded project on negotiated settlements (with Douglas Gibler). He is also co-authoring the textbook *Puzzles in International Relations* (with Alex Mintz and Glen Biglaiser, Cambridge University Press, forthcoming).

Understanding Foreign Policy Decision Making

Alex Mintz

IDC-Herzliya, Israel

Karl DeRouen Jr.

University of Alabama

CAMBRIDGE UNIVERSITY PRESS
Cambridge, New York, Melbourne, Madrid, Cape Town, Singapore,
São Paulo, Delhi, Dubai, Tokyo

Cambridge University Press
32 Avenue of the Americas, New York, NY 10013-2473, USA

www.cambridge.org
Information on this title: www.cambridge.org/9780521700092

First published 2010

Printed in the United States of America

A catalog record for this publication is available from the British Library.

Library of Congress Cataloging in Publication data

Mintz, Alex, 1953–
Understanding foreign policy decision making / Alex Mintz, Karl DeRouen.
    p.   cm.
Includes bibliographical references and index.
ISBN 978-0-521-87645-2 (hardback) – ISBN 978-0-521-70009-2 (pbk.)
1. International relations – Decision making.   2. International relations – Psychological
aspects.   I. DeRouen, Karl R., 1962–   II. Title.
JZ1253.M56   2009
327.101'9 – dc22   2009014315

ISBN 978-0-521-87645-2 Hardback
ISBN 978-0-521-70009-2 Paperback

Dedicated to Yael and Haidee

Contents

Acknowledgments

We are grateful to the Yaakov Agam Chair in Public Diplomacy at the IDC-Herzliya, Israel and the College of Arts and Sciences Leadership Board Faculty Fellowship at the University of Alabama. We would also like to thank Alex Fiedler and Jenna Lea for research assistance. Ed Parsons, Acquisitions Editor at Cambridge University Press, was wonderful to work with, and we appreciated his professionalism and encouragement.

PART ONE

INTRODUCTION

1

Why Study Foreign Policy from a Decision-Making Perspective?

Foreign policy choices range from the dramatic to the mundane. Leaders make decisions to go to war, make peace, form an alliance, establish diplomatic relations, implement a position on nuclear nonproliferation, impose economic sanctions, or ratify global environmental agreements. The focus of this book is this broad range of decisions.

We approach this topic from a number of directions. We consider, among others, the type of the decision (one-shot, sequential, interactive, group), the level of analysis in foreign policy decision making (the individual, group, coalition), the processes and dynamics that lead to the decision, biases and errors, and, of course, models of decision making (rational actor, cybernetic, bureaucratic politics, organizational politics, poliheuristic theory, and prospect theory). We examine the determinants of foreign policy decisions (the decision environment, psychological factors, international factors, and domestic influences). We look at a host of psychological factors that shape decisions, such as images and belief systems, emotions, analogies, the personality of leaders, leadership style, miscalculations and misperceptions, and environmental factors such as time constraints, ambiguity, stress, and risk. We then look at the effect of international and domestic factors such as deterrence, the arms race, the regime type of the adversary, strategic surprise, economic conditions, public opinion, and electoral cycles on foreign policy decision making. We conclude with a case study of the U.S. decision to invade Iraq in 2003, analyzed through five decision models.

FOREIGN POLICY DECISION MAKING

Foreign policy decision making (FPDM) refers to the choices individuals, groups, and coalitions make that affect a nation's actions on the international stage. Foreign policy decisions are typically characterized by high stakes, enormous uncertainty, and substantial risk (Renshon and Renshon 2008, 509). Most of what we read about international affairs concerns only the actions of

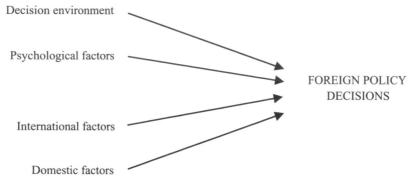

Figure 1.1. Determinants of Foreign Policy Decisions.

states and their leaders. It can be illuminating to understand what goes into the decisions that presage the actions and events. FPDM is an important avenue of research because the way decisions are made can shape the eventual choice. That is, an actor could arrive at different *outcomes* depending on the decision *process*. Moreover, significant cognitive limitations often distort information processing. Some decisions are calculated carefully, whereas others are more intuitive.

The course of world politics is shaped by leaders' decisions. The uncertainty involved in foreign policy making can pertain, for example, to an opponent's motives, beliefs, intentions, or calculations (ibid., 514). If we can understand how decisions are made, we can better understand and, perhaps more important, predict outcomes in the international arena. Figure 1.1 displays key determinants of foreign policy decisions.

Many foreign policy decisions resemble a chess game. Consider, for example, the moves and countermoves, and subsequent moves and countermoves in reaction to prior moves and decisions of Saddam Hussein and George H. W. Bush before the First Gulf War; the interactive sequence of decisions of U.S. and European powers vis-à-vis Iran on its nuclear program; or the discussions and negotiations between Israel and Syria and Israel and the Palestinian Authority. The essence of many foreign policy decisions is a decision process taken in an interactive setting and consisting of a sequence of decisions. As in chess, players learn from prior moves. When playing with the same opponent for many years, they also learn from game to game. This can also result in bluffing behavior and attempts to mask signals. Just like in professional chess, many foreign policy decisions are taken under stress of time. FPDM consists of four components:

1. identifying the decision problem,
2. searching for alternatives,
3. choosing an alternative, and
4. executing the alternative. (Robinson and Snyder 1965, 437)

We make decisions every day. Some of these decisions require little thought. For example, if one is required to wear a uniform to work, one spends little time deciding what to wear. Some decisions must be made quickly. For example, if the traffic reporter on the radio says there is an accident just a mile ahead on the road on which you are driving, you would need to think of a course of action quickly. However, this decision can become clouded by uncertainty if taking a detour around the accident places you on roads you do not know. The situation becomes even worse if the street signs on your detour are missing or if pranksters have turned them around. In contrast, on your normal route to work, there is little time spent deciding on which route to take. Decisions are more or less automatic and made in an environment of certainty. In the event of an accident, you could be faced with time constraints, uncertainty, and incomplete information. These are two very different decision environments.

Although the stakes are much higher, these everyday decision dynamics also occur at the foreign policy level. In our driving analogy, the actor could try to compare the costs and benefits of several alternatives. The options could include waiting until the accident clears or taking the first possible exit in hopes of saving time. In the face of uncertainty, comparing costs and benefits may be more difficult. The actor might, however, think back to some previous experience that approximates the current situation. The use of analogies might provide a mental shortcut that can save time and effort. Perhaps in a similar past experience, the driver detoured and was easily able to navigate back to the main road. As we will show using historical and contemporary examples, analogies can also work in foreign policy but are sometimes misleading and can lead to suboptimal outcomes.

WHY STUDY FOREIGN POLICY DECISION MAKING?

As one recent article (Renshon and Renshon 2008, 511) pointed out, no crisis or war can be understood "without direct reference to the decision making of individual leaders." Scholarly attention to FPDM generally dates back to the 1954 publication of *Decision-Making as an Approach to the Study of International Politics* by Richard C. Snyder, Henry W. Bruck, and Burtin Sapin – the first systematic look at the determinants of government FPDM. This seminal work focused on the decision process itself by merging aspects of organizational behavior, communication, and motivation (Hudson 2005, 6). The book introduced an ambitious framework for the study of decision making, but it did not create enough momentum to carry the discipline into mainstream international relations.

An analysis of foreign policy decisions can uncover the cognitive processes that lead to foreign policy making and "get into the minds" of leaders who make the decisions. It can also help identify unique and general patterns of decisions and generate insights about leadership styles and personalities that cannot be revealed through a systemic approach to foreign policy analysis.

Such an approach to foreign policy analysis has the potential to make a broad and important contribution to the study of international relations. FPDM can provide deeper understandings of biases, motivations, and perceptions. Moreover, the growth and development of theories of cognitive psychology and decision theory directly spurred advances in FPDM (Voss and Dorsey 1992, 5–6). These advances comprise the basis of this book.

Other factors also make FPDM an inviting approach. For example, many international relations theories apply specifically to great powers. An FPDM approach, in contrast, can speak to issues that affect all nations (M. Hermann 2001). Nations have security considerations, trade disputes, and myriad other agenda items – environmental, political – that require decisions. Joe Hagan has outlined several other compelling reasons for the study of foreign policy from a decision-making perspective (Hagan 2001). First, FPDM can add to grand systemic theories of war by helping us to understand how uncertainties shape decision makers' responses to systemic and military capacity ratios. Hagan tells us uncertainties, value trade-offs, and dispersion of authority are important influences on FPDM. Security decisions, for example, involve a great deal of uncertainty because policies are often sorted out in debate between moderates and hard-liners, as is the case, for example, within the current Iranian leadership. Decision-making theories can help us to understand this debate and the decisions that are made to implement the position of the winning side.

Traditional models of foreign policy decision making assume that security matters are paramount. However, many note that domestic issues can shape foreign policy. Value trade-offs refer to how domestic values such as the desire of leaders to stay in power can drive foreign policy. Domestic politics can shape foreign actions. Decision-making models can help us understand why this happens. As we show, the rational actor model, cybernetic theory, prospect theory, poliheuristic theory, and other decision models shed light on the subject of domestic politics influencing foreign behavior. For example, according to the poliheuristic theory of decision, domestic politics is "the essence of decision."

Finally, we come to the unitary actor assumption. The decision-making approach to foreign policy analysis often has been overshadowed by the unitary, rational actor assumption commonly used in international relations. Nevertheless, a slow but compelling body of literature in FPDM has emerged over the decades highlighting the *psychology* of foreign policy decision making of groups, coalitions, and, of course, leaders. It is standard for pundits, politicians, and scholars alike to speak in terms of "Canada doing" this or "Australia doing" that. However, such language obscures what really goes on behind the scenes. Most foreign policies emanate from diffuse sources of power. There are coalition governments in which competing parties debate over policy. There are also legislative, mass public, special interest group, and judicial constraints on executive power. Bureaucracy also can be an important source of power.

For example, the United States Department of Defense, Central Intelligence Agency, National Security Agency, and other security agencies can be expected to express a strong voice in national security decisions, whereas the Office of Management and Budget will have greater influence in budgetary decisions. As we show in the next chapter, the size and composition of the decision unit have important implications for decision making. These implications are easily ignored if we only consider systemic unitary actor assumptions.

Given the complexities involved in foreign policy making, it becomes clear that an approach to foreign policy analysis focusing on decision making is vital to a comprehensive understanding of foreign policy behavior, our world, and the specific policies of nations. FPDM is equipped with theories and models that help us understand how biases and errors, uncertainty, domestic politics, and various decision units can shape decisions. In this sense it takes us into the nuts and bolts of international relations. FPDM is a "peek under the hood" at what underlies international affairs.

THE RATIONAL AND COGNITIVE SCHOOLS

Many scholarly analyses of FPDM proceed from the **rational actor** assumption. The realist paradigm, in particular, assumes that states, as unitary actors, act to maximize gains and minimize losses while navigating an anarchic international system (Waltz 1979; Mearsheimer 1995). This perspective is often referred to as the ideal type – many consider it the most desirable form of decision making. The rational actor assumption is a hallmark of microeconomics. Individual economic decision makers want to buy low, sell high, and maximize wealth. Stated more formally, the rational decision maker chooses from among a set of alternatives, the alternative that maximizes utility. Buying a new car is a frequently used example. There are several important dimensions (criteria) in the decision: price, safety, fuel efficiency, warranty, and so on. The alternatives could include a fuel-efficient import, an expensive sports car, and a gas-guzzling SUV. Information about the cars is typically readily available and fuel efficiency and warranty guidelines are clearly stated on the window tag. Price may or may not be clearly stated on the window tag. Buyers determine their objectives beforehand and then compare the payoffs of each of the alternatives. As we will describe, the means of searching the information (for example, by type of car vs. by key decision criteria) has implications for the decision.

The rational model has much to recommend it. It is open to new information and casts a wide net in search of information. Decisions can be made by a person or small group searching for the optimal outcome. The executive relies on bureaucrats to provide information for the decision process, and after the decision is made the bureaucracy implements the decision (Rosati 1993, 268). Indeed, there are historical cases of bureaucratic reorganization with an eye toward optimizing the process. After World War II, the National Security

Act merged the departments of War and Navy into the Defense Department under one secretary. Similarly, the act created a new Executive Branch entity, the National Security Council, headed by the National Security Advisor. The object of these endeavors was to centralize the security realm as the United States redefined its international role.

Centralization has its critics. After 9/11, the Department of Homeland Security was created. This enlarged bureaucracy subsumed, among other entities, the Federal Emergency Management Agency (FEMA) – the agency in charge of disaster response. In the wake of Hurricane Katrina in August 2005, FEMA was widely criticized for its inability to manage the disaster response. In hearings that followed, the former head of FEMA, Michael Brown, complained that the agency had been hamstrung by its new position as part of the new Department of Homeland Security. FEMA now had to go through too many bureaucratic layers.

The rational model is useful in situations such as the strategic analysis of deterrence and nuclear weapons. It has been applied in game theory settings to show how certain decisions have been made. For example, the rational actor assumption employed in the Prisoner's Dilemma game demonstrates why actors who cannot or do not communicate make suboptimal decisions in a one-shot interactive game.

Psychological theories help us understand *how* leaders make foreign policy decisions. The core focus of cognitive psychology is on "how people acquire, process, and store information," which has direct relevance to decision making (Van Wagner 2008). Personality theories help us understand the effects of personality traits and personality profiles on FPDM, whereas affective theories are relevant to the study of the role of emotions in foreign policy decision making.

Cognitive models generally posit that the rational actor assumption is not realized in practice. Robert Jervis influential book *Perception and Misperception in International Politics* (1976) is perhaps the most important work in this area. Various dynamics are indicative of cognitive approaches. These dynamics feature mental shortcuts and other processes indicative of the mind's inability to carry out the complicated calculus of the rational model. Many of these processes are indicative of bias and error. Cognitive processes are not to be understood as "irrational" but rather as more realistic interpretations of how the human mind really works. Cognitive models also take into account the high costs of information gathering, time pressure, ambiguity, memory problems, misperceptions, organizational structure, and other factors that enter into most decisions (Mandel 1986, 252). We look in further detail at the cognitive-rational debate in Chapters 4 and 5 when we discuss the rational actor model and alternatives (bounded rationality, prospect theory, and poliheuristic theory).

Political psychologist Rose McDermott (2004b, 691) has observed that "recent advances in neurosciences offer a wealth of new information about how the brain works and how the body and mind interact." According to

McDermott (p. 692), **cognitive neuroscience** can help answer one of the critical questions in political science and international relations: "under what conditions do emotions help explain decision making?" The tools of cognitive neuroscience have been applied only recently to understanding foreign policy decision making. The work has largely focused on the effect of emotions on decision making, judgment, and learning as well as on how domestic and international events provide feedback, which in turn can influence leaders' decisions.

This book builds upon these studies and presents a **psychological** approach to decision making. The benefits of such an approach are its ability to explain not only outcomes of decisions but also the processes and distortions that lead to decisions and the decision dynamics. In contrast to other approaches such as rational choice, a psychological approach to decision making focuses on process validity as well as outcome validity. Furthermore, the psychological approach deals with information search and processing as well as with biases and errors in decision making. The rational choice approach does not fully describe how decision making is affected by cognitive biases. However, if we are to understand decision making, we need to understand how information processing is limited and how various biases, search patterns, and decision rules affect decision making. Existing textbooks do not present such an explicit approach to foreign policy decision making, American foreign policy, and comparative foreign policy.

COMPARATIVE FOREIGN POLICY

Foreign policy decisions often are studied by focusing on a single country (e.g., a decision on the use of force by a U.S. president) or by conducting research across nations (e.g., comparing environmental decisions by leaders of the United States, United Kingdom, Germany, France, and Italy) or across time (e.g., comparing decisions of U.S. presidents in the first and second Iraq wars). The unit of analysis in such comparative studies is the event – "who does what to whom, how" in international affairs (Hudson 2005, 9). Events are compared along behavioral dimensions and other influences on foreign policy, such as the regime type of the adversary, domestic conditions, the arms race, whether it was a strategic surprise, a threat, and so on (ibid.).

For example, we can examine how leaders of different countries make foreign economic decisions on trade, aid, and arms transfers or on global environmental challenges such as pollution controls. The advantage of the comparative foreign policy approach is that it allows the student of foreign policy analysis not just to examine one case, but to compare similarities and differences across multiple cases using a comparative case-study approach. Thus, from a methodological point of view, the comparative foreign policy approach can enhance the validity of a single case study.

Limitations of the Decision-Making Approach

The importance of decision making to foreign policy can hardly be over-stated. However, the decision-making approach to foreign policy analysis is not without limitations. Decisions are critical in foreign policy making, but understanding decisions does not provide a complete analysis. International, domestic, cultural, and social changes affect foreign policy in both the short and the long run. Systemic factors and unique state-level factors affect decisions. In this book we discuss the effects of key international, domestic, and cultural factors on foreign policy decision making as well.

PLAN OF THE BOOK

This book attempts to explain how and why foreign policy decisions are made. It considers key psychological, environmental, international, and domestic factors that shape foreign policy decision making. The goal for us as observers of foreign policy is to be able to understand how and why decisions are made. We accomplish these tasks by describing the theories, models, and concepts of FPDM while illustrating them through examples and case studies.

We intersperse many brief examples of decision principles, concepts, and theories throughout the book. In addition, we offer several longer case studies that provide greater detail on decision-making processes and dynamics. These cases come from a wide variety of polities, societies, and cultures: the United States, Cuba, New Zealand, Iraq, Israel, the Palestinian Authority, Argentina, the United Kingdom, Iceland, and other countries. The longer cases are U.S.-Cuban relations (1954–1967), the Israeli-Palestinian negotiations at Camp David in 2000, New Zealand's decision to stop allowing nuclear visits and thus end its defense alliance with the United States, the Falkland Islands War between England and Argentina, and the U.S. decisions not to invade Iraq in 1991 and to invade Iraq in 2003.

This introductory chapter has provided a broad outline of FPDM. We have explained our approach, the rationale for studying foreign policy from a decision-making perspective, and introduced a few basic concepts that are needed before we proceed. We discuss theories and models and provide relevant examples throughout the remainder of the book.

Chapter 2 covers types of decisions, the levels of analysis in foreign policy decision making, and key characteristics of the decision environment, such as time constraints, information problems, uncertainty, ambiguity, risk, accountability, dynamic versus static settings, and other conditions that are generally beyond the influence of the decision unit. We also cover information search patterns and decision rules.

In Chapter 3, we show how a series of cognitive biases affects decision making in foreign policy. We introduce the "wishful thinking" bias, the "shooting from the hip" bias, the "preference over preference" bias, the "poliheuristic bias," and other biases and errors in decision making. The chapter also discusses the effects on decision making of group dynamics known as groupthink and polythink, as well as the group polarization effect.

In Chapter 4, we introduce the rational actor model of FPDM. We look at the expected utility model of war and cover some game-theoretic models such as the Prisoner's Dilemma, the Chicken Game, and the Tit-for-Tat strategy.

In Chapter 5, we introduce alternative models to the rational actor model. We summarize the main concepts and models such as cybernetic theory, bureaucratic politics, organizational politics, prospect theory, and the poliheuristic theory of decision. These models provide competing explanations of the decision process. We apply these models to a case study of the decision *not* to invade Iraq in 1991. The chapter covers the mechanics of how choices are made from among a set of alternatives using different decision models. We also introduce Applied Decision Analysis, a procedure that aims to uncover leaders' decision patterns. The chapter refers the reader to the Appendix, which includes creative exercises that can be used to understand FPDM from various perspectives.

Chapter 6 focuses on psychological factors shaping foreign policy decisions. Decisions are influenced by emotions, images, beliefs and belief systems, cognitive consistency, the use of historical analogies, and the personality of leaders and leadership style.

Chapter 7 considers domestic and international determinants of foreign policy decisions. Topics here include deterrence, arms races, alliances, regime type of the adversary, strategic surprise, economic conditions, public opinion, and electoral cycles. This chapter also looks at decisions about the use of nonmilitary tools of foreign policy such as economic aid, trade, mediation, and negotiation.

In Chapter 8, we cover the framing and marketing of decisions. This takes in elements of politics, as decision units move to "market and sell" their decisions to the public. We also look at media effects on foreign policy decision making.

Chapter 9 concludes the book with a summary and overview. It also provides a case study of the U.S. decision to invade Iraq in 2003. The Appendix contains a decision-making exercise that can be used in the classroom or as a research tool for scholars. Such policy scenarios can be used to simulate decision-making processes.

PART TWO

THE DECISION ENVIRONMENT

2

Types of Decisions and Levels of Analysis in Foreign Policy Decision Making

TYPES OF DECISIONS

One can speak of a variety of decision types. Some decisions are simple and, once made, can be forgotten. Other decisions must be revisited every so often and might be dependent on what a rival does in response. Some decisions are small but are part of a series of related decisions. This section introduces a number of important concepts related to decision type. These decision types are listed in Table 2.1 below.[1]

One-shot or **single decisions** are rare in international affairs because most decisions are part of a sequence of decisions and/or decisions that are made interactively with other actors. However, scholars of foreign policy decision making (FPDM) often focus on the analysis of a single decision, such as the U.S. government's decision not to invade Iraq in 1991 or its decision to invade Iraq in 2003. As another example, the U.S. decision not to provide militarily aid to the French at Dien Bien Phu in 1954 was a one-shot decision. Although perhaps not a perfect example, the U.S. decision not to ratify the Kyoto Protocol might be considered another example of a one-shot foreign policy decision.

Strategic, interactive decisions are those involving at least two players who make decisions that affect and are affected by the other player's decisions. For example, Yasser Arafat, while president of the Palestinian National Authority, had to decide whether to accept, counter, or reject the offer made to him by Israeli prime minister Ehud Barak at Camp David in 2000. The classic Prisoner's Dilemma provides a prime example of a one-shot **interactive decision**. In this scenario, two suspects are arrested on suspicion of carrying out a serious crime. The suspects are interrogated separately. They each have one choice over time. They can accept a plea bargain deal offered by the police. This deal would mean testifying against the other suspect. Or they can refuse the deal and stay loyal to their partner.

---

[1] Any model of decision making needs to explain each of these decision types. The models are introduced in Chapters 4 and 5.

Table 2.1. *Types of decisions*

One-shot (single) decisions
Interactive decisions
Sequential decisions
Sequential-interactive decisions
Group decisions

Assuming a single decision to explain foreign policy acts may be unrealistic. For this reason, some scholars turn to **sequential decision making**. Sequential decisions involve a series of interrelated decisions, such as whether to attack Iraq; occupy Iraq; increase or decrease troop levels; whether to withdraw or to stay; and, finally, when the operation should end.

Foreign policy making consists of many decisions that involve a **sequence of interactive decisions**. For example, the arms race (e.g., between the United States and the Soviet Union, or NATO and the Warsaw Treaty Organization (WTO) during the Cold War, or Israel and its Arab neighbors, or India and Pakistan, or North and South Korea) is a sequential and interactive process of decisions by at least two countries responding to each other's decisions on armament or disarmament. Chess is a game of strategic and sequential interaction as one player's move affects the other player's as well as her own subsequent moves.

Foreign policy decisions are influenced by group dynamics (Maoz 1990a, 1990b). The Cuban Missile Crisis is a prime example. Groups can be ad hoc combinations of individuals, bureaucratic agencies, or coalitions. **Group decision making** can be complicated because group members may have different agendas, interests, and preferences for ordering structures and policy options. Thus, group processes often involve bargaining among group members. There is substantial difference between individual and group decision-making dynamics. Examples of group decisions include decisions of presidential advisory groups, UN Security Council members, or the U.S. National Security Council.

Decisions can also be conceptualized as "impulse-driven (emotional) actions, ends-means (instrumental) actions, or interaction-oriented (strategic) actions" (Walker and Schafer forthcoming, 4). As for foreign policy and political decision making, there are two types of decisions: impulse-driven (the psychological approach) and ends-means (the rational choice approach). Both consider strategic interaction.

Unilateral, Negotiated, Structured, and Unstructured Decisions

Sometimes, decisions are **unilateral**, such as Libyan leader Muammar Qaddafi's decision to abandon Libya's nuclear program in 2003 or New Zealand's 1985 decision to prohibit visits to its ports by ships carrying nuclear cargo.

Negotiated decisions result from interaction between at least two players, and sometimes more, such as the decision by North Korea, after intensive multilateral talks and negotiations, to offer to abandon its nuclear program in exchange for massive aid.

There are structured, semistructured and unstructured decisions. **Structured decisions** are repetitive, routine decisions, involving relatively high certainty, and a definitive procedure. **Semistructured decisions** involve more risk and are unstructured in one or more of the factors. **Unstructured decisions** involve complexity and have no ready or routine solution. Structural features such as goals and choices can be poorly specified or missing, putting the decision maker in a somewhat uncertain situation.[2]

Herbert Simon (1960) pointed out that the decision making process consists of the following stages:

1. intelligence (collect information and identify problem),
2. design (identify alternatives, and select criteria),
3. choice (use criteria to evaluate alternatives and make a decision), and
4. implementation (put decision into effect and allocate resources).

Holistic, Heuristic and Wholistic Decisions

Decisions can be made based on holistic, heuristic, or wholistic search (Sage 1990, 239–242). Holistic search involves a thorough examination of all the alternatives, dimensions, and implications of the decision. Heuristic decisions are made while employing cognitive shortcuts. Wholistic decisions are made while disregarding the components of the decision. Such decisions are intuitive, involving standard operating procedures (SOPs) and/or the use of analogies (ibid.). Heuristic and wholistic searches are more process oriented than holistic searches (ibid.).

For example, in making interest rates decisions, the U.S. Federal Reserve typically evaluates alternatives in a comprehensive manner based on multiple decision criteria in a holistic fashion. The 1961 U.S. decision to invade the Bay of Pigs is an example of a nonholistic process because implications for each alternative were not carefully assessed (Neustadt and May 1986). Some decisions regarding the 2003 Iraq War relied on historical analogies – wholistic search – stemming from the 1991 Gulf War. Many budgetary decisions, such as changes in defense spending, also follow SOPs, such as incremental increase in spending or "fair share" allocation of resources.

Trade-offs in Decision Making

Leaders often face difficult dilemmas in making foreign policy because numerous foreign policy decisions involve trade-offs between competing alternatives.

---

[2] See http://dssresources.com/glossary/177.php.

Table 2.2. *Levels of analysis in foreign
policy decision making*

Individual
Group
Coalition

Source: M. Hermann (2001).

For example, given the repeated threats Iranian president Mahmoud Ahmadi-nejad has made against Israel, including the direct threat that Iran will wipe Israel from the map, Israeli leaders are confronted with a dilemma of whether to use force to halt (or at least slow down) the Iranian nuclear program. Given a fixed amount of resources, policy makers have also to decide whether to allocate more resources to "guns" (defense spending) or "butter" (welfare programs) with all the attended ramifications.

Trade-offs can also appear among dimensions (criteria) of a decision – for example, trade-offs between economic and electoral consequences of an alternative course of foreign policy or between security and human rights concerns. Trade-offs affect information processing and choice.

THE LEVEL OF ANALYSIS IN FOREIGN POLICY DECISION MAKING

One can examine foreign policy decisions from three main levels: the individual, the group, and the coalition[3] (see Table 2.2). Decision processes and actual choices are shaped by who makes the decision – the **decision unit**. Both the size and composition of the decision unit directly influence foreign policy decision making. The decision-making process taken by a single person is not expected to follow the same dynamics as a group decision or a coalition decision. If there are several groups involved, the process will be different from the other processes. In this section, we discuss how the decision unit shapes foreign policy decision making.

Individual-Level Decisions

The premise of the decision-making approach to foreign policy and international relations "assumes that leaders matter in the explanation of foreign policy decisions by acting on their definitions of the situation in the domain of world politics" (Walker and Schafer, forthcoming, 2). The decisions of individuals aggregate into the behavior of groups, coalitions, and states. Individual-level

[3] The levels of analysis in FPDM are somewhat different from those in international relations, a discipline in which scholars typically talk about the individual, the state, and the system as the main units of analysis. In FPDM the units specifically refer to entities making decisions (leaders, groups, coalitions).

decisions are more likely when leaders have an inordinate amount of power within a state. Powerful leaders typically do not need to seek consensus. Examples here include Mao Tse-tung of China, Fidel Castro of Cuba, Joseph Stalin of the USSR, Napoleon of France, Kim Jong-il of North Korea, and Saddam Hussein of Iraq. Institutional constraints are not a major factor for these decision makers.

Individuals are critically important during times of crisis. Political psychologist Margaret Hermann (2001) notes that crises, high-level diplomacy, and leader interest increase the probability of individual-level decision making. For example, decisions to go to war or participate in international summits are often associated with decision making by a dominant individual (M. Hermann 2001). Studies of individual decision making focus on psychological factors such as the personality of the decision maker, operational codes, learning, evoked set, cognitive consistency, and misperception (Cashman 1993). On 9/11, then-mayor of New York City Rudolph Giuliani made critical decisions seemingly on the spur of the moment. In the following chapters, we carefully explore the dynamics of decisions made by individual leaders.

Group-level Decisions

Here, numerous foreign policy decisions are made by groups, not by all-powerful individuals (Maoz 1990a). Such concepts as groupthink, polythink, group polarization, and advisory group influence show the importance of small-group dynamics in foreign policy decision making. They also demonstrate the potential biases and errors that group decision making can lead to. There are a variety of group-level decisions. There are the prototypical groups such as President Kennedy's Executive Committee (EXCOM), which dealt with the Cuban Missile Crisis. This is an example of how a group can deal with an ad hoc problem. Other examples of groups, such as the Soviet Politburo and the American Joint Chiefs of Staff, contend with ongoing policy debates and operational issues (M. Hermann 2001). The group comprises members whose allegiance is primarily directed within the group, and the respective actors do not have to consult others outside the group (ibid.). The decision reached by this unit is a group decision that emerges after debate. The group might reach a conclusion on the basis of concurrence (groupthink), unanimity, or plurality (C. Hermann et al. 2001). Unlike the individual-level model, certain group dynamics can influence the decision process. For example, members strive to avoid the conflict that often occurs in groups and work toward concurrence (ibid.). The groupthink dynamic identified by Irving Janis (1982) is a classic example of how group dynamics can affect decisions.

Decision making within agencies or presidential cabinets can also be considered group decisions in a bureaucratic politics decision setting. Long, drawn-out policies that deal with international terror, AIDS in Africa, or global warming usually involve bureaucratic agencies (Mingst 2002). Decisions made here involve a fair amount of political power struggle and debate between agencies and influential bureaucrats. Actors recognize that political conflict and differences of opinion, even differences of philosophy, are inevitable (M. Hermann 2001). To take an example from a domestic issue, the federally funded program designed to combat coastal erosion in Louisiana is managed by a task force of several state and federal agencies. The process involves a great deal of political infighting, compromise, and political give and take as the various agencies act on their interests, agendas, and preferences. Agency representatives are typically loyal to their agency first and foremost, and this can sometimes present a challenge to executives.

Coalition Decision Making

Coalition decision making represents a third type of decision unit. Individual units within a coalition cannot make decisions on their own, thus there is some level of bargaining and leverage between relatively independent actors. No single actor in the unit can make the decision unilaterally. Here, the first level of allegiance is directed outside the group toward the party or constituency of the coalition members. In the context of international politics, this means no one actor can decide state policy (M. Hermann 2001). For example, the government of Israel relies on coalitional decision making. The members of coalition cabinets owe their immediate allegiance to their parties and constituencies. Decisions here might reflect coalition dynamics such as majority rule and minimum-winning coalitions. Another example of this type of decision making, this one in a nondemocratic society, occurred during the Iranian hostage crisis of 1979–1981. No one actor (that is, the students, the government, or the Ayatollah) could alone decide the fate of the crisis (ibid.).

The coalition decision unit is also quite common. Coalition dynamics are shaped by size factors. Minimum-winning coalition refers to the minimum number of parties needed to keep the coalition in power. The coalition is generally not interested in including more parties than necessary because credit and resources would then have to be shared, and there would be more groups to please when making any decision (Hagan et al. 2001). A surplus coalition, in contrast, can lose a party and still remain in power.

Michael Ireland and Scott Gartner (2001, 562) observe that cabinet coalition structure is a strong indicator of the likelihood of conflict initiation. In other words, are surplus parties (those that can withstand the loss of at least one party) more or less likely to initiate force than minimum-winning coalitions (those that cannot survive the loss of any party)? The role of veto players is an important variable in cabinet structures; in this context, a veto player is a party "whose agreement is necessary for a change in the status quo" (Tsebelis 1999, 593). Significant policy change is harder with more veto players.

Coalition governments are more likely to reciprocate force with force because with so many parties involved, the blame is shared if things go wrong (Prins and Sprecher 1999). If the policy is a success, all can claim credit. However, as the number of veto players within the coalition increases, initiation is less likely (Ireland and Gartner 2001, 551). Veto players (parties that can stop an action by threatening to leave the government) are less important in a surplus setting (Tsebelis 1999; Ireland and Gartner 2001). Glenn Palmer, Patrick Regan, and Tamar London (2004) also find that surplus governments are more forceful.

Coalition decision making involves invoking certain rules and guidelines to reach a decision. A decision can be reached as a consensus but often will be based on a simple majority rule. Coalition dynamics are important. For instance, small parties in a coalition can be "pivotal" if they have the capacity to bring down the government with their defection. Another variation occurs if there are no set rules for reaching a decision. In these extreme cases, the decision process is one of anarchy (Hagan et al. 2001; M. Hermann 2001).

If the executive and legislative branches are controlled by opposing parties, presidential systems resemble coalitions (Hagan et al. 2001). Such was the case during the Nixon Administration, which culminated in the passage of the War Powers Act over the president's veto. The three main coalition models are the unit veto, minimum winning, and anarchy (Hagan et al. 2001). Different institutional factors such as laws or constitutions establish the rules of the game for decision making. If the rules dictate that unanimity is required for the coalition to reach a decision, then the coalition will tend toward the unit veto or minimum-winning coalition models. In the unit veto system, any actor can put up a roadblock. In the minimum-winning coalition model, the pivotal party dynamic becomes an issue. In the anarchy model, there is no official rule for decision making. As noted, the Iranian decision model during the hostage crisis reflected an anarchic process (Hagan et al. 2001). We take up coalitions in greater detail in the case studies in the next sections.

CASE STUDY: ISRAEL'S FOREIGN POLICY MAKING BY COALITION

The Israeli Cabinet often provides a good example of the effect of political coalitions on foreign policy decision making. Israel has a wide range of parties that cover the political and religious spectra. For a government to form, a major party must establish a coalition with other parties. Small, pivotal parties often keep the government in power. Defection of coalition partners can threaten the survival of the government.

Former Israeli Prime Minister Ehud Olmert's government embarked on negotiations with the leaders of the Palestinian Authority, President Mahmoud Abbas (Abu-Mazen) and Prime Minister Salem Fayad. The highlight of the negotiating process was the Annapolis Summit held at the Naval Academy outside of Washington, D.C., in November 2007. As Verter (2007) and others pointed out, however, Olmert's decisions about the extent and timing of concessions to the Palestinians were heavily constrained, influenced, and determined by the views of Olmert's Kadima party's coalition partners, Shas and Israel Beytenu. In a coalition government consisting of Kadima, Labor, Shas, Israel Beytenu, and the Pensioners' Party, Olmert simply could not make meaningful territorial concessions to the Palestinians on Jerusalem and elsewhere without risking the downfall of his government. Thus, whereas the president of the Palestinian Authority wanted to finalize the principles of the final agreement prior to the Annapolis Summit, Olmert pushed for a vaguer statement that left the main issues off the table for future discussions.

Knesset member Eli Yishai, leader of the Shas party (and deputy prime minister and minister of industry, trade, and labor) had indicated that Shas would not stay in the Olmert government should the sensitive Jerusalem issue be on the agenda at the summit or even be discussed with the Palestinians. Such a move by Shas would topple Olmert's government and lead to early elections. Minister Avigdor Liberman, head of the Israel Beytenu party and then minister of strategic threats and a coalition member, warned that should Israel make concessions to the Palestinians, his party also would quit the government (Liberman resigned from the government shortly after Annapolis). As then U.S. Secretary of State Rice discovered in her many visits to the region, there are serious limits to the prime minister's power in Israel, a power that is constrained by coalition calculations and domestic political considerations.[4]

As Verter pointed out (2007), Olmert's stand at Annapolis ensured that his government would stay in power – for the time being. The failure to discuss sensitive issues at the summit, such as the status of Jerusalem, enabled the leaders of the Shas and Israel Beytenu parties to claim credit in front of their constituencies for preventing Olmert from reaching an agreement on sensitive territorial issues at Annapolis. Unable to conclude a deal with the Palestinians because of domestic coalition constraints, Olmert and his Palestinian partners decided to *start* the negotiation process instead of agreeing on key issues.

Secretary of State Rice, who met with the Shas and Israel Beytenu leaders in Israel before the summit at Annapolis, quickly realized that Olmert could not make such concessions because of coalition limitations and threats to the survival of his government, despite plans by Kadima ministers Ramon and Livni to further the talks. In fact, the Shas spiritual leader and chief rabbi, Ovadia Yossef, was not discouraged from meeting with the head of the opposition, Benjamin Netanyahu, to signal to Olmert that the Shas party had the option to form a government led by the opposition (Verter 2007). It was the degree of

---

[4] One should also recall that leaders of Israel and Egypt who made bold concessions, Yitzhak Rabin (with the Oslo agreements) and Anwar Sadat (with the Camp David agreement), were both assassinated by their own people.

political flexibility of Olmert's coalition partners that determined Israel's stand on concessions to the Palestinians and the outcome of the Annapolis summit.

Turning to the Palestinian side, the situation is not much different. Challenges to the president of the Palestinian Authority from such Palestinian groups as Hamas and Islamic Jihad have been serious and even violent. Some Palestinian factions have even participated in a counter-Annapolis summit organized by Iran to denounce and challenge the Annapolis meeting.

ANOTHER EXAMPLE OF COALITION DECISION MAKING: ICELAND'S COD WAR, 1971–1974[5]

From the late 1950s to the late 1970s, the governments of Iceland and the United Kingdom faced off several times over fishing rights. In the wake of diminished catches in 1967, Iceland extended its territorial waters from twelve to fifty miles in opposition to fishermen from other European countries – especially Britain. What made this crisis especially interesting was that Iceland and the UK were both democracies, members of the NATO alliance, and strong trade partners. Nevertheless, the Icelandic Coast Guard ships and British naval vessels had serious encounters.

The government of Iceland was ruled by a three-party, left-leaning coalition during the 1970s fisheries crisis. The three parties were the centrist Progressive Party (which had 25 percent of the vote), the Socialist Popular Alliance (20 percent), and the Organization of Leftists and Liberals (9 percent). In the early 1970s, the government had to contend with two related issues: territorial limits and the continued presence of U.S. troops in the strategically important North Atlantic. The Progressives and the Leftists and Liberals favored continued NATO membership but were divided on the issue of U.S. troop deployment in Iceland. The Popular Alliance did not support NATO membership or U.S. troops. Thus, there were very serious policy differences within the coalition. Valur Ingimundarson (2003) notes that the dominant theme for agreement was that U.S. troops should leave and that the territorial waters should be extended beyond twelve miles. These two policies were expressions partly of nationalism and partly of solidarity with the Third World. The main disagreement was over how Iceland should align itself geopolitically. The moderate parties supported continued NATO involvement, whereas the leftist Popular Alliance favored a new direction.

The Fisheries portfolio was held by Lúdvík Jósepsson of the far-left Popular Alliance. Jósepsson was in charge of the negotiations with Britain that ensued after Iceland unilaterally extended its territorial waters to fifty miles. He was very popular, and his forceful actions in this arena garnered favorable public

---

[5] This section borrows heavily from Ingimundarson (2003).

attention and support. His political clout in dealing with the fisheries issue seems to have come at the expense of Foreign Minister Guoni Ágústsson. Jósepsson attempted bold moves during the crisis that had to be superseded by the prime minister. The prime minister and foreign minister, both of the Progressive Party, also favored the extension to fifty miles and were aware of the nationalistic overtones surrounding fisheries, but were also keen on keeping a U.S. military presence in the country. The Popular Alliance wanted the U.S. forces out and Iceland out of NATO. Thus, the parties shared a relatively similar position on fisheries but differed drastically on foreign policy.

One key difference of opinion was over how to negotiate with Britain. The crisis escalated almost to the point of warfare. Iceland deployed special ships that cut fishing lines of British vessels and, in return, the British fishers demanded and obtained protection by British frigates. Icelandic and British ships rammed one another, but no shots were fired by either side. Nevertheless, this crisis provides a rare example of two democracies on the brink of war.

The Cod War crisis of 1971–1974 is a good example of how one party can have inordinate power in a coalition setting. The Popular Alliance was forcing the government to act aggressively by linking the debate over the fisheries to the debate over U.S. troops. The leftists were more willing to anger the United States by directly linking these two issues. The collision of these two issues and the presence of a party in government that was willing to upset both British and American allies made it difficult for the moderate prime minister and foreign minister to deal effectively with the United States. The Americans perceived that Foreign Minister Ágústsson was incapable of facilitating the troops deal. The prime minister also had a hard time striking a deal with Britain over fisheries because the Popular Alliance did not want such a deal and did not want to be excluded from any such talks.

When foreign policy issues emerge that cut across coalition parties, it can be difficult for governments to make decisions. Several times during the crisis, the Popular Alliance threatened to leave the coalition. The Alliance had effectively linked troops and fisheries. The extension of the territorial limit had broad national support. The U.S. troops issue was not so clear cut. By linking the two issues, the Popular Alliance played the part of a pivotal party. It used the fisheries issue, which the other two coalition parties generally supported, to drive their more radical position on the troops policy.

Within the framework provided by Margaret Hermann (2001), the Icelandic coalition is an example of a multiple-autonomous-actors decision unit rather than a single decision unit. The Popular Alliance was acting almost in a renegade manner and overstepping the bounds of the Fisheries portfolio by delving into foreign policy. The more moderate foreign minister had little credibility in dealing with the Americans, who did not believe he could deliver on his promises.

THE DECISION ENVIRONMENT

A decision problem typically consists of a set of decision alternatives (for example, do nothing, apply sanctions, or attack) and a set of decision dimensions or criteria (for example, political, diplomatic, military, and economic considerations).

Many foreign policy decisions must be made in a relatively short time frame, under stress and ambiguity of information. Characteristics of the **decision environment** affect the decision strategies used by leaders and their ultimate choices (Kahneman and Tversky 1982; Payne, Bettman, and Johnson 1993). Specifically, uncertainty, stress, familiarity or lack of familiarity with the decision task, risk and threat perception, and accountability all influence decision strategy and choice. Some scholars have argued that stress and external threats may even lead to increased "rigidity in decision making" and overreliance on standard operating procedures in decision making (Renshon and Renshon 2008, 515).

The common denominator of the factors that mediate the onset of decision strategies centers on the cognitive demands (load) imposed by the decision task. The heavier the demand (for example, the more ambiguous and unfamiliar the decision task is to the decision maker), the more likely the decision maker is to employ simplifying heuristics (cognitive shortcuts).

Decision-making environments are often in a state of flux (Anderson 1983; Vertzberger 1990). Foreign policy crises are characterized by an evolving choice set out of which policy alternatives emerge during the process (Mintz et al. 1997). National security and foreign policy crises are marked by a somewhat chaotic situation wherein information is presented to and received by a leader in a rather complex and varied fashion.

Most decisions in foreign policy are taken in interactive settings: Bush versus Saddam, Olmert versus Nasrallah, and, during the Cold War, NATO versus the WTO. The foreign policy decision-making environment is also characterized by ambiguity of information, uncertainty about opponents' motivations and intentions, dynamic settings, and high risk (see Table 2.3). Foreign policy decisions often have important consequences for nations, their allies, and rival countries. Furthermore, they can affect the survivability of leaders in power.

Time Constraints

One of the hallmarks of crises is that time is limited and decisions might be rushed. Time pressure may take the form of a short deadline for a decision or, more likely, "an uncertain deadline that is believed to necessitate a quick decision" (Renshon and Renshon 2008, 513). Crisis decision makers do not have the luxury of waiting to see how decisions play out. Because time is limited, the rational actor model is typically compromised. It becomes difficult to carry

Table 2.3. *Environmental factors
affecting foreign policy decisions*

Time constraints
Information constraints
Ambiguity
Familiarity
Accountability
Risk
Stress
Dynamic vs. static setting
Interactive setting

out rational calculations. This does not necessarily mean that a bad decision will be made. Sometimes time constraints and pressure can force a decision maker to stop and devote full attention to the problem at hand and actually enhance a decision (see Maule and Andrade 1997).

Time constraints are more likely to lead to nonholistic search, the use of simplified heuristic and SOPs, and satisficing decision making. We further discuss time pressures when we take up the effects of stress on decision making in Chapter 6.

Information Constraints

The rational actor model requires solid information if it is to work as designed (Allison 1971). Without reliable information, it is difficult to compare alternatives, conduct a cost-benefit analysis, and determine utilities. However, foreign policy is rife with incomplete and inaccurate information.

Producer-consumer problems abound in foreign policy. Producers are the information gatherers in the field. For example, intelligence agencies have field operatives who send intelligence back to headquarters where consumers use it to inform decisions. The process is prone to problems. For example, producers may generate biased information. One motivation for this behavior is that producers want their information to be noticed.

The Vietnam War was characterized by well-known information problems. President Johnson was repeatedly told that the war was going according to plan and that incremental increases in troops could lead to victory. The president was being given biased information that was not entirely accurate. This made it difficult for the president to compare alternatives and utilities realistically. Israeli Prime Minister Menachem Begin received inaccurate information about troop level and deployment in Lebanon in 1982. The information he received led to decisions he would later regret. This does not equate, of course, to being irrational, but it does mean the conditions required to make an optimal decision were not met.

Ambiguity

Ambiguity occurs when information has multiple, often competing, meanings, or when a situation can have multiple possible outcomes. Ambiguity might, for example, result when an adversary sends a signal that can be interpreted as either hostile or conciliatory, leaving the ultimate move of the adversary in doubt. Ambiguous information is more likely to be ignored or discounted (Vertzberger 1990). For example, in the week before the Yom Kippur War in 1973, information about Soviet advisors and their families leaving Syria and Egypt was discounted by Israeli intelligence analysts in part because it could be indicative of either defensive or offensive intentions (ibid., 58). Information supplied by U.S. intelligence agencies about Iraqi offensive force posture before the August 1990 invasion of Kuwait was ignored by the U.S. administration largely because it contradicted assessments of U.S. allies in the region, such as Egypt and Saudia Arabia. Ambiguity typically increases the complexity of foreign policy decisions, causing decision makers to use cognitive shortcuts to simplify the decision-making process.

Familiarity

Familiarity with the decision problem is present when decision makers encounter a situation that is similar to one that they have seen or experienced before. In these situations, foreign policy decision makers often employ heuristics or SOPs because they believe that what worked before will work again (Payne, Bettman, and Johnson 1993) and tend to rely on prior acts and decisions. Familiarity with the decision problem often leads to the use of intuitive decision making. Instead of examining the components of the decision, the decision maker jumps to conclusions based on prior experience with a similar situation before even assessing the costs and benefits of alternatives. Often, familiarity with the decision task can be helpful in simplifying and facilitating a decision and allows a leader to choose an alternative quickly, without having to consider all of the information again. However, this process may lead to the discounting of inconsistent information as well as biases and errors in decision making; it can even result in overgeneralization (for example, Kruglanski and Ajzen 1983; Vertzberger 1990; Hirshberg 1993).

Dynamic Setting

Dynamic settings are those in which the choice set (meaning alternatives) or dimension set (criteria) that is available to the decision maker changes in the process of the decision, as opposed to static settings in which the decision maker is aware of all alternatives upfront and these alternatives remain fixed during the decision process. A dynamic setting could involve the emergence of a new alternative (for example, an avenue of diplomatic communication opening up during a crisis) or an old alternative being taken off the table (for example, the closing of a diplomatic channel by the adversary). Alternatives can also disappear and later reappear during a crisis. Mintz et al. (1997) showed that dynamic choice sets can change the way decision makers process information and arrive at a decision: the emergence of a new option may cause it to be compared to the previous options in an alternative-based manner.

Interactive Setting

Leaders make decisions that affect and are affected by the decisions of other players or leaders. As we pointed out in Chapter 1, an example of a game in an interactive, sequential setting is chess. Understanding the strategic interactive context of a decision is a crucial part of understanding foreign policy prefer-ences, processes, judgment, and choice, because previous and future reasoning of the opponent will have an effect on the payoffs. Failure to consider the inter-active setting of the foreign policy decision is likely to result in an incomplete understanding of the decision.

Risk

Risk is an important component of foreign policy decision making because the stakes in the foreign policy arena tend to be high (Astorino-Courtois and Trusty 2000). The amount of risk leaders are willing to take affects their foreign policy decisions. Risk can be thought of as the probability that an actor associates with receiving a negative outcome. A high-risk alternative is one in which the probability associated with failure is large enough that the expected utility of the action is negative. At the individual level, attitudes toward risk are an important determinant of a decision maker's actions because those attitudes will influence the level of uncertainty with which a decision maker is comfortable acting. Although these attitudes are in part a function of individual idiosyncrasies, they are also affected by the individual's level of satisfaction with the status quo: those who are more dissatisfied are more willing to take risks (Kahneman and Tversky 1979). Prospect theory centers around the risk orientation of decision makers. Risk acceptance is assumed in the domain of loss, and risk avoidance in the domain of gain.

Stress

Stress can be conceptualized as "an excess of demands over capacity" (Renshon and Renshon 2008, 512). International crises entail high levels of perceived threat. Decision makers are faced with situations that must be dealt with right away because ignoring them could lead to an unfavorable outcome. For example, the Thatcher government had to act quickly after Argentina invaded the Falkland Islands. The stress level was heightened by the fact that it would take a number of days for British ships to reach the islands. Such time constraints introduce an element of stress to decision making.

Robert Mandel (1986, 257) and Ole Holsti (1972; cited in Dougherty and Pfaltzgraff 1990, 496–499; see also Holsti 1989) have summarized some of the impacts that a stressful environment can have on decision makers during crises. Stress caused by time constraints or uncertainty can unleash feelings of shame or anxiety. It can also influence information processing by causing decision makers to ignore certain information and alternatives, oversimplify, and rely more on historical analogy. Stress also has been found to frequently cause leaders to overestimate the capabilities of their opponents. Taken to the extreme, stress can even cause panic. Studies have revealed that stress leads to decreased focus, regression to primitive or very elementary decision styles, an increase in errors, and tendencies toward random behavior.

In their influential book on conflict and choice, Irving Janis and Leon Mann (1977) view psychological stress as a situation involving high levels of unfavorable emotion, such as guilt or fear, that make information processing more difficult (cited in Sage 1990, 35). In turn, the risk and uncertainty associated with the decision make the stress more profound. Janis and Mann (1977) identify several behaviors that result from stress (also cited in Sage 1990, 35). If the decision maker thinks that avoiding a major loss will be hard because of severe time constraints, there is a greater likelihood of panic. If all alternatives seem risky and finding a reasonable one seems unlikely, decision makers maintain a **defensive avoidance** posture.

However, some research has shown that low levels of stress can actually lead to good decisions. Janis and Mann (1977) observe that if stress is moderate during an important decision and it does not induce severe time constraints, quality alternatives can be identified and carefully assessed.

McDermott (2004a, 173–177) claims that acute stress brought on, for example, by a deadline elicits a hormonal reaction in the brain that can be beneficial. The effects of the hormones are felt throughout the body and short-term performance improves. Chronic stress, by contrast, can have detrimental health effects if the threat does not subside. This form of stress is heightened if it comes on unexpectedly. Civil war is an example of a situation that can lead to chronic stress, and accordingly we would expect stress levels to be higher in countries experiencing civil war.

The ultimate effects of particularly stressful events such as terrorist attacks might not emerge until long after the event is over. This syndrome has come to be known as posttraumatic stress disorder (PTSD), and symptoms include numbness, guilt, flashbacks, and exaggerated reactions to surprise.

Susceptibility to PTSD varies by individual and typically affects leaders and their decisions.

Accountability

A decision maker is accountable if she must explain, or is expected to explain, a decision and believes that she can be rewarded or punished because of it. When a decision maker is held accountable for a decision, she is likely to be more careful and, as such, will be more likely to procure and evaluate information in a more holistic manner. These tendencies are even more pronounced in situations in which the leader commits publicly to a course of action. Payne, Bettman, and Johnson (1993), however, point out that accountability does not necessarily make one less likely to rely on cognitive heuristics (because these heuristics can become the justification) and will not automatically reduce bias.

   The effects of accountability are also apparent when individuals must answer for mistakes they have made. Experimental work has shown that subjects who are held accountable for bad decisions in the face of unforeseen circumstances are likely to defend themselves on the grounds that if they had known, they would not have made the poor decision (Markman and Tetlock 2000). The tendency of managers to display certainty of hindsight bias can be reduced or prevented when individuals are held accountable and can defend their actions (ibid.).

   One study looked at the impact of political accountability on performance of Israeli leaders in the Yom Kippur War of 1973. It found that differences in performance resulted from individual differences in personal accountability and available social support networks (Bar-Joseph and McDermott 2008, 144). Specifically, the degree to which a leader "feels responsible for the crisis, prepared for the challenges, and . . . accountable for the outcome affects that person's quality of decision making" (ibid., 145).

   A common assumption is that good behavior is to be expected from individuals who are being held accountable (Lerner and Tetlock 1999). However, the relationship may not be quite so simple. Research on the effects of accountability on decision making finds that it varies widely depending on the context (ibid.). For example, legitimate accountability (being accountable to a friend or appropriate authority figure as opposed to a cruel person) leads to better behavior than its illegitimate form. The latter can lead to stress and decline in motivation, which obviously affect decision making.

   David Brulé and Alex Mintz (2006) found that U.S. presidents are affected by public opinion on the use of force (because they prefer to be accountable to the public), but that the effect of public support and opposition is not symmetrical. Public support above 50 percent is typically seen as allowing for presidential use of force, whereas public opposition over 80 percent restrains leaders in most situations from using force against adversaries.

THE ROLE OF ADVISORY GROUPS

Many consequential foreign policy decisions involve several decision makers and advisors (Renshon and Renshon 2008, 518). Advisory groups can shape foreign (and domestic) policy by helping set the agenda, manipulating information, framing alternative courses of action, controling the flow of information, preventing contradictory and nonsupportive information from filtering in, interpreting incoming information for policy makers in certain ways, and serving as gatekeepers. Advisory groups (for example, to the president or prime minister) can be powerful and influential, or not so influential.

Steven Redd (2002, 335) studied how advisory groups shape foreign policy decisions and concluded, "decision makers are highly sensitive to and cognizant of the political ramifications of their decisions." Specifically, political information provided by advisors and advisory groups influences both information processing and foreign policy choices (ibid.). Thomas Preston (2001; see also George and George 1998, ch. 6) showed that presidents with foreign policy expertise (for example, Eisenhower, Kennedy, George H. W. Bush) are less likely to rely on advisory staff when making foreign policy decisions. For those with less foreign policy experience (for example, Clinton, Truman, Johnson), advisors are much more important.

At the time of 9/11, the U.S. Defense Policy Board was led by Richard Perle. The board played a key role in shaping U.S. policy on Iraq prior to the war and during the early stages of the war (Perle was replaced by Tillie Fowler in June 2003). According to its official charter:

> The Defense Policy Board "will provide the Secretary of Defense, Deputy Secretary and Under Secretary for Policy with independent, informed advice and opinion concerning major matters of defense policy. It will focus upon long-term, enduring issues central to strategic planning for the Department of Defense and will be responsible for research and analysis of topics, long or short range, addressed to it by the Secretary of Defense, Deputy Secretary and Under Secretary for Policy" Membership in the U.S. Defense Policy Board consists primarily of private sector individuals with distinguished backgrounds in national security affairs, but may include no more than four government officials. Membership will be approximately thirty. From time to time, associate members may be appointed to the Defense Policy Board to participate in an assessment of a particular issue.[6]

Another group, the Baker-Hamilton Committee, submitted a bipartisan report to President George W. Bush on the U.S. war in Iraq, providing the president with a face-saving strategy for withdrawing all U.S. combat forces by

---

[6] http://fl1.findlaw.com/news.findlaw.com/hdocs/docs/dod/dpbac80201chrtr.pdfww.findlaw.com.

Table 2.4. *Information search patterns*

Holistic vs. nonholistic
Order sensitive vs. order insensitive
Alternative based vs. dimension based
Maximizing vs. satisficing
Compensatory vs. noncompensatory

the beginning of 2008. The Baker-Hamilton report favored, among other things, direct negotiations with regional players such as Iran and Syria and an increase of U.S. advisors embedded within Iraqi troops. President Bush, however, almost immediately distanced himself from key proposals in the Baker-Hamilton report.

A key recommendation of the Winograd committee, which studied the performance of Israeli political and military leaders in the second war in Lebanon in the summer of 2006, was the bolstering of Israel's National Security Council as an advisory group to the prime minister and cabinet members so it could provide policy makers with systematic and detailed assessments of policy options and their implications and would counterbalance the opinion and recommendations of the Israel Defense Forces.

INFORMATION SEARCH PATTERNS

Policy makers perceive and access information in a number of ways. These perceptions, in turn, can determine how information is processed and decisions are made. The way information is gathered, processed, and framed affects foreign policy. In this section, we cover several of the most prominent patterns of information processing.

Andrew Sage (1990, 232–242) describes the various processing characteristics of the rational and cognitive approaches. The rational actor model can be considered holistic because the decision maker considers all information at hand and makes extensive use of comparison. However, this section also focuses on heuristic decision-processing characteristics and concepts because we discuss explanations of foreign policy decision making that do not rely on the classical rational assumptions. Sage notes that these approaches most directly address the decision process because they set out to explain and understand the limitations of human cognition.

Significant cognitive limitations affect information search. The use of heuristic decision rules generally means the use of simplified cognitive shortcuts in decision making. There is a wide variety of patterns to consider here, from order-sensitive searches and noncompensatory search rules to dimension or alternative-based search patterns (see Table 2.4).

Holistic versus Nonholistic Search

Holistic search simply means reviewing all the information on the alternative courses of action, the dimensions that influence the decision, and the implications of each alternative on each dimension.

While employing nonholistic search, the decision maker only reviews part of the information about the decision. Nonholistic searches are associated with the use of heuristics in decision making because simplifying cognitive shortcuts imply that not all the information is accessed and evaluated.

Order-Sensitive versus Order-Insensitive Search

Both the sequence of dimensions and the order of alternatives can affect our decisions (Redd 2002). For example, in searching for a used car, the order of viewing cars may affect the choice; we may only look at the first few cars we were considering buying because of the costs and efforts associated with traveling to see other cars on our list. Consequently, we will likely select one of the first few cars we see rather than look at all the cars. However, if we had reversed the sequence of car shopping, we may have purchased a different car.

Research has shown that the order in which information is presented to leaders affects foreign policy decision making. Political leaders are sensitive to negative political information and may discard alternatives that are presented to them by their advisors before other important criteria (economic, diplomatic) have been presented to them. If a political advisor sets the agenda prior to input from the military advisor, the outcome may be different from a reversed sequence of events.

Alternative-Based versus Dimension-Based Search

Decision makers can also base their search for information on alternatives or on dimensions. A search is considered alternative based if the decision maker considers in turn each of the possible implications for each alternative. In a dimension-based search, the payoffs for each dimension across alternatives are considered one at a time. For example, an individual conducting an alternative-based search for a new car would look closely at all information for each potential car in succession. In a dimension-based search, the person would proceed by assessing the implications of each dimension across alternatives. Alternative-based searches are sometimes referred to as **interdimensional** and dimension-based searches as **intradimensional**. As we will discuss, search patterns are important because they can influence how a decision is made and which alternative is selected.

Maximizing versus Satisficing Search Patterns

Rational decision makers attempt to **maximize**, which means that they select the best alternative out of a set of alternatives by evaluating the benefits and costs of each alternative and selecting the one that has the highest net gain (total benefits minus total costs).

In contrast, when employing a **satisficing** decision rule, the decision maker selects the alternative that is "good enough" but not necessarily the best. Once an alternative is acceptable to the decision maker, subsequent alternatives are not even considered. Seminal work by Nobel laureate Herbert Simon (1957; 1959) suggests that instead of optimizing gains, humans follow a pattern of satisficing in which decision makers select the first acceptable alternative rather than carry out a search and comparison. Because information costs are high, decision makers evaluate the possible alternatives and accept the first that meets a certain minimum requirement. Simon argued that decision makers are more likely to select the alternative that satisfies some minimum threshold. This rule is much less demanding than the rational ideal version of utility maximization.

Compensatory versus Noncompensatory Rule

We can now delve more deeply into the nuances of FPDM as we discuss two broad categories of information search patterns: **compensatory** (or linear) and **noncompensatory**. In the **compensatory** model, a low score on one dimension can be compensated for by a high score on another dimension. For example, if an executive is deciding whether to use force, a low score on the political dimension can be compensated for with a high score on the military dimension.

A **noncompensatory** search means that if an alternative has a low score in one dimension, then no other score along another dimension, or dimensions, can compensate. For example, during the Cuban Missile Crisis, the "diplomatic pressure" option scored so low on the political dimension that nothing could compensate. The noncompensatory approach is nonadditive and relies on cognitive shortcuts or heuristics because not all information is reviewed.

Compensatory processes are generally marked by interdimensional searches, typically using a constant amount of information per alternative (Billings and Marcus 1983, 333). The compensatory model is alternative based because the decision maker considers all dimensions of an alternative before moving on to another alternative (Payne et al. 1988, 536).

The noncompensatory model is dimension based. The process is simplified by sequentially eliminating alternatives that do not meet a certain threshold using one, or a few, criteria, as opposed to compensatory processes that entail the comparison of alternatives across dimensions (Mintz 1993). Noncompensatory models do not consider all alternatives on all dimensions before an

Table 2.5. *Noncompensatory decision rules*

Conjunctive
Disjunctive
Elimination by aspect
Lexicographic

acceptable solution is found (Mintz, Geva, and DeRouen Jr. 1993). Noncompensatory selection procedures usually imply an intradimensional component that is attribute based, rather than alternative based (Payne et al. 1988, 536). Some scholars suggest that noncompensatory, rather than compensatory, linear models, are used in more complicated decision environments because they are cognitively easier (Einhorn 1970, 1971; Payne 1976; E. Johnson and Meyer 1984; Brannick and Brannick 1989). The definitive feature of the noncompensatory models effectively rules out compensation between variables (Brannick and Brannick 1989).

The idea behind the noncompensatory models, then, is to eliminate alternatives quickly to simplify the information search and evaluation phases of the decision process (Payne 1976, 384; Payne et al. 1988, 534). Additive compensatory models present explanations of foreign policy decision making that do not necessarily capture the motivations for political survival and the constraints of public opinion.

Broadly speaking, the rational model is associated with compensatory searches. This process fits with the classic model's exhaustive search. Cognitive models, in contrast, are typically linked with noncompensatory, heuristic processes. Two main noncompensatory procedures that are used when decisions are made based on multidimensional criteria are the conjunctive and the disjunctive procedures. In the former, evaluations are made on the basis of the existence of more than one dimensional threshold that must be satisfied; in the latter, evaluations depend on the existence of one dimension that is of paramount importance (Dawes 1964).

NONCOMPENSATORY DECISION RULES

Research has shown that decision makers use a variety of decision rules while making decisions. The main noncompensatory decision models, listed in Table 2.5, are the conjunctive (CON), disjunctive (DIS), elimination by aspect (EBA), and lexicographic (LEX) (Sage 1990).

Conjunctive Decision Rule (CON)

The conjunctive decision rule (CON) procedure, by definition, implies noncompensatory logic in which values must be above a certain level on each dimension. The CON model posits the existence of multiple thresholds. The least relevant dimension has the greatest impact on the selection procedure because all dimensions must surpass the threshold. For example, having an excellent heart, liver, and lungs cannot compensate for the fact that the body's sole remaining kidney is dysfunctional (Dawes 1964, 105).

Under the CON decision rule, the decision maker sets a minimum acceptable value for each dimension of the decision. To be accepted, the alternative, or alternatives, have to be above the minimum acceptable value for all dimensions. An alternative is rejected if it fails to exceed any minimum value.

Disjunctive Decision Rule (DIS)

The disjunctive decision rule (DIS) is the mirror image of the conjunctive rule. Using the disjunctive rule, the decision maker sets a minimally acceptable value for each dimension. To be retained, an alternative has to pass the threshold value for at least one dimension. Alternatives that fail to meet this critical value are rejected.

The DIS procedure eliminates alternatives on the basis of the most important dimension. Robyn Dawes (1964, 105) gave the example of the football player who is selected based on his exceptional ability in one aspect of the game, be it passing, kicking, running, or blocking. A disjunctive process is followed if a team that needs a quarterback eschews an average quarterback who can kick quite well in favor of an excellent passer. The key to the DIS process is the most relevant dimension (Einhorn 1971, 3).

Elimination-by-aspect (EBA) Decision Rule

The elimination-by-aspect (EBA) decision rule is a sequential elimination decision heuristic. In this procedure, each attribute or dimension is given a different weight reflective of its importance. The dimensions are selected for their use in comparing alternatives with a probability proportional to their weight. Alternatives that do not score above a certain threshold on a key dimension are then sequentially discarded. Then a second dimension is chosen and the process is repeated until only one dimension remains (Payne et al. 1988). EBA is inherently similar to other noncompensatory models, but it differs mainly as a result of its probabilistic nature – meaning that the order in which elimination proceeds may vary from case to case as weights change (Tversky 1972a, 285; 1972b, 349–350).

Lexicographic (LEX) Decision Rule

The lexicographic decision rule (LEX) involves the selection of the alternative that provides the greatest utility on what has been deemed the most important dimension (Payne et al. 1988); for example, imposing economic sanctions on the adversary because it produces weapons of mass destruction. Other examples include buying a stock based on a report on favorable future earnings, selling a stock because one needs the money, and buying a car because one likes its color. Search patterns and decision rules obviously influence FPDM because the use of a specific decision rule can lead to a different outcome than the use of another rule.

CONCLUSION

There are a number of interesting avenues for exploring the FPDM environment. This chapter outlines a number of them: decision types, levels of analysis, environmental factors, information search patterns, and decision rules. Taken together, these perspectives provide a rich tapestry for exploring how and why foreign decisions are made.

3

Biases in Decision Making

One of the main problems that leaders may encounter in crises is their tendency to be influenced by biases and errors in decision making because of cognitive limitations (Forman and Selly 2001). In fact, decision making for most complex, crucial foreign policy decisions takes place under constraints of information-processing limitations (ibid.). Biases often lead to **misperception**. Leaders see the world in ways that are subconsciously filtered by previous beliefs and experiences. In his seminal study of bias and misperception, Robert Jervis (1976) argues that decision makers generally do not perceive the world accurately and that we can understand and identify the sources of the misperception. Biases are listed in Table 3.1.

Saddam Hussein's misperceptions following Iraq's invasion of Kuwait in 1990 provide a textbook example (Mingst 2002). Saddam likely perceived that the United States would not react too strongly to the invasion, a perception based on a meeting he had with U.S. Ambassador April Glaspie. Many contend that Glaspie signaled to Saddam that the United States would not intervene in the border dispute between Kuwait and Iraq.

Saddam also might have expected that the Arab world would unite behind him as he tried to make Israel a party to the conflict. He might well have perceived that the world was focused on events in Europe as the Cold War was ending and the Soviet Union was breaking apart.

In 2008, the Hamas leadership miscalculated when it failed to anticipate Israel's forceful response to Hamas's continued rocket attacks on the Jewish state. The Hamas leadership did not expect Israel to retaliate prior to an election. It suffered from the **wishful thinking** bias that the Israelis would not dare enter Hamas-controlled Gaza.

Analysis of decisions in Pearl Harbor, the Bay of Pigs, Operation Barbarossa, the Yom Kippur War of 1973, and the Israel-Hezbollah war of July 2006, to name just a few historical and contemporary examples, reveals the common nature of biases and errors that influence the decisions of leaders. Ironically, despite the fact that many biases in decision making are known, leaders are continually

Table 3.1. *Biases in decision making*

Focusing on short-term benefits rather than longer-term problems
Preference over preference
Locking on one alternative
Wishful thinking
Post-hoc rationalization
Relying on the past
Focusing on a narrow range of policy options rather than on a wide range of options
Groupthink
Overconfidence; over-estimating one's capabilities and underestimating rival's capabilities
Ignoring critical information; denial and avoidance
Focusing on only part of the decision problem
Turf battles leading to suboptimal decisions
Lack of tracking and auditing of prior decisions and plans
Poliheuristic bias
Shooting from the hip
Polythink
Group polarization effect

Source: This table is an extension of a list in Forman and Selly 2001.

influenced by biases and sometimes repeat the same mistakes. Surprisingly, such biases are even resistant to **debiasing** – the attempt to reduce or eliminate biases from the cognitive calculus of decision making (Bazerman 2006, 193; Renshon and Renshon 2008, 527).

For example, Israeli leaders were susceptible to known cognitive biases in their decision to retaliate for the Hezbollah infiltration into Northern Israel on July 12, 2006 (Winograd Interim Report 2007). Published testimonies of Israeli policy makers who served in key leadership positions during the war in Lebanon, given before a commission studying the war, provide a rare testimony to how decisions are made and how biases influence such decisions.

For example, the chief of staff of the Israeli Defense Forces during the July 2006 war in Lebanon, Lieutenant-General Dan Halutz, advocated almost exclusively for air strikes as the preferred policy during the war. His **preference over preference** bias toward this alternative course of action influenced the political echelon and military's decisions. The architects of the Israeli retaliation to Hezbollah's attack also hoped that by putting pressure on Lebanon, its government would disarm Hezbollah and force it to withdraw from the Lebanese border – a "wishful thinking" bias. And before the Yom Kippur war of 1973, Israeli military planners focused on two key alternatives available to their Arab opponents – the "war option" and the "no war option" – while they ignored the possibility of the "limited war option" available to Egypt and Syria (see Levy 1989a, 283). Consequently, they ignored the possibility of a limited attack by their enemies. Egypt and Syria surprised Israel in October 1973 with a limited offensive.

Another study, using an experimental methodology, demonstrated that U.S. policy makers are susceptible to the preference over preference and the **locking on one alternative** biases when making decisions on technologies for combating terrorism (Mintz and Redd 2007). Specifically, officers who participated in the experiment wanted to "do something" and ignored supportive information in favor of "doing nothing." They had a preference for one alternative (border crossing sensors) over other alternatives (such as emergency responders), assigned greater weight and importance to their domain (the military dimension), and virtually ignored the economic costs of the program.

Leaders want to make high-quality decisions, but "their motivated (i.e. affect-driven) and unmotivated biases (e.g. cognitive predisposition)" significantly influence their judgment and, consequently, their decisions (Levy 2003, 38). Leaders are susceptible to the groupthink bias. For example, during the 2006 war in Lebanon, Lieutenant-General Halutz wanted the military to talk in one voice, rather than present multiple viewpoints and challenges to launching an attack. This has elements of the **groupthink** bias.

Leaders tend **not to track and audit their decision processes** (Forman and Selly 2001), to see how previous results of their decisions and actions can be adjusted or modified. In contrast, during the Yom Kippur War of 1973, Israeli military planners were quick to adjust and modify their ground force campaign. This approach resulted in the crossing of the Suez Canal and the encircling the Egyptian Third Army by General Ariel Sharon's forces. Critics point out that such creative revision of Israel's battle plans did not take place in the campaign of summer 2006, which largely relied on air strikes.

Leaders become involved in **bureaucratic politics and turf battles that lead to suboptimal decisions**. Prior to 9/11, the Federal Bureau of Investigations (FBI), the Central Intelligence Agency (CIA), and other governmental agencies of the United States did not share critical information that could have made such an attack by the terrorists much more difficult. Implicit in the work of several leading analysts of the foreign policy decision-making process (Jervis 1976; George 1980a; Jervis, Lebow, and Stein 1985; Holsti 1990), is the assumption that there are cognitive limits on the rationalist microeconomic theory of foreign policy decision making.

How do biases affect foreign policy decisions? Table 3.1 lists biases in decision making.[1] To answer this question, we turn to a case study of the U.S. decision to invade Iraq in 2003.

---

[1] See Forman and Selly (2001) for a list of cognitive biases in decision making, including some biases listed in Table 3.1 and discussed in this chapter.

CASE STUDY: THE U.S. DECISION TO INVADE IRAQ IN 2003 — THE
EFFECT OF COGNITIVE BIASES ON FOREIGN POLICY MAKING[2]

The invasion of Iraq was justified by the Bush administration on the basis of
intelligence reports that Iraq had weapons of mass destruction (WMD) and
threatened the security of the Middle East and the United States. A 2004 CIA
report pointed out, however, that the Bush administration paid little attention
to a prewar U.S. intelligence prediction that ethnic and tribal turmoil in Iraq
would result from an invasion. The report said that the administration was
more worried about Iraq's weapons program and added, "in an ironic twist,
the policy community was receptive to technical intelligence (the weapons
program) where the analysis was wrong, but apparently paid little attention
to intelligence on cultural and political issues (post-Saddam Iraq) where the
analysis was right" (*USA Today* October 12, 2005). The report "rebukes the
Bush administration for not paying enough attention to prewar intelligence
that predicted the factional rivalries now threatening to split Iraq" (ibid.).

The Bush administration suggested before the invasion and early in the Iraq
War that American forces would be greeted as liberators by the Iraqi people.
Which biases influenced Washington's decisions? We look at several examples.

Leaders typically **focus on short-term benefits rather than longer-term
problems**. For example, when he declared "mission accomplished" in May
2003, President Bush was focusing on the results of the military campaign
and its short-term, immediate consequences while ignoring the long-term
problems of insurgency and political violence in Iraq.

Leaders tend to have **preference over preference** for an alternative course
of action. For example, although in the months before the invasion of Iraq
in 2003 UN weapons inspectors reported that they did not find evidence
of WMD in Iraq, the Bush administration and the public largely ignored the
inspectors' reports because they contradicted the administration's preferences,
agenda, and plans to invade Iraq. Leaders and the public often attribute "bad"
behavior to nondemocratic countries, especially the leaders of those countries.

Many in the U.S. administration expected Iraq to turn into a democracy,
but they ignored the religious, ethnic, tribal, cultural, and political cleavages
that already existed in Iraqi society and the threat the invasion posed to some
key Iraqi groups (for example, the Sunnis). This is an example of the **wishful
thinking bias**. Leaders often have unrealistic expectations and are overly optimistic about the outcome of a foreign policy act. Moreover, they often engage
in **post-hoc rationalization** of their choices and actions.

Leaders often **rely on the past** and make decisions that are similar to decisions
they made "last time" even though circumstances may have changed (ibid.).
For example, President Bush applied to Iraq the same policy (invade using

[2] We thank Tracy Long for research assistance on this section.

ground forces) as he ordered in Afghanistan (Yetiv 2004, 231), ignoring the fact that Iraq is completely different from Afghanistan in its social, ethnic, and religious background and composition. Likewise, when the administration focused on the occupation stage of the Iraq War, it expected an occupation along the lines of post–World War Europe or the presence of U.S. troops in South Korea. However, Iraq is not a "friendly" area and, as such, the strategy for relinquishing control that was modeled on past events and cases has not been effective in dealing with the insurgency. We call this the **historical analogy** bias.

Leaders tend to **examine a narrow rather than a broad range of policy options**. The Bush administration focused only on the set of possibilities that suggested Iraq had an intact WMD program. It did not evaluate the alternative that Iraq did not possess WMD. Consequently, any new information on Iraq was interpreted with the bias that it possessed them. As a result, the administration only looked at the range of alternatives that would minimize the WMD threat. As Yetiv (2004, 230) points out, the dynamics of Bush's inner circle "did not favor a serious evaluation of different options for dealing with Iraq."

The **groupthink** bias was at work within the administration. It is well documented that President Bush advocated the removal of Saddam Hussein by force. Other members of the administration were reluctant to voice serious objection to this view (Yetiv 2004, 230), although Secretary of State Colin Powell was the voice of discontent on the policies surrounding the Iraq War (Woodward 2004, 25). As the war continued and Powell's discontent became more and more vocal, he was gradually excluded from the decision-making process, and when the first term of the Bush presidency ended, he resigned (ibid.).

Leaders are often **overconfident** in their foreign policy and national security decisions. For example, U.S. military planners predicted that the "Shock and Awe" attack on Iraq by U.S. forces would defeat the Iraqis. The battle plan was based on the Shock and Awe concept developed at the National Defense University. It focused on psychologically destroying the enemy's will to fight rather than solely on the physical destruction of its military forces. Deputy Secretary of Defense Paul Wolfowitz argued that the United States should get rid of Saddam Hussein and that this action would be relatively easy to do (Woodward 2004, 21). Although this part of the war was, indeed, executed almost perfectly from the perspective of U.S. military planners, the challenges involved in rebuilding postwar Iraq have turned out to be enormous.

Leaders often **overestimate their country's capabilities and underestimate their opponent's capabilities**. When the United States was considering invading Iraq, it overestimated its ability to deal with the subsequent insurgency and downplayed its possible effectiveness, even suggesting that it would fall apart after the war. Then it said that the insurgency would end when the interim government was formed. Next, it claimed that the insurgency would end with the ratification of the constitution and, more recently, with the strategy shift and troop enhancement to Iraq known as the Surge.

Leaders often **ignore critical information**. When gathering evidence and making its case before the UN to justify the invasion of Iraq, the Bush administration tended to focus on and highlight information that supported and fit the alternatives suggesting that Iraq might have had an active WMD program (Yetiv 2004, 224). At the same time, when UN weapons inspectors conveyed information suggesting that Iraq had no WMD, the administration gave this information considerably less weight and exposure. If one assumes President George W. Bush's 2002 State of the Union address to be indicative of his administration's intentions, it is easy to see that the administration decided early on to invade Iraq and therefore accepted supportive information and largely ignored negative information about the invasion and its potential consequences (Woodward 2004).

Leaders often **consider only part of the total decision problem**. As the administration made its case to the American public, it focused primarily on the invasion aspect (Woodward 2004). Much of the discussion of the war focused on how the American Occupation Forces would not be viewed as conquerors but as liberators, and, as such, they would be met in the streets with dancing and cheering Iraqi civilians. However, the administration did not pay enough attention to the occupation aspect of the war.

Leaders tend to partake in **turf battles and politics, which typically lead to suboptimal decisions**. Before the war, the idea that an occupied Iraq could be the cornerstone of a democratic Arabian peninsula was discussed by Secretary of Defense Rumsfeld and National Security Adviser Rice. These key members of the White House staff formed a war coalition. Opposed to them was the section of the staff led by Secretary Powell. Powell was adamantly opposed to attacking Iraq as a response to the 9/11 terrorist attacks. According to Woodward (2004, 25), Powell saw no real link between Saddam and 9/11. Many White House reporters noted that the turf battle between these two groups for the president's ear was almost epic in proportion.

Leaders often **fail to track and audit decisions**. For a long period after the invasion of Iraq, the administration did not articulate a clear exit strategy or a detailed plan for Iraqi reconstruction. The United States incrementally increased troop levels over time, but there was no careful and honest assessment as to whether these increments were succeeding. Vietnam is another frequently cited example of the incremental approach gone amok.

Policy makers demonstrating the **poliheuristic** bias tend to avoid alternatives that are likely to hurt them politically or personally. This may lead to suboptimal decisions. For example, once the United States invaded Iraq and became embroiled in the war with all the sunk costs incurred, it became difficult for President Bush to reverse his policy and withdraw from Iraq. However, as the United States approached its 2008 election and candidates sought to appeal to the center of the electoral map, more voices in the administration called for a timetable for withdrawal from Iraq.

It is clear that biases, decision pathologies, and decision dynamics have affected U.S. decision making vis-à-vis Iraq. Rational actors are expected to make informed decisions by comparing the costs and benefits of alternatives, a process that is expected to lead to high-quality decisions. These conditions and dynamics characterize certain economic and voting decisions (see Lau and Levy 1998). Indeed, economists conducted much of the pioneering work on rational decision making. Application of this approach to FPDM had to deal with the uncertainty and incomplete information that characterize many foreign policy decisions. What rational actor models do not do is focus on biases in decision making and information processing.

Psychological approaches lend themselves to the study of decisions in the face of these mitigating circumstances. The effect of these biases magnifies foreign policy decisions because options must be "identified and constructed" by the decision maker in the midst of great uncertainty (Lau and Levy 1998, 31). In voting decisions and many economic decisions, the options are clearly laid out a priori.

The first generation of cognitive models represents decision makers as "consistency seekers." The world is a confusing place and contains a tremendous wealth of available information, and policy makers must deal with this overload by reducing it to a manageable level. A more recent conception of decision making treats individuals as "cognitive misers" who use mental shortcuts known as *heuristics* (Fiske and Taylor 1991). These approaches are not necessarily mutually exclusive but do differ in their specific focus. In many foreign policy situations, groups are involved in the decision-making process.

GROUPTHINK

Again, group dynamics can influence how information is processed and decisions are made. The structure, cohesion (or lack of cohesion), internal processes and dynamics, and management of the group, affect decisions (George 1980a, 82; quoted in Renshon and Renshon 2008, 518). Irving Janis (1982) introduced the concept of groupthink. The group making the decision seeks consensus at the expense of exploring a variety of alternatives. Conformity to the group's views is an overarching concern for all members, so dissent is stifled and in some instances even punished. The group exhibits self-censorship and feelings of invulnerability and does not tolerate contrary viewpoints as it seeks to consolidate its unanimity. The group vilifies outside groups and sees itself as morally superior. Groupthink obtains when members of the group come to disregard information that does not conform to the majority position. For the United States during the Cold War, the outside enemy group was the Soviet

Union and its allies. In summarizing this phenomenon, Greg Cashman (1993, 112–115) notes that groupthink situations have certain hallmarks. The syndrome is usually linked to groups in which members are of similar background and age.

Groupthink situations are more likely if the group is isolated from outside input. It is also more likely if the group lacks an impartial leader who can tolerate dissent. A lack of norms or procedures for decision making also leaves the group vulnerable to a groupthink dynamic. Groupthink provides safety and security for decision makers and these qualities can be inviting if the situation at hand is a crisis or has moral overtones, or if there was a recent policy failure. Consequently, it is not surprising to find that decision making during major crises are susceptible to groupthink, because members rely on each other for support and validation.

Janis notes several reasons groupthink is normally expected to be deleterious to foreign policy decision making. The most obvious problem is that the search for information and alternatives is inadequately carried out. Outside experts are not solicited and thinking is conformist. After a decision is made, it is not likely to be vetted for possible problems and undesired outcomes. Because the group often has an unrealistically high opinion of itself and its ability to succeed, it is less likely to have a backup plan in case of failure or the ability to monitor past decisions.

The Cuban revolution provides an interesting, yet extreme, example of groupthink outside the U.S. context. After Castro's revolutionaries came to power in 1959, the leadership was dominated by the more radical hardliners such as Castro, his younger brother Raul, and Ernesto "Che" Guevara. The charismatic rebel Camilo Cienfuegos favored a more moderate path, including free and fair elections. Soon after this rift became apparent, Cienfuegos disappeared in a mysterious plane accident. Even if he was not in fact murdered, he clearly had become shut out of the inner group. Hubert Matos, another moderate voice in the early days after the revolution, began voicing his displeasure with the growing number of communists in government. He later resigned after he was accused of being an enemy of the revolution, and Castro had him imprisoned for twenty years. This is an extreme case of punishment for an expression of dissent from the group.

Groupthink in American Foreign Policy

Foreign policy in the United States is often a "victim" of the groupthink syndrome. Examples of this challenge to optimal decision making are listed in Table 3.2.

A classic example of groupthink emerges from the Johnson administration's conduct during the Vietnam War. Jerel Rosati (2004, 269) notes that a small group of high-level decision makers with a strong leader at the helm demonstrated a strong tendency to conform and achieve consensus. The result was

Table 3.2. *Some examples of*
groupthink in American
foreign policy

Vietnam
Bay of Pigs
Rescue Mission in Iran
Iraq 1991
Iraq 2003

an artificial conformity to, and a lack of thorough evaluation of, alternatives that were contrary to the president's position. The group underestimated the enemy's capabilities and overestimated the United States' ability to win the war. There was also a lack of policy adjustment and insufficient monitoring of past decisions. This resulted in a Vietnam policy that became very unpopular with the American public and ultimately gave way to American withdrawal and a communist victory.

The Bay of Pigs invasion provides another classic example of groupthink. President Kennedy inherited the plan from the Eisenhower administration. Some of the CIA personnel involved in the 1954 Guatemalan coup thought that a plan based on this analogy would work (this case is explored in detail in Chapter 6). None of Kennedy's advisors spoke out against the Bay of Pigs plan even though they had many doubts. The conditions were conducive to groupthink. Also, the presidential advisors were all elites who had attended prestigious universities and had similar backgrounds. A young and new president, Kennedy did not challenge the plan and later harbored deep dissatisfaction with the CIA.

The shunning that individuals experienced when going against the group was evident during the decision to launch a rescue operation to save the American hostages in Iran. In the later years of the Carter administration, Secretary of State Cyrus Vance and National Security Advisor Zbigniew Brzezinski had begun to disagree openly on pivotal foreign policy issues. The president increasingly came to rely on his national security advisor at the expense of his secretary of state. For his part, Brezinski perceived Vance to be not enough of a realist when it came to dealing with the Cold War (Berger 2002). In fact, Vance was very moderate and subdued, preferring negotiation to aggressive confrontation. The differences of opinion and philosophy between the two advisors to the president on several high-profile matters culminated in Vance being kept out of the loop in classic groupthink style during the decision and planning of the secret rescue mission in Iran. Vance was openly opposed to the mission, the decision for which was made in his absence. Vance, who over his career had built up a very solid reputation as a statesman, resigned in disgust.

As we pointed out earlier, there was little dissent among administration officials over the decision not to invade Iraq at the end of the 1991 Gulf War. As

General Norman Schwarzkopf (1993) points out, the option of invading Iraq was not even considered, although the U.S. military had the manpower and equipment in place to continue the march to Baghdad. The opinion of the so-called neoconservatives in the post-9/11 environment with respect to removing Saddam Hussein from power represents a typical groupthink syndrome. The backgrounds, worldviews, beliefs, mind-sets, and images of members of the group were to a large extent similar. General Colin Powell, an outsider to the neocons, expressed his opposition to the invasion but was left in the minority. He was more or less left out of discussions regarding the invasion of Iraq in the immediate aftermath of 9/11 (Sciolino and Tyler 2001).

It is possible to prevent groupthink. One way, Janis notes, is for the leader actively to seek diverse options. Of course, this is what Kennedy did during the Cuban Missile Crisis. He specifically told his executive committee to come up with a variety of alternatives and advocated thinking "outside the box." Including a devil's advocate in meetings can also help elicit more options. Finally, groups can avoid a groupthink bias if the leader of the group keeps the search process untainted by refraining from giving her opinion at the outset.

BEYOND GROUPTHINK

The traditional groupthink model has been refined and expanded over time to include additional group processes and pathologies. In *Beyond Groupthink*, Paul 't Hart, Eric Stern, and Bengt Sundelius (1997a) point out that small groups working in an advisory process are varied in composition and role, and that there are political and institutional factors that operate above the level of the group that define and shape its role (ibid., 12). The authors (1997b) raise additional questions regarding the groupthink model. First, it is unclear how applicable the model is. Most of the extant research on the model is confined to the U.S., raising the question of the model's applicability outside of the presidential system and its rather unique presidential advisory system. 't Hart and colleagues (1997b, 11) also caution that groupthink should not be confused with the study of group decision making. In short, they strongly assert that there is more to small-group decision making than the groupthink bias.

One of the overarching findings in *Beyond Groupthink* is that there may be multiple group dynamics overlapping at any point in time. For example, Stern's (1997) reanalysis of the Bay of Pigs suggests that Janis's groupthink model does not perfectly account for events in 1961. Instead, Stern opts for an explanation of the outcome based on the concept of "newness" – meaning Kennedy and his advisors made the decisions they did because they were new to the workings of the presidency. Essentially, the newness explanation states that new groups are vulnerable to group bias and other dynamics that can lead to less desirable outcomes. Groups have various stages of development. Traits, such as group norms, cohesion, power structure, roles, and decision rules, may not be well developed in the early stages of a group and may change over time. In short, the newness of Kennedy's group prevented it from questioning and challenging the CIA's assessment of the situation. This explanation works in tandem with Janis's rather than supplanting it. It is a key example of the *Beyond Groupthink* research agenda and how it combines and interacts with various group processes.

In another example of post-groupthink work, Preston and 't Hart (1999) link bureaucratic dynamics in groups to leadership characteristics in two decisions made during the Vietnam War. They asked why the president did not change his mind on Vietnam until 1968 when there were so many signals that things were not going well. The authors attribute part of the problem to the nature of the bureaucratic culture established under Johnson. The bureaucratic system in place was a reflection of the president's low cognitive complexity, lack of expertise in foreign policy, and great need for power (ibid.).

Groupthink and Multiple Advocacy

Alexander George (1980a) developed another possible solution to groupthink. His **multiple advocacy** model posits a loose decision structure in which the executive moderates a diversity of views. The central element of the model is that the person in charge, wanting to ensure that no decisions are reached before a policy leaves a department through a purely internal bargaining process, uses a "mixed-system" approach in which he or she advocates competition between agencies or individuals (Dougherty and Pfaltzgraff 1990, 472–473). The leader then chooses from among several policy options that have been openly debated by various agencies. A leader who fails to do this risks missing out on policy options that have been discounted before they can reach the top decision-making level.

The multiple advocacy model of the executive works best when three conditions are met: (1) intellectual (information, competence, technical support) and bureaucratic (bargaining skills, status, power) resources are evenly distributed; (2) the executive actively monitors the multiple-advocacy process; and (3) there is adequate time for debate and bargaining (George 1980a, 194).

George (1980a, 126–128) offers an example of the multiple advocacy model. In 1964, President Johnson had to decide whether to go forward with NATO's planned Multilateral Force (MLF). Prior to the decision, advisors had thrashed out a pro-MLF agreement among them and then presented a final proposal to the president after coercing other elements of the bureaucracy. If McGeorge Bundy, the president's special assistant for national security affairs, had not intervened, the president would not have been privy to the full menu of alternatives concerning the MLF. Bundy was able to divert the advisors' "end run" and invoke multiple advocacy by calling on presidential advisor Richard Neustadt to provide the president with an independent appraisal of the alternatives. The ultimate result was that the MLF plan was rejected.

Following the Bay of Pigs disaster, Attorney General Robert Kennedy suggested to President Kennedy that a devil's advocate be present at meetings to give an opposing opinion on a given situation. A devil's advocate is intended to limit the effect of groupthink on consensus-seeking behavior in groups.

POLYTHINK

Polythink is defined by Alex Mintz, Shaul Mishal, and Nadav Morag (2005) as a plurality of opinions, views, and perceptions of group members.[3] Polythink is the antithesis of groupthink. In their study, the authors asked the Israeli participants at the Camp David summit of 2000 among the Israelis, Palestinians, and Americans to "sketch" the decision matrices of the late Palestinian leader Yasser Arafat and Israeli prime minister Ehud Barak. To the authors' surprise, the interviews revealed the polythink syndrome – "multiple and varied perceptions of and opinions on the same issue by different group members" during Camp David 2000 (ibid., 3).

Polythink is characterized by varied and multiple views, opinions, and perceptions of the same goals and alternatives among group members. Polythink means "poly (many) ways of perceiving the same decision problem, goals and solutions." (ibid., 6). Polythink reflects group heterogencity. It can be contrasted with the homogenous, uniform, monolithic worldview of group members that characterizes groupthink.

Two symptoms of polythink are independence of thought and the existence of contradictory interests among group members. These may create a situation in which it becomes virtually impossible for group members to reach a common interpretation of reality and common policy goals (ibid.).

Polythink can be measured. One can determine empirically whether polythink exists in a group. "This can be done by comparing the content of the responses, as well as by examining the number of overlapping choice sets of alternatives and dimension sets (or considerations) of group members" (ibid., 8). Such an analysis can reveal the extent of overlap in the matrices, that is, "whether the alternative sets and dimension sets are (1) completely or (2) partially identical, or whether (3) there is little overlap between the choice sets and the dimension sets. Particularly disjointed delegations may produce the extreme opposite effect of groupthink, namely polythink" (ibid.).

---

[3] This section and the polythink case study that follows are based on Mintz, Mishal, and Morag (2005).

CASE STUDY: POLYTHINK AT CAMP DAVID, 2000

Mintz and colleagues (2005) asked each member of the Israeli delegation to consider each of the following issues:

1. The decision alternatives of President Arafat (the specific question was: What were Arafat's policy alternatives at Camp David 2000?)
2. The decision criteria (dimensions) of President Arafat (the specific question was: What were Arafat's decision dimensions at Camp David 2000?)
3. The decision alternatives of Prime Minister Barak (the specific question was identical to Question 1 but referred to Barak)
4. The decision criteria (dimensions) of Prime Minister Barak (the specific question was identical to Question 2 but referred to Barak)

On the basis of the delegates' responses, the authors generated eighteen decision matrices and compared the alternatives and dimensions of all delegates to determine whether members of the group exhibited similar (as with groupthink) or dissimilar (as with polythink) decision matrices.

The authors revealed that members of the delegation

lacked agreement regarding the Palestinian delegation's alternatives (acceptance of a permanent agreement, reaching a partial agreement, doing nothing, ensuring physical survival, etc.). Members of the delegation were also divided on how they viewed the dimensions or issues that the Palestinians had focused on during their talks with Israel (commitment to the Palestinian cause, regime survival, fear of an American/Israeli trap, Arafat's historical role, territorial concessions, domestic Israeli considerations, relations with the US, fear of physical attacks on negotiators, Jerusalem, Temple mount, the refugee problem, historical precedence of territorial withdrawals, and a Palestinian state). Some delegates sketched Arafat's choice set in a binary mode, while others in multi-categorical terms. A few identified decision dimensions and criteria in a binary mode while others in a non-binary, multi-dimensional framework. Some delegates sketched a comprehensive decision matrix for Arafat while others a relatively narrow one. There is little evidence that members of the Israeli delegation had homogenous and consistent, collective conception of what dimensions and issues were motivating the behavior of the Palestinian delegation or what alternatives the Palestinians could reasonably choose from. (ibid.)

To a lesser extent, members of the Israeli delegation

did not share a common conception as to which alternatives also constituted the actual choice set of former Prime Minister Barak and which dimensions and factors had the greatest impact on Israel's negotiating stance (e.g. desire for peace, regional considerations, domestic political considerations, the need to deny Arafat room for maneuver, the need to reveal true Palestinian intentions, Barak's historical role and personal considerations, pan-Arab coalitions, Israeli public opinion, security arrangements, Israel's international standing, or demographic considerations).(ibid.)

As is the case with groupthink, polythink may lead to the following problems:

1. Suboptimal decisions
2. Limited review of alternatives, objectives, and risks
3. Selective use of information
4. Paralysis in decision making

Several consequences of polythink are very different from those of groupthink (Mintz et al. 2005, 16–18):

1. There is greater likelihood for group conflict: because group members have different, sometimes even opposing views of the situation and of potential solutions, there is greater likelihood for group conflict due to polythink compared with groupthink, in which group members share more common views.
2. There is greater likelihood for leaks: because group members do not hold uniform views of the situation under polythink, they are more likely to leak information (e.g., to undermine positions that they oppose) than if it is a groupthink situation.
3. There is less likelihood for the group to speak in one voice: under polythink, there is greater likelihood that group members will talk to their counterparts, constituencies, and even the media in different voices, whereas under groupthink, in which members share a more uniform, common view of the situation and/or the solution to the situation, they are more likely to speak in one voice.
4. There is greater likelihood for framing effects: under polythink, some members may frame offers, proposals, counter-proposals and even disagreements in different ways. Some may give it a positive spin, whereas others may give it a negative spin. The likelihood of group members framing it in opposite directions when there is a group consensus as in groupthink is limited.
5. There is no room for error: compared with groupthink, under polythink, the group is less likely to revise its offers if and when they are turned down or presented with a counteroffer, because any updating of offers and proposals is less likely to result in a consensus relative to a groupthink situation, in which members share more or less the same position on things.
6. There is adoption of positions with lowest common denominator: polythink may create decision situations in which the lowest common denominator becomes the dominant product of the group. This is the

case because each member of the group needs to make concessions in his normative worldview and organizational and political agendas to reach an accommodation with other group members.

7. There is broader vision because of the plurality of opinions among group members: on the plus side, polythink is less likely to lead to the "narrowing of vision" syndrome that often characterizes groupthink."

The Camp David talks of 2000 revealed that constituencies, parties, bureaucracies, worldviews, beliefs, group leaders, and expertise place significant constraints on the freedom of action of negotiators and that the "psychological presence" of these audiences act to curtail the cognitive processes and information search by negotiators. Collective considerations had to compete in the mind of each delegate with other interest-based considerations (institutional, domestic political, and personal).

Did Polythink Lead to the Collapse of the Camp David Talks?

The authors' interviews with members of the Israeli delegation to Camp David 2000 showed that "they had a heterogeneous array of perceptions as to Palestinian and Israeli policy options and intentions at Camp David. There is no evidence to suggest however, that polythink among members of the Israeli delegation at Camp David 2000 was the reason for the collapse of the Camp David talks" (Mintz et al. 2005, 25). Polythink was not directly causal of the collapse of talks, but it certainly had an important influence in decisions.

Polythink created for the Israeli delegates a reality in which negotiations between and among Israelis themselves became no less important than the negotiations with the Palestinians (ibid.). Prime Minister Barak had to take into account the standing (in terms of domestic and bureaucratic politics and worldviews) of each of the Israeli delegates. His ability to assign authority and affect each of the Israeli delegates was therefore more limited (Sher 2001). Thus, whereas Barak required the help of aides in terms of expertise and information, he had limited the overall influence of these aides on the negotiating process (ibid.). In fact, it is well documented that some members of the Israeli delegation learned about some of Barak's proposals and plans only *after* he introduced them at Camp David (Pundak 2001).

Cannon-Bowers, Salas, and Converse (1993) claim that shared mental models increase the speed, accuracy, and flexibility in decision making by emphasizing the most salient dimensions. By contrast, the existence of multiple mental models within the collective body may create a bewildering array of considerations that each delegate must take into account. As coalitions are more brittle and issues more controversial, polythink becomes more relevant. Furthermore, the existence of multiple power bases, diverse institutional interests, and bureaucratic agendas within a delegation may serve as an "advance warning" for unsuccessful outcomes in negotiations. (Mintz et al. 2005)

The polythink model may potentially serve as a useful tool to explain negotiation processes of other countries and perhaps even help predict their outcomes. For example, in an April 2005 seminar organized by the Middle East Institute, four of the top U.S. officials who played a role in the peace negotiations during the Clinton administration (Dennis Ross, Robert Miller, Martin Indyk, and Rob Malley) each presented different views regarding the reasons for the failure of the Camp David talks, essentially pointing to the polythink syndrome among members of the American officials who played a role in the peace process. (ibid.)

In contrast, the Annapolis Summit in November 2007 triggered the opposite of what occurred at Camp David 2000. This is because in this round of negotiations the Palestinian leadership was more divided (Fatah vs. Hamas) and the Israeli government was more ideologically and politically centered, with a larger majority in parliament than the coalition Barak had during Camp David 2000. Hence, it is not surprising that in this round of negotiations, the Israeli leadership exhibited more signs of a homogenous position, whereas the Palestinian side exhibited signs of polythink. (ibid.)

Biases such as polythink affect information processing, perceptions, and misperceptions, and ultimately the choices leaders make.

GROUP POLARIZATION EFFECT

A risky shift phenomenon occurs when a group collectively agrees on a course of action that is more extreme than the course group members would have selected if asked individually. For example, members of an advisory group to the chief executive may have some negative views about a foreign policy act directed at a certain country. After deliberation, the group as a whole advocates even more aggressive acts toward that country.

Consider the case of the United States versus Iraq in the early 2000s. Members of the neoconservative advisory group to the Secretary of Defense, known as the U.S. Defense Policy Board Advisory Committee,[4] made negative assessments of Saddam's intentions (Sciolino and Tyler 2001). After deliberations that took place soon after 9/11, the group took a strong stance that advocated the removal of Saddam Hussein from power (ibid.).

Group polarization can also happen when each member of a group has peaceful attitudes in foreign policy. Together, such a group would typically advocate an even more dovish approach to the situation than would individual members alone. Consider the case of the United States and the Palestinian

[4] DPBAC, more commonly known as the Defense Policy Board.

Authority under Abu-Mazen (Mahmoud Abbas). Individual members of the Bush administration had positive opinions about Abu-Mazen. Collectively, after the group concluded its deliberations, it advocated even more supportive measures for Abbas than individual members would have recommended.

CONCLUSION

Humans see the world through various lenses that cause degrees of misperception and defective decision processes that are collectively known as biases. This chapter has outlined a number of these decision biases. We illustrated the influences of such biases on foreign policy decisions with several cases studies. Any analysis of FPDM that ignores bias will likely paint an incomplete picture.

PART THREE

MODELS OF DECISION MAKING

4

The Rational Actor Model

In this chapter, we look at models and approaches to FPDM that proceed from rational actor assumptions. We examine the expected utility model of war and some game-theoretic models such as the Prisoner's Dilemma, Chicken Game, and the Tit-for-Tat strategy.

The rational actor model is a linchpin of FPDM. Paul MacDonald (2003, 551) contends that many see it "as the most plausible candidate for a universal theory of political and social behavior, whose simple and intuitively plausible assumptions hold the promise of unifying the diverse subfields of political science." Whereas many scholars criticize the model, others strongly defend it. Before a model can be proposed based on its tenets or its underlying assumptions criticized, we must first understand it.

A rational approach extensively used in foreign policy analysis today, **expected utility theory** (EUT) sprang from the work of von Neumann and Morgenstern in the 1940s. The approach has its roots in microeconomics. The decision maker is assumed to be able to rank preferences "according to the degree of satisfaction of achieving these goals and objectives" (Sage 1990, 233). The rational actor is also expected to be able to identify alternatives and their consequences and to select from these alternatives in an effort to maximize satisfaction. In this setting, the rational economic decision maker is expected to be able to access a set of objectives and goals.

Allison Graham (1971, 30) defines rationality as a "consistent, value-maximizing choice within specified constraints." According to Allison (ibid., 29), and as mentioned in Chapter 2, the rational decision maker chooses the alternative that provides the consequence that is most preferred.

The brevity of this definition belies the strength of the model. The rational actor model is parsimonious. This means that a few rather straightforward assumptions, taken together, can explain a wide range of foreign policy decisions and actions (Schelling 1961; Powell 1987; B. Bueno de Mesquita et al. 2003). The model is primarily useful in explanations of economic behavior. MacDonald (2003, 552) summarizes the three parts of the rationality assumption. First, actors are assumed to employ **purposive action** motivated by goal-oriented behavior and not simply by habit or social expectations. The decision maker must be able to identify an a priori goal and move with the intention of reaching that objective. An unemployed person looking for a job is behaving purposively if he or she actively searches for work.

Second, actors display **consistent preferences** as manifested in the ability to rank the preferences in transitive order. **Transitivity** means that if Outcome 1 is preferred over Outcome 2, and 2 is preferred to 3, then 1 is preferred to 3. For example, if diplomacy is preferred to sanctions and sanctions are preferred to use of force, then diplomacy is preferred over the use of force (McDermott 2004a, 52–57). **Invariance** means that a decision maker's preference holds steady in the face of various means of information presentation (McDermott 2004a, 52–57). For example, sometimes information can be framed in a particularly leading manner. William Riker (1995, 24) observes that preference ordering is a hallmark of purposive behavior so that taken together these first two assumptions mean that actors must know what they want and be able to rank outcomes in relation to the goal. In other words, you need to know your destination if you hope to get there. Finally, and as noted by Allison (1971), **utility maximization** means that actors will select the alternative that provides the greatest amount of net benefits.

Greg Cashman (1993, 77–78) provides a useful set of steps in the rational model:

1. Identify problem
2. Identify and rank goals
3. Gather information (this can be ongoing)
4. Identify alternatives for reaching goals
5. Analyze alternatives by considering consequences and effectiveness (costs and benefits) of each alternative and probabilities associated with success
6. Select alternative that maximizes chances of selecting best alternative as determined in step five
7. Implement decision
8. Monitor and evaluate

A careful consideration of policy alternatives using the rational actor model does not automatically ensure a sound outcome. Experts and advisory groups often analyze policy dilemmas thoroughly but arrive at a suboptimal outcome. In general, the analytic process of the rational model should lead to better decisions, although not always to better outcomes (see Renshon and Renshon 2008).

Scholars distinguish between "thin" and "thick" rationality (Ferejohn 1991). **Thin rationality** simply denotes the strategic pursuit of stable and ordered preferences. Such preferences can be of any kind: selfish, self-destructive, or other. **Thick rationality** assumes, in contrast, that actors have specific preferences, in practice "mostly material self-interest or the preservation or augmentation of power; for politicians typically perpetuation in office" (Huber and Dion 2002, 1). Consequently, thin rationality can be applied in the study of a much wider range of human behavior and decisions than thick rationality can (ibid.).

As we describe in the next chapter, several alternative models challenge and question the rational actor model of FPDM. Although the rational actor model is parsimonious and elegant, its assumptions are often construed as unrealistic (Allison 1971, 30–31).

CASE STUDY: NEW ZEALAND'S DEFIANCE OF THE
UNITED STATES AND ANZUS

Sometimes leaders make decisions that seem to defy the rational ideal. For example, it may appear that Saddam Hussein was not rational in his defiance of the United States in 1990–1991 and again in the wake of 9/11. Is it rational for leaders of a small country to make a decision knowing it will undermine the credibility of its major military alliance? Was it rational for Argentina to attack a British possession (the Falkland Islands) in 1982? New Zealand made a decision in the 1980s that seems to defy rationality. We explore this decision and its implications in this brief case study.

For decades New Zealand was a full member of the tripartite Australia, New Zealand, United States Security Treaty (ANZUS) alliance. New Zealand is a democratic state with a strong record of cooperation with the United States. Since World War II, it served as a base for American planes and ships. The ANZUS treaty, signed in 1951, is a mutual defense pact in which each signatory agrees to come to the aid of any member that is under threat. New Zealand's goal in signing the Treaty was obviously to be secure. However, leading up to the ANZUS crisis, many New Zealanders came to oppose the nuclear deterrence doctrine being played out in the region.

Changes became apparent in the 1980s. The new Labour government of David Lange adopted a policy of preventing nuclear ship visits. This policy was reflective of a widespread opposition to nuclear weapons in the country. Such a policy meant that all visiting ships would be required to declare any nuclear capabilities. The United States put the new policy to the test in early 1985 with the request to allow a visit by the USS *Buchanan* (Pugh 1989). The New Zealand government formally rejected the request in February 1985 because the United States (per its policy) would neither confirm nor deny nuclear capability. New Zealand viewed this request as unreasonable and the ANZUS Treaty soon began to unravel. In August 1986, the United States informed New Zealand that it would no longer honor its mutual defense commitment (Pugh 1989, 2). As a result of the ANZUS crisis, the United Kingdom also backed away from its New Zealand security commitments. Thus, the decision to prevent nuclear visits undermined New Zealand's security during the Cold War. However, a more circumspect view is that by establishing itself as a promoter of international peace, New Zealand had conceivably increased its security and saved money that might otherwise have gone to expensive defense systems.

To an outside observer, it may not have appeared rational for New Zealand to walk away from the ANZUS Treaty and thereby signal that it did not consider U.S. protection essential to its security. This move was surprising to many because, even though New Zealand was geographically removed from the front lines of the Cold War, it did not have strong defenses against an attack. In addition, its actions threatened to precipitate negative economic actions from the United States. In the aftermath of the ANZUS break, U.S.–New Zealand relations deteriorated, and as of 2008 have not returned to pre-crisis levels.

The ANZUS break illustrates that domestic politics can be an important determinant of foreign policy decision making. Rational actor models depict states as unitary actors negotiating in an anarchic international system and constantly taking stock of their security status vis-à-vis rivals and other threats while maximizing their goal. Security decisions are informed by rational assessments of the security environment. If New Zealand had acted in the manner anticipated by the rational model, it would not have made a decision that conceivably undermined its security at a time when the Cold War was still active and the Soviets had recently invaded Afghanistan. In fact, what appears to have happened in New Zealand is that foreign policy became democratized and public opinion helped consolidate the antinuclear policy (Pugh 1989). If these domestic political considerations are taken into account, the break from ANZUS was not so surprising.

The debate over ANZUS continues today within New Zealand politics. Some New Zealanders feel vulnerable without U.S. protection in the post-9/11 world, whereas others feel it is safer to distance New Zealand from the United States and its wars in Afghanistan and Iraq. This latter stance is dramatically different from Australia's willingness to support the United States in these conflicts. The nuclear-free policy has become something of a sacred cow in New Zealand despite the country's chronic energy concerns. However, if the goal of New Zealand is to become environmentally green, then the decision makes sense.

THE EXPECTED UTILITY MODEL OF WAR DECISION MAKING

One of the most significant research programs that uses rational choice to predict international behavior was carried out by Bruce Bueno de Mesquita (1981) and colleagues. In his book *The War Trap* (1981) Bueno de Mesquita uses rational actor assumptions to create an expected utility theory (EUT) of international conflict. EUT assumes that decision makers "attempt to maximize expected utility in their choices between risky options: they weight the utilities of individual outcomes by their probabilities and choose the option with the highest weighted sum" (Levy 1992, 172–173). Thus, utility is maximized. In the EUT model, the utility scores associated with each outcome are multiplied by the probability of that outcome obtaining. The cells are summed for each alternative, and the alternative with the highest sum is selected to maximize utility (Maoz 1990a, 167). The EUT model is methodical, orderly, and comprehensive in its assessment of alternatives and implications (Maoz 1990a).

B. Bueno de Mesquita's EUT model posits that states will not go to war if the expected gains are smaller than expected losses. He tests the theory against data from the nineteenth and twentieth centuries, and his basic hypotheses are strongly supported. Rational, compensatory behavior processes are at the heart of the EUT model of decision making.

OPPORTUNITY COSTS

Economists tell us that costs matter. However, there are often trade-offs in decision making (Arrow 2007). Barry Schwartz (2004) makes the interesting observation that having too many choices can be bad. He notes that the high living standard in the United States comes with a cost. The myriad choices available to Americans in terms of recreation, jobs, food, living arrangements, cars, movies, music, and clothing can elicit opportunity costs that loom as losses. These losses are manifested as unhappiness. Thus, for some, there is a paradoxical relationship between higher living standards and lower feelings of contentment. The bad feelings are worse for those who try to maximize along the lines of the rational model. Individuals who are more likely to satisfice will not be as strongly affected.

At the height of the Cold War, nations had to decide whether to ally with the Soviet bloc (Warsaw Treaty Organization) or with the United States and its allies in NATO. Choosing one over the other entailed opportunity costs. Whereas the Bush administration called for stiff sanctions against Iran as a deterrent of its nuclear program and defiance of UN resolutions, the Russians and Chinese have emphasized the opportunity costs of not dealing with this oil-rich country.

Opportunity costs are likewise important in the context of civil war. For example, when a rebel army is beginning to form, each rebel (unless coerced) makes a decision about whether to join the rebellion. If the rebel has little educational or economic opportunity available to him, then opportunity costs to joining the rebellion are very low. The decision becomes harder (and the opportunity costs higher) when the potential rebel has to choose between going to university and living a life on the run in the jungle or mountains. This is one reason why there are fewer civil wars in developed countries.

Decisions by leaders of developing countries to spend large amounts of money on military equipment and soldiers carry with them high opportunity costs. The money that goes to defense could help bring the country out of poverty and provide educational opportunities for children (see UNICEF 1996).

Opportunity costs also affect the probability of interstate war. Jack Levy (2001) notes that the Kantian argument that trade promotes peace is based on opportunity costs. Each country in a trade relationship derives some utility from the arrangement. War would disrupt this arrangement, so opportunity costs of war are higher for trading states.

GAME-THEORETIC MODELS

Game theory is more a method that can help us understand decision making than it is an actual theory. Simply put, game theory helps us to see the choices states have when dealing with each other. It puts their choices into a strategic perspective because it lets us see how an actor's decision is contingent on the other actors' past or expected behavior. The game format simplifies complicated relationships by uncovering equilibria among the players (Maoz 1990a, 26). It can also help us to understand or predict behavior between states that is sometimes counterintuitive.

All game models must identify,

> at least implicitly, the players, the rules of the game (i.e., what choices the actors can make, when, and with what information), the outcomes associated with every combination of possible moves, the players' payoffs for these outcomes, and solution concept (a set of axioms specifying the considerations that guide behavior and the characteristics of the predicted result of the play of the game). (Morgan, 2004, 33)

Game theory is built on the rational actor assumption. Studies that use game theory to understand FPDM usually portray states as the unit of analysis, although much recent game-theoretic work in international relations treats nonstate actors as players as well. Game theorists often analyze policies as influenced by both domestic and international factors. Some games are modeled with two levels to capture actions at both domestic and international arenas (Putnam 1999).

In making foreign policy decisions, leaders look inside at domestic politics – elections, public opinion, the bureaucracy, and many other internal factors – as well as international factors that influence foreign policy decisions – deterrence, the arms race, the regime type of the adversary, and so on. For example, game theory has shown why democratic leaders are less likely to back down in crises. The game reveals that the threats made by democracies are more credible because of audience costs (Fearon 1994a). Democracies stand to lose more if they send a costly signal to an adversary – such as a threat – and then back down. This behavior by democratic states can account in part for the relations between democracies (Fearon 1994a). The signaling of audience costs has also been used in a game theory approach to model decisions made by challengers and defenders in an immediate deterrence setting (in which there are three states: defender, challenger, and protégé (Fearon 1994b). In this case, "costly signals" sent by both challenger and defender to domestic audiences are important. If the defender is more powerful, the challenger is more likely to threaten a nonvital interest of the defender. This situation enables a costly signal that the defender is committed to protecting the protégé. It is this costly signal that does the actual deterring. These influential studies of crisis behavior demonstrate the importance of understanding the strategic foreign policy behavior of states over and above standard explanations of balance of capabilities and national interests.

With regard to game-theoretic work on nonstate actors as players, one influential study examines the selectorate (voters who put leaders in office) and the government (B. Bueno de Mesquita et al. 2003). The selectorate is the group that is responsible for keeping a leader in office. It expects benefits from the leader it put in office. In a democracy this group is, by definition, rather large. Dictators, in contrast, rely on a much smaller selectorate. The size of the selectorate has important implications for foreign policy behavior. Democratic leaders have a more tenuous hold on their selectorate, and this scenario should make for better government and, subsequently, more sound foreign policy decisions. The reverse is true for autocracies. The paradox is that democratic leaders provide better leadership and are more prone to peace but have shorter tenures (ibid.). The game can also be applied to a host of applications beyond foreign policy such as welfare spending, civil liberties, and corruption.

Another application of game theory is to demonstrate how foreign policy decisions might be swayed by election prospects. If a government is facing a close election, it is more likely to favor bold foreign initiatives. For this reason, its potential target states will be on their best behavior when a potential attacker is facing a close election (Smith 1996). This model can help us to understand foreign policy decision making in both states.

Game theory has been used to demonstrate that opposition parties are important players. When a democratic government has strong support from the public – including the opposition – a strong signal is conveyed to potential adversaries. The resolve of the democracy is perceived as very credible, potential adversaries are likely to back down, and there is no war (Schultz 2001). However, Saddam Hussein could not be compelled to withdraw from Kuwait despite the threat of a U.S.-led attack.

Game theory has been applied to the analysis of decisions by terrorists and the government. One of the puzzling observations about terrorists is that many are educated and relatively prosperous. This belies the common conception of the poverty-stricken, uneducated suicide bomber driven to acts of desperation. One study uses game theory modeled with the government, the terrorist organization, and a number of volunteers as the players, for insights to this seeming paradox (E. Bueno de Mesquita 2005). The study finds that terrorists are screened from among a number of volunteers and that more educated ones get selected. In other words, there is a bias inherent in looking at only the actual operatives who carry out missions. For every completed mission, there are several volunteers who were not chosen. The author argues that socioeconomics are a factor in terrorism that should be considered when agencies and governments are making counterterrorism and economic aid decisions.

Prisoner's Dilemma

The most common game is the **Prisoner's Dilemma**, an example of one-shot decision making. In this scenario, two suspects are arrested on suspicion of carrying out a serious crime. The suspects are interrogated separately. They each have one choice. They can accept a plea bargain deal offered by the police. This deal would mean testifying against the other suspect. Or they can refuse the deal and stay loyal to their partner. Staying loyal to the partner might be costly because there is no guarantee the partner will reciprocate.

This simple decision example takes place in an environment of incomplete information. This means that neither suspect knows what the other is doing. They cannot communicate before making their decision. Because the players do not know what the other is doing, they will choose the best outcome regardless of what the other player does. The result is that each will choose to take the plea bargain. This is known as **minimax** behavior. Each player is acting to avoid the worst outcome that could result from the other player's actions. Because each takes the deal, the police do not need to offer a generous deal to either. If the players could have communicated, they could have agreed not to take the deal, and both would have done better because there would have been no testimony to link either to the serious crime.

Figure 4.1 depicts the prisoner's dilemma and its payoffs. Each player has one decision: to cooperate (with the other prisoner) or defect (and give testimony against the other prisoner).

Payoffs:

−5 This is the worst payoff. The prisoner who gets this is a sucker because he will get harsh punishment for the serious crime after the other prisoner testifies against him.

		Prisoner 2	
		Cooperate	Defect
Prisoner 1	Cooperate	2, 2	−5, 5
	Defect	5, −5	−2, −2

Figure 4.1. The Prisoner's Dilemma.

−2 This is better than the sucker payoff but still represents a loss because it results in a short jail sentence after being charged with a lesser crime.

2 This payoff represents a slightly positive outcome because the prisoner takes the deal offered by police and is offered leniency.

5 The prisoner who takes the deal offered by the police gets this favorable payoff if the other prisoner refuses the deal and cooperates with his partner.

The payoffs are arbitrary numbers that convey a general sense of the utility of each outcome. A payoff of −5 represents significant loss. This payoff represents a long jail sentence. The cell highlighted in gray in Figure 4.1 represents the Nash equilibrium, which means neither prisoner could improve payoff with a unilateral shift (Maoz 1990a, 393). Each player has a dominant strategy to defect because without knowing what the other player will do, defecting avoids the worst outcome. The equilibrium can be better understood by looking only at Player 1's payoffs. A 5 is better than 2 in the first column and a −2 is better than −5 in the second column. Thus, defecting results in a better outcome regardless of what the other player does. The same exercise can be done from Player 2's perspective by covering Player 1's payoffs in the rows. If the players could communicate, they might have ended up in the upper left cell, each receiving the second best outcome. Viewing the actual game structure helps us to see this.

Of course, examples like this rarely, if ever, obtain in the real world, but researchers use such games to help explain and understand the underpinnings of decision. In this case, the Prisoner's Dilemma game can help us to understand why decision makers could choose a less-than-optimal option. The game is an excellent example of how being rational does not necessarily lead to the best outcome. As simplifications of reality, games are often criticized as too simplistic. For example, the one-shot assumption is quite unrealistic, and it is not easy to identify such cases in the real world.

Chicken

The **Chicken Game** is commonly used to depict strategic and rational behavior. The popular narrative for this game is as follows. Two drivers are facing each other in cars. They will drive toward each other head-on, and whoever swerves is the loser. If they both swerve, they each lose but avoid the worst outcome of a head-on crash. If only one driver swerves, he loses relatively more than if both had swerved. The driver who does not swerve in that situation would be the winner. So the payoff structure is ranked as: winner (other driver swerves), survivor (both swerve), sucker (other driver wins), and crash (neither swerve).

Chicken is more complicated than Prisoner's Dilemma. Although it would seem that swerving is the right thing to do, if the player wants to win, he could risk thinking the other player would choose the rational alternative of swerving. For this reason the game provides two Nash equilibria – one for each outcome in which one driver swerves (Maoz 1990a). These equilibria represent outcomes in which neither player can gain by changing strategy while the other player maintains his.

To win at Chicken, a player must signal that he is willing to pay any cost to avoid losing. This signaling is known as **precommitment** ("Chicken Game," wikipedia.org). In the case of Chicken, the most obvious precommitment signal would be disabling your steering wheel. These signals establish credibility by showing the other driver that you will not swerve. For this reason, the Chicken game has implications for **brinksmanship** behavior between states. Essentially, brinksmanship means a continuous escalation of threat to prevent the other player from defecting (not swerving). Brinksmanship was a policy of the superpowers during the Cold War.

Tit-for-Tat

Robert Axelrod (1984) convened a tournament to determine the winning strategy for dealing with the Prisoner's Dilemma. The winner of the tournament would be the computer program that generated the most points in an iterated setting. This means that the game was played over time rather than in the typical one-shot mode. The tournament's winning strategy was a simple **Tit-for-Tat** program. It cooperated in the first move and simply repeated the other player's move thereafter. Tit-for-Tat rewarded cooperation and immediately punished defection. The game showed that even if two states had slipped into uncooperative behavior, over time cooperation could emerge as long as each player expected a long time horizon (B. Bueno de Mesquita 2003).

There may be short-term benefits to not cooperating, but unlike the one-shot Prisoner's Dilemma, over the long run, cooperation becomes a reward if Tit-for-Tat is used in an iterated setting. Cooperation becomes a stable equilibrium.

The key to the success of Tit-for-Tat is that it creates credibility so that cooperative moves will be seen as shows of good faith as long-term strategies become transparent (B. Bueno de Mesquita 2003, 142). A cooperative equilibrium cannot be reached using Tit-for-Tat if the game only lasts for a few rounds. As the game of known length approaches its last move, it is rational for each player to want to defect. In fact, each party will defect in the first round out of fear; they will never be able to avoid being the sucker in the future (recall in the original game that this was the prisoner who rejected the deal from police) and gain the cooperation payoff (ibid).

CONCLUSION

This chapter probed the rational actor model. The model is central to the study of politics, economics, psychology and several other fields. It is attractive because of its parsimony and predictive power. That is, it relies on only a few relatively straightforward assumptions to explain and predict a wide variety of decisions. Among other models, the rational model is the basis of game theory and EUT. For all of its merits, the model continues to attract criticisms. This is the subject of the next chapter.

5

Alternatives to the Rational Actor Model

In this chapter, we look at alternatives to the rational actor models (see Table 5.1). We focus on bounded rationality and the cybernetic model, bureaucratic politics, organizational politics, and prospect theory.[1] Next we take an in-depth look at a model that combines elements of the rational and cognitive schools – poliheuristic theory. We then analyze the case study of the 1991 U.S. decision not to invade Iraq through six models of decision making. Finally, we discuss the Applied Decision Analysis (ADA) procedure.

BOUNDED RATIONALITY AND THE CYBERNETIC MODEL

The cognitive and rational schools offer different understandings of decision making. Herbert Simon (1985) came up with interesting anthropological-like terms to distinguish rational and cognitive decision makers. He coined the terms *Homo economicus* to refer to the former, and *Homo psychologicus* to refer to the latter. Simon distinguished cognitive models on the basis that they assume decision makers have limited information-processing capabilities. Instead of objectively searching all information for the best outcome, decision makers will select an alternative that is acceptable. This is the satisficing behavior described in Chapter 2. Whereas the rational school focuses on the maximizing behavior and the comparison of costs and benefits, the cognitive school probes how humans make decisions and learn in a bounded rational environment. Furthermore, the cognitive school takes into account that humans are selective in the information they use in decision making, use incomplete search processes, and are more likely to select a satisfactory rather than an optimal alternative (Simon 1985, 295).

---

[1] Mintz (2005a; 2007b) introduced **behavioral international relations** (BIR), which is a unified paradigm consisting of "everything which is not rational choice theory": prospect theory, poliheuristic theory, cybernetic theory, operational code analysis, leadership psychology, emotions, biases and misperceptions, images, information processing, framing effects, etc. Behavioral IR is process oriented and involves satisficing.

Table 5.1. *Alternatives to the rational actor model*

Bounded rationality and the cybernetic model
Bureaucratic politics
Organizational politics
Prospect theory
Poliheuristic theory

Simon argues that humans are boundedly or procedurally rational. **Bounded rationality** is **procedural** in that it is behavior "adaptive within the constraints imposed both by the external situation and the capacities of the decision maker" (Simon 1985, 294). Classical rationality, in contrast, can be thought of as **substantive** because it relates to the nature of the outcome rather than the substance of the process of arriving at an outcome. Miriam Steiner (1983) notes that bounded rationality is still rational but that the biological and psychological limits humans face make it more likely that we will take cognitive shortcuts and quite possibly not find the optimal outcome.

If decision makers do not consider all information in exhaustive search processes, how does the human mind make sense of the complicated world? Simon argued that classical rationality applied in "slow—moving situations where the actor has a single, operational goal," but in more complex situations, rational explanations are inadequate (Simon 1959, 279). High information costs drive actors to evaluate alternatives and accept one on the basis of satisficing (Simon 1959, 262–263).

In the **cybernetic** decision-making model, uncertainty is minimized through the use of information feedback loops (Steinbruner 1974, 51). The cybernetic approach suggests that decision makers lack the fundamental cognitive skills needed to carry out the rational model during complex problem-solving situations (Steiner 1983, 423). The cybernetic paradigm precludes the need to calculate optimal procedures and alternatives on the basis of preferred outcomes by eliminating alternatives and ignoring the environment and the issue of variety (Steinbruner 1974, 56–57). The decision maker understands the decision as a simple one that does not require elaborate mental processing. There is no need to dwell on the calculation of the probability of all possible outcomes because there is not expected to be a wide variety of outcomes (Dougherty and Pfaltzgraff 1990, 479–481). The cybernetic decision maker filters out extraneous information and therefore is only focused on a narrow range of incoming information. With only a few options available, the cybernetic approach takes on the appearance of a programmed response.

John Steinbruner notes that the rational paradigm is a powerful one, but has limitations. Some actions cannot be easily accounted for with rational explanations. For example, the Japanese attack on Pearl Harbor and the Egyptian advances on Israel in 1967 seem to defy rationality (Steinbruner 1974, 47).

The cybernetic paradigm is designed to address these seemingly complex and counterintuitive decision processes. The rational framework largely ignores uncertainty as it assumes that "the range of possible outcomes is known, and thereby eliminates the possibility that an outcome might occur which was not even visualized in advance. It assumes that [in] complex problems neither of these assumptions can be held" (Steinbruner 1974, 18). The cybernetic approach is necessary because decision makers lack the fundamental cognitive skills needed to carry out the rational schema during the structural, uncertainty–laden policy problems of our time (Steiner 1983, 423).

The cybernetic model can also be applied at the group level. Agencies do not undertake wholesale reevaluation and self-monitoring but rather only make adjustments at the margins (Cashman 1993). With this framework in mind, decisions that must go through large agencies are broken into smaller units that are then handled by subunits of the agency (Dougherty and Pfaltzgraff 1990, 480–481).

Steinbruner (1974; see also Dougherty and Pfaltzgraff 1990, 479–480) provides several examples of cybernetic decision making in the everyday world. The tennis player striking the ball without consciously making hundreds of mental calculations each time a shot is made is an excellent example. There is no need to make complicated calculations each time a shot is made because the player relies on information stored in feedback loops. As we discuss elsewhere, organizational decision making also has elements of the cybernetic process to the extent that choices are made on the basis of minor tweaking of policies.

The rational paradigm might explain the tennis player's actions by wrongly assigning him the ability to make unconscious calculations every time the ball is struck. This explanation, however, is an example of the tautology that lies beneath the surface of many rational explanations. This is because rationality is often described in terms of the final outcome. However, if the outcome cannot be measured independently of the decision process, a tautology obtains. We cannot be sure the tennis player was acting rationally just because he or she hit a lob over the opponent's head – the ball may have been mishit. Put differently, if there is not a means of establishing utility values independently, the postulate that decision makers will always choose the alternative that maximizes utility is a tautology (Steinbruner, 1974: 28).

BUREAUCRATIC POLITICS

Despite its applicability to many situations, a host of factors disrupt or cloud the rational ideal. In his classic work on the Cuban Missile Crisis, Graham Allison (1971, 257) notes that the rational model leads analysts to ascertain the nature of the problem and the alternatives, costs, and benefits associated with each alternative. However, Allison notes other questions might be just as important and shows us how international events can be understood using two other decision models. Analysts might be interested in determining which organizations constitute the government and how these agencies collect the necessary information to perform their duties. Another category of questions might probe the identity of the key players involved, as well as their personalities and political clout. These additional two models are the **bureaucratic politics** and **organizational politics** models. Unlike the rational actor model, these models represent decentralized processes that involve various actors in various agencies. Bureaucratic decision models look at the impact of organizational structure on decision making. These models do not focus on factors such as perception, personality, and rationality (Mandel 1986, 258).

The bureaucratic politics model (sometimes called the **governmental model**) looks at how decisions involving various bureaucracies can elicit political competition. Max Weber pointed out these facts more than a century ago. The key to this model is that there is no overarching master plan and that decisions emerge from political struggle and bargaining between groups (Dougherty and Pfaltzgraff 1990, 477). Thus, foreign policy decisions emerge through an abstract political space rather than a formal decision procedure that relies on a formal chain of command. The actors in the bureaucratic politics model are key individuals sitting atop key organizations, each of which is trying to maximize its interests, agendas, and goals. In contrast to the rational actor model described by Allison (1971), however, the bureaucratic politics model assumes multiple organizations and bureaucracies rather than a single actor.

Bureaucracies are hierarchical organizations that jealously protect their own turf by controlling policy in their area of expertise. Decision makers even have the incentive to negotiate internally with each other before presenting alternatives to the executive (George 1972). The process may affect which information is presented to the leader and may even restrict information on additional policy options available to the leader. As Jonathan Renshon and Stanley Renshon (2008, 518) point out, bureaucracies are likely to limit the search for information and alternatives. Bureaucracies strive to grow so their expertise monopoly can be further consolidated. Turf wars can even result in one agency being swallowed up by a larger agency. The U.S. Arms Control and Disarmament Agency (ACDA) was created as a small, independent executive branch agency in the early 1960s. After at least one failure, the State Department was successful in pushing through legislation that put the ACDA in the State Department.

When an issue comes along that straddles more than one agency, personalities and agency clout become deciding factors. Larger-than-life figures, such as J. Edgar Hoover or Henry Kissinger, have inordinate power in these situations.

Bureaucratic decisions are not cut and dry. There are winning coalitions/individuals and losing coalitions/individuals. The losing side might not accept its loss and attempt to prevail despite the reality of the situation. This can lead to fragmented decision making (Cashman 1993). General Douglas MacArthur, for example, made decisions that went against his civilian superiors in Washington during the Korean War. Ultimately he was relieved of duty by President Truman. The bureaucratic politics model is most applicable when there is time for political wrangling to take shape. Jerel Rosati (1981) refers to the process as pluralistic because it is generally open to input from various agencies and individuals. The outcome is a result of a compromise.

Issues that cut across policy areas will often elicit political struggles within and among agencies. Agency pursuit of self-interest affects how information is searched and how decisions are made.

Midlevel policy decisions are well represented by the bureaucratic politics model. There is typically not enough time for bureaucratic politics to play out during crises. However, decisions such as President Bush's long-term policies of dealing with terror in the wake of 9/11 involve multiple agencies and important reorganizations. For example, as discussed in Chapter 1, the Federal Emergency Management Administration (FEMA) became part of a new cabinet agency known as Homeland Security. Like ACDA, FEMA had been autonomous before this reorganization. In the wake of Hurricane Katrina in 2005 and its devastating impact on New Orleans, evidence of turf wars and the difficulties of reorganization became apparent.

Morton Halperin (1974) provides an interesting bureaucratic politics model of presidential decision making and policy implementation. He notes that presidents, except during rare events such as the Cuban Missile Crisis, usually do not indicate specific actors, methods, or timetables when they make decisions. Presidents make vague decisions after considerable delays and typically do not offer a coherent plan that is applicable to a range of related issues.

Halperin provides an example of his model using President Johnson's decision on the antiballistic missile system (ABM) in the 1960s. The decision reveals the politics and coalition building inherent in the bureaucratic model. The decision involved great discretion in the president's release of information and his stand on the issue, and the president sent out mixed signals throughout the decision process. These mixed signals were manifested in three apparently different purposes for the system. Ostensibly, the president wanted funding for the system but would delay deployment pending an arms talk with the Soviets; Secretary of Defense Robert McNamara argued for the system for protection against the Soviets; the Joint Chiefs of Staff and key senators on the Armed Services Committee wanted it for protection against the Chinese; and the system eventually authorized was designed to protect cities against a Soviet attack. Halperin demonstrates that President Johnson was able to use vague decision making to maintain a coalition between Secretary of Defense McNamara, the Joint Chiefs of Staff, and Senate Armed Services Chairman Richard Russell. The president played his cards close to his chest so that each side thought he was championing its cause. In this sense, the bureaucratic model took on conflict-solving properties.

In Halperin's ABM example the president leaned toward a particular strategy, but he did not overtly fight for it or release specific details or implementation strategies. He simply let his general view and position be known and then allowed the bureaucracy and Congress to fight over it with the assumption that the final policy or decision would pass over his desk for ultimate approval (Halperin 1974). This approach is similar to Churchill's famous order during World War II that reports be brought to him on index cards because he had no time for details.

In Halperin's bureaucratic politics model, the president is reined in by the bureaucracy. Presidential policy goals must be communicated to department heads to begin the implementation process. There is no direct and simultaneous presidential policy mechanism. The result of this effect is evidenced by the ABM policy decision. The ABM decision was shaped by the president's general policy desires, which in turn set the process in motion. The ambiguous nature of the president's goals served to preclude any single actor's views from dominating the decision process (ibid., 306).

"Where you stand depends on where you sit" (Allison 1969, 711). When Ariel Sharon was national infrastructure minister and housing minister of Israel, he was the force behind the settlements movement in the West Bank and Gaza. However, as a prime minister, Sharon's famous quote was, "things that you see from here [(i.e., the prime minister's office)], you don't see from there." Conversely, Ehud Barak, as Israel's prime minister, offered the Palestinians deep concessions at Camp David 2000. However, as a defense minister in Prime Minister Olmert's government, he has highlighted the danger of giving up territory to the Palestinians in the West Bank because it can endanger Israel's security.

ORGANIZATIONAL POLITICS

Decisions are also made within agencies. The key dynamic in the **organizational politics** model is **standard operating procedures** (SOPs). SOPs tend to govern mundane issues that low-level bureaucrats can handle. However, important decisions, such as long-term budget making, might be considered through the organizational lens. Often governmental decisions involve little uncertainty, are not crisis decisions, and are made on the basis of some a priori guideline or administrative rule. Graham Allison (1971; cited in Dougherty and Pfaltzgraff 1990, 487) pulls several examples of this form of decision making from the Cuban Missile Crisis. Upon installing the missiles in Cuba, the Soviets did not make immediate efforts to hide the medium-range ballistic missiles despite the fact they were aware of America's ability to use high-altitude U-2 surveillance planes. Further, the Soviets did not preinstall radar or surface-to-air missiles to defend the missile sites. Allison interprets this as a clear example of organizational decision making with its attendant SOPs. In the past, the

Soviets had installed similar missile sites in the USSR without attention to radar or camouflage. These were not seen as vital on Soviet soil. So when the time came for the same agency to install missile sites, they followed SOP. In this instance, SOP was a miserable failure for the Soviets.

David Braybrooke and Charles Lindblom (1963) describe an organizational decision dynamic known as **incrementalism**. This dynamic is conservative in that it entails only minor fine tuning of past decisions rather than a broad exploration of policy alternatives. Incrementalism leads to decisional inertia because the same alternatives are accepted over and over (Mandel 1986, 259). Because there is no large deviation from past choices, there is little chance of catastrophic failure resulting from one decision. Although low-risk, if left unmonitored, incrementalism can get out of control. Many have attributed the U.S. experience in Vietnam to incrementalism run amok (Cashman 1993). Most budgeting decisions can be characterized as incremental. The hugely complicated U.S. defense budget in any given year, for example, might largely be a reflection of last year's budget with minor adjustments for inflation and other reasons. Note that incrementalism does not ensure that utility is maximized as it is in the rational actor model.

Because incremental decisions only make for small changes in the status quo, they rarely completely solve problems, but rather provide temporary solutions. Braybrooke and Lindblom (1963, 71) assert that this is the typical kind of problem solving encountered in everyday politics. Decision makers using incremental approaches can compartmentalize problems so that problems can be isolated and politically acceptable solutions found. In this regard, the American two-party system provides abundant examples of incrementalism. A policy is decided on for a certain problem, the policy is altered by the other party, then tried, then altered again, and so on (ibid., 73). The two-party system yields slow, incremental solutions to policy problems, exemplified by the recent debate on immigration in the United States.

Graham Allison's *Essence of Decision* (1971) had a major impact on the study of FPDM. Two criticisms of Allison's three models stand out. The first critique, by Stephen Krasner (1972), mainly questioned the bureaucratic politics model. Krasner strongly challenged the notion that the president's power could be circumvented by the bureaucracy. He makes the point that several key members of Kennedy's Executive Committee (e.g., Dean Acheson and Robert Kennedy) were not representing bureaucratic interests but rather were more directly answering to the president. Krasner notes that bureaucracies are beholden to the president and that makes them less likely to maintain private agendas. He concludes that President Kennedy was firmly in control of events.

A more recent critique of Allison painstakingly dissects each of the three models (Bendor and Hammond 1992). These authors conclude that the rational actor model is poorly specified and was practically set up to fail. Because the ensuing two models are compared to the rational model, this problem is magnified. In the organizational model, Allison wrongly assumes SOPs are constraining when the literature typically considers them to be enabling. The bureaucratic politics model is excessively complicated. Furthermore, studies of bureaucracies often employ rational choice models. Bendor and Hammond conclude that *Essence of Decision* is still relevant but that readers should use caution. In conclusion, the bureaucratic politics model has supporters and detractors and is best applied to midlevel policy decisions.[2]

PROSPECT THEORY

Since its formulation by Daniel Kahneman and Amos Tversky (1979), **prospect theory** has become a leading psychological theory of decision making. Prospect theory holds that people are risk-averse with respect to gains and risk-acceptant with respect to losses (Kahneman and Tversky 1979). Prospect theory was posited as an alternative to EUT (described in Chapter 4) and other rational models that are based on levels of assets. Prospect theory is built around deviations from a reference point. Gains and losses of asset levels are critical (Levy 2000, 194).

Prospect theory has broad implications for international relations. Karl DeRouen Jr. (1995) invoked prospect theory to account for uses of military force when presidents are in political trouble. Rose McDermott (1992) used prospect theory to describe the events surrounding President Carter's attempt to rescue hostages in 1980. The rescue operation was risky, but Carter was in a domain of political loss leading up to the 1980 election. Glen Biglaiser and Karl DeRouen Jr. (2004) show that Latin American leaders in domains of political loss (high inflation) are more likely to adopt the risky option of liberal economic reform (see also Weyland 1996).

As mentioned, the domain of the decision maker is central to prospect theory. An example Jack Levy (1992, 174) draws from Kahneman and Tversky's experimental work illustrates this point. One group of subjects was presented with a scenario that invoked a domain of gain. These subjects were told to choose from among a guaranteed outcome of $3,000, a 20 percent chance of nothing, or an 80 percent chance of receiving $4,000. Eighty percent chose the sure outcome. Another group was presented information in a domain of loss. They chose from among an 80 percent chance of losing $4,000, a 20 percent chance of losing nothing, or a certain loss of $3,000. Ninety-two percent took the gamble. Levy notes that while EUT would have predicted preference for higher value outcomes, in both cases subjects tended to prefer

---

[2] For example, many scholars rely on principal-agent models to explain the relationship between managers (principals) and subordinates (agents) in the midst of information asymmetries and different interests (see, e.g., De Groot 1988).

the outcome with a lower value. This experiment provides evidence of **loss aversion**. Prospect theory suggests that avoiding loss is more important than securing gain. Individuals cherish what they possess and are wary of losing what they already have. The **endowment effect** is the name given to the high value people place on what they currently possess.

Prospect theory comprises two phases (Levy 1992). In the **editing phase**, the decision is presented and options are identified. The outcomes and their associated probabilities are also ascertained. **Framing** effects occur in this phase because prospect theory asserts that the way the decision information is presented can affect the choice. This assertion runs counter to the rational model's insistence that the order and method of information are not critical determinants of the choice (McDermott 2004a). Thus, information can be framed in such a way as to change the decision outcome.

Levy (2000, 195–197) provides an example, based on work of Kahneman and Tversky, of how framing can shape a choice. In this example, subjects are presented two very different versions of a scenario. In one version, subjects are told that an Asian disease has broken out and is predicted to kill six hundred people. There are two programs being considered for dealing with the crisis. The first program will save two hundred people. In the second program, there is a 33 percent chance that all will be saved and a 67 percent chance no one will be saved. In the second version, one program will result in four hundred deaths, and in the other, there is a 33 percent probability that no one will die and a 67 percent probability that all six hundred will die. The difference in the two scenarios is that the first group receives information framed in terms of survival. The second group receives information framed in terms of mortality. The results from the experiment reveal how framing can change the dynamics of the decision. The survival-framed group overwhelmingly selected the less risky first choice. The results were reversed when information was framed in terms of mortality. The subjects were more likely to select the riskier second option. Thus, this experiment provides empirical evidence that decision makers are more risk averse in the domain of gain and risk acceptant in the domain of loss. Framing is taken up in greater detail in Chapter 7.

In the second phase of prospect theory, the **evaluation phase**, a choice is made. This choice is based on the reference point and the value or utility function. As stated, prospect theory considers changes from the reference point as critical. EUT is not sensitive to change from a reference point. The example McDermott (2004a, 71) supplied involves a person who ended up with $1,001. From a prospect theory perspective, if the person started with $1, he would be much happier than if he had started with $1,000. Change from the starting value would not factor into the EUT account. The value curve for individuals can take different shapes depending on risk propensity. The curve is concave for gains, reflecting an aversion to risk. The curve is convex for losses, reflecting a willingness to take risk to recover losses (Levy 1992, 173). If the actor is risk neutral the value/utility curve is linear.

Arab and Israeli students in Israel participated in an experiment on the effect of negative versus positive framing on the consequences of peace between Israel and Syria. When the situation was framed as a gain (Israel withdrawal from the Golan Heights will lead, with 90 percent certainty, to peace), more students supported the withdrawal alternative than when the situation was framed as a loss (Israeli withdrawal from the Heights would lead, with 10 percent certainty, to war; Mintz and Geva 1997).

Sunk Costs

Related to prospect theory is the concept of **sunk costs**. Such costs often cause leaders to continue on a certain path even when circumstances change for the worse. Examples include presidents Lyndon Johnson in Vietnam, George W. Bush in Iraq, and Israeli leaders in Lebanon following the 1982 invasion. This process is known as "irrational escalation of commitment." It occurs when leaders "continue to persevere in losing or failing ventures, often pouring more and more valuable resources into them, in the hopes of eventual success. This is nonrational because cost-benefit calculations should not include resources *already* expended (i.e., sunk costs), and yet individuals have a very difficult time disregarding this factor" (Renshon and Renshon 2008, 538). In other words, throwing good money after bad does not make sense.

The costs already incurred by the U.S. involvement in Iraq represent sunk costs, which are typically difficult to reverse. The war in Iraq is an example of how sunk costs can influence subsequent decision making. Barry Schwartz (2005) observes that President Bush invokes the deaths of the thousands of Americans who have died in the war to justify continued U.S. military involvement. He also notes similar statements made during the Vietnam War to support prolonging that action. Sunk costs make it harder to reverse an unsuccessful move.

Terrorist organizations that build infrastructure for their actions and recruit members often have difficulty stopping acts of terrorism even when circumstances change because of the sunk costs incurred in building the organization.

Once the purchase of an item has been made, it has a "sunk cost." Expensive military projects such as the Israeli Lavi fighter jet show how sunk costs influence important policy decisions. In this case, the Israeli government kept funding the program long after it became clear the project was not cost effective. Eventually, it terminated the project. Sunk costs can translate to opportunity costs. For example, in funding the Lavi, the Israeli government did not fund many other programs that could have contributed to the strength of Israel Defense Forces.

INTEGRATING THE RATIONAL AND COGNITIVE MODELS:
POLIHEURISTIC THEORY

Allison (1971, 258–259) argues that elements of the rational, organizational, and bureaucratic politics models should be combined to explain decisions. Rather than using the three models side by side, Mintz suggests combining the cognitive and rational schools to form the **poliheuristic** decision model. The poliheuristic model is a two-step process. In the first step, the decision maker reduces the set of alternatives while using cognitive shortcuts. In the next step, the rational approach is used to select from the remaining alternatives. Thus, a decision has two components. The poliheuristic model is innovative in that decision makers simplify their environment in the face of stress and time constraints by making decisions in two steps.

The leading decision paradigm in international relations is the rational actor, expected utility theory (see B. Bueno de Mesquita 1981). Another influential paradigm is the bounded-rational cybernetic approach (see Steinbruner 1974; 2002). Poliheuristic theory is a bridge between rational and cognitive perspectives. Some decisions involve vital national interests. Other decisions are not as critical. Some situations are familiar to leaders; other challenges are less familiar. Some decisions are made in a static context; others in a dynamic setting.

The first stage of poliheuristic theory involves a noncompensatory, nonholistic, satisficing search. It uses decision heuristics and primarily corresponds to the cognitive school of decision making. The second stage involves rational processing of surviving alternatives. It corresponds to rational choice theory. Cognitive political heuristics are more important in the first stage of the decision, whereas rational, maximizing calculations are more applicable to the second stage of the poliheuristic decision process.

Poliheuristic theory is applicable to single decisions made by leaders, group decisions, sequential decisions, and decisions in strategic settings. It explains how and why leaders make decisions. A key premise of poliheuristic theory is that leaders use more than one decision strategy when making decisions, including strategies that are suboptimal (Mintz et al. 1997). For example, political leaders will avoid policies that are likely to result in an electoral defeat. They then consider remaining options analytically.

According to poliheuristic theory:

1. Foreign policy decisions are often made in a hyperbounded environment; leaders typically focus only on a narrow set of policy alternatives and decision dimensions while making decisions.
2. In making decisions, leaders use a two-stage decision process.
3. Although international factors are important, domestic politics is "the essence of decision."

4. Decision making in foreign affairs involves multiple heuristics, is non-compensatory with respect to key dimension(s) and involves framing and counterframing efforts.
5. Most foreign policy decisions are taken in an interactive (strategic) setting. Many foreign policy decisions are interactive and sequential.

What is Poliheuristic Decision Making?

The term poliheuristic can be broken down into "the roots poly (many) and heuristic (shortcuts), which alludes to the cognitive mechanisms used by decision makers to simplify complex foreign policy decisions" (Mintz et al. 1997, 554).[3] "Poli" also refers to the notion that political leaders measure gains and losses in political terms. Poliheuristic theory postulates that when making decisions, policy makers employ a two-stage decision calculus consisting of (1) rejecting policies that are unacceptable to the policy maker on a critical dimension or dimensions and (2) selecting an alternative from the subset of remaining alternatives while maximizing benefits and minimizing risks (see Mintz 1993, 1995, 2003, 2004a; Mintz and Geva 1997; Mintz et al. 1997; Payne et al. 1993). Table 5.2 presents indicators of noncompensatory political loss aversion.

Poliheuristic theory is also applicable to decisions by nondemocratic, autocratic leaders (James and Zhang 2004; Kinne 2005). These leaders are also concerned about threats to regime survival, political power, and legitimacy and therefore also adopt the "avoid major loss," noncompensatory principle. According to Brandon Kinne (2005, 16), the theory is applicable to single-party autocracies, personalist autocracies, and military dictatorships. The "avoid major political loss" principle varies according to the type of autocracy: leaders of single-party systems eliminate alternatives that "do not sufficiently appease the interest of the party"; leaders in personalist autocracies "eliminate decision alternatives that do not satisfy the leader's need to maintain political status"; and leaders of military regimes eliminate alternatives that "do not sufficiently appease the ruling military cabal or junta" (ibid.).

Whereas military and economic considerations can be noncompensatory for leaders, poliheuristic theory sees domestic politics as "the essence of decision." High political audience costs are nonadditive. Avoiding major loss is noncompensatory (Goertz 2004). Domestic political audience costs are an integral part of foreign policy making. Policy makers are political actors whose self-interest in political survival is paramount (Russett and Barzilai 1992; Sathasivam 2003). Consequently, policy makers are likely to reject outright any alternative that poses potentially high costs, particularly on the political dimension, even if that same alternative also yields potentially high benefits on other dimensions

---

[3] This section is taken from Mintz (2004a).

Table 5.2. *Indicators of noncompensatory political loss aversion*

Prospects of an electoral defeat
Threat to a leader's survival
Significant drop in public support for a policy
Significant drop in popularity
Domestic opposition
Threat to regime survival
Intra-party rivalry and competition
External challenge to the regime
Potential collapse of the coalition, government, or regime
Threat to political power, dignity, honor, or legitimacy of a leader
Demonstrations, riots, and so forth
The existence of veto players (e.g., pivotal parties in parliamentary systems)

Source: Mintz (2004a).

(although military and strategic considerations are also often noncompensatory). This process can lead to a poliheuristic bias.

Because it is based on decision shortcuts and rules of thumb that leaders use, poliheuristic theory can explain complicated foreign policy decisions.

> It is unique in its ability to deal with multiple players, multiple alternatives, and multiple dimensions, such as those characterizing multiplayer arms races, alliance decisions, and environmental decisions. It is inherently built on the assumption that policy makers simplify complicated decision problems by first using simple cognitive shortcuts and then applying a more detailed analytic decision calculus to arrive at a choice. (Mintz 2004a, 8)

Poliheuristic theory is dimension based, noncompensatory, nonholistic, satisficing, and order sensitive. This set of characteristics distinguishes it from other theories of decision making (expected utility theory, cybernetic theory, and prospect theory).[4]

---

[4] Mintz (2004a, 8) has noted that in strategic settings

> such as those that characterize many war and peace decisions (see Morrow 1997), the Poliheuristic leader eliminates, in the first stage, not only his or her non-compensatory alternatives but also alternatives perceived to be politically infeasible for an opponent (for an example, see Astorino-Courtois and Trusty 2000). The reduced choice sets can then be subjected to a standard game-theoretic analysis in the second stage of the decision (Mintz and Astorino-Courtois 2001). In sequential settings, each decision in the sequence of decisions involves a two-stage poliheuristic decision calculus. Thus, Saddam Hussein's decisions in fall 2002 and spring 2003 can be viewed as a sequence of poliheuristic decisions on whether to cooperate (minimally) with United Nations inspectors. In sequential and interactive (strategic) situations, each decision is part of a sequence of decisions by both players in a strategic interaction, each employing a poliheuristic calculus in each decision node in a strategic setting (see Eisenband 2003). According to this thesis, Saddam Hussein and George Bush have engaged in a sequential and interactive poliheuristic game consisting of numerous mini-decisions.

CASE STUDY: THE DECISION NOT TO INVADE IRAQ IN 1991 — AN
APPLICATION OF VARIOUS DECISION-MAKING MODELS TO A
FOREIGN POLICY EVENT

Background

The Bush administration's decision to stop the Gulf War in February 1991, one hundred hours after the ground campaign was launched and six weeks after air bombardment began, aroused considerable public debate in the United States. In a poll taken January 2–5, 1992, two-thirds of Americans surveyed said that the U.S.-led coalition should have continued fighting to force Saddam Hussein from power. News reports indicated that U.S. allies in the war (e.g., Britain, France, Saudi Arabia) were likewise surprised by the president's decision to stop the war (*Newsweek* January 20, 1992). Further, although congressional leaders were initially thrilled over Bush's declaration of victory in the Gulf War (Moss and Rodriguez 1991), the initial euphoria turned into a sense of disappointment that the White House lost its best chance to oust Saddam Hussein when it stopped short of invading Baghdad.

The first admission within the administration that it may have "misplayed" the end of the war came as President Bush denied that the commander of Operation Desert Storm, General Norman Schwarzkopf, wanted the fighting to continue a little longer. Schwarzkopf said that continuing the war for a little longer could have "closed the door" on Saddam (Bedard 1991). The ouster of Saddam before the 1992 election also might have prevented Saddam from undermining Bush's reelection effort (ibid.).

On November 29, the UN Security Council passed Resolution 678 authorizing the use of "all necessary means," including military force, to force Iraq out of Kuwait (Strong 1992, 227). The United States played a leading role in the formulation and confirmation of the UN resolutions and in the building of a multinational military force capable of enforcing them. Operation Desert Storm began with a massive air war against military targets in Iraq and Kuwait. The air war was followed by a swift and successful ground campaign that finally drove the Iraqi forces out of Kuwait (ibid.).

On February 27, 1992, President Bush told the American people that Kuwait was liberated and that the Iraqi army had been defeated. A permanent cease-fire resolution was imposed. It included not only "international supervision of the destruction of chemical and biological weapons and the use of oil revenues for reparations, but also [called for] Iraqi recognition of the permanent borders of Kuwait, the release of all Kuwaiti detainees and provisions for an international peace keeping force along the Iraq—Kuwait border" (Balz 1991).

In this chapter we apply six models of decision making to President Bush's decision to stop Operation Desert Storm: the rational actor model, cybernetic theory, prospect theory, poliheuristic theory, organizational politics, and bureaucratic politics. We do not expect all six models to explain the decision. We look at models that do account for the Bush administration's decision, models that partially explain the decision, and a model that does not provide a good explanation of the 1991 decision.

A Rational Actor Interpretation

The administration's alternatives were "stop the war" or "continue the war." The rational actor model calls for detailed cost-benefit calculations along each dimension of the decision. A decision is made by selecting the alternative with the highest "net gain" – the best alternative.

A "stop the war" termination decision differs considerably from one made to initiate conflict, when costs and utilities are typically more uncertain. Actual participation in a conflict allows the leader to more lucidly perceive "what the war is actually costing him in its social, economic, military and political dimensions" (Staudenmaier 1987, 27).

Escalation, deescalation, or termination of conflicts entails the calculation of benefits and costs along several dimensions. Military, strategic, political, economic, and diplomatic factors, the balance of forces, and other conditions are important factors affecting such decisions. Moreover, on the basis of premises of strategic calculation, theorists argue that in order to terminate war, at least one of the participants "must revise his estimate of the relative advantages and disadvantages of continuing hostilities" (Stein 1975, 6). A change in the calculus is therefore an essential prerequisite to the termination of war. However, the process of making compromises and reaching agreement on the termination of hostilities may be hindered by loss aversion because each side may view its own concessions as losses that loom larger than the gains achieved by the concessions of the adversary. The very willingness of one party to make a particular concession (e.g., to propose a ceasefire) immediately reduces the perceived value of the concession.

This interpretation of the decision to stop the war in the Persian Gulf is consistent with the historical record. Alexander George (1993), for example, notes that the removal of Saddam Hussein from power was not explicitly authorized by the UN Security Council. It was "not among the military objectives formally assigned to General Schwarzkopf's forces, nor was it an official military objective of the Bush administration" (91; see also Hybel and Kaufman 2006).

George (1993, 97) noted that coalition support for the war was geared to limited military objectives and might have eroded quickly if the administration had embarked on more ambitious goals. To continue the war meant "that Washington and its allies will escalate the military and political objectives they had set for themselves" (ibid.). However, there were important limitations to the political objectives. The UN coalition did not want to weaken Iraq "to the point of being unable to resist pressures from Iran and Syria. Rather, although a much weakened Iraq would emerge from the war, it should be capable of contributing to maintaining a regional balance of power" (ibid., 93). In addition, the U.S. "intentionally refrained from destroying the entire Iraq Army so that enough soldiers would be left to topple the dictator and hold the country together. Under new and stable leadership, the theory went, Iraq would not disintegrate into another Lebanon" (George 1993).[5]

When faced with the decision of when to stop the war and with his popularity skyrocketing, the president selected the risk-averse alternative of stopping the war and rejected the risky alternative of invading Baghdad and ousting Saddam from power. The political and military risks involved in continuing the war could not have been compensated for by increasing the gap in the military balance between the Allied Forces and Saddam's forces. The president had decided that the potential costs might be excessive in relation to possible future gains and therefore decided to terminate hostilities. The success of the military operation placed the president in the domain of gain both politically and militarily and led to the rejection of the "continue the march to Baghdad" alternative.

A Cybernetic Explanation

The cybernetic, bounded-rationality model of decision making is based on the premise that decision makers will not necessarily seek the best alternative but rather one that is good enough – that is, satisfactory.

A cybernetic explanation of the Bush administration's decision not to invade Iraq in 1991 points to a decision that is indeed good enough for the international coalition and most (if not all) of its members. Arab nations objected to occupation and invasion of a capital of an Arab state and there was the danger that they would withdraw from the coalition. The "stop the war" alternative was satisfactory from their point of view compared with continuing onto Baghdad. This was also the goal of the military campaign and, more important, followed the mandate the coalition received from the United Nations.

---

[5] George (1993, 93–98) notes that a lesser option, with fewer of the disadvantages and risks of a march to Baghdad, was available.

> It was discussed within the administration in early March and rejected for many of the same reasons. The proposal, which originated with members of a high-level interagency committee, was that allied forces remain indefinitely in southern Iraq, a fairly lightly populated area under which lay most of Iraq's oil fields. The object would be not only to put pressure on the Iraqi government to comply with cease-fire terms but also to encourage efforts to remove Saddam. U.S. military chiefs are said to have voiced strong and decisive opposition to the proposal. For them, as well as for some civilian officials, it was enough that all the military objectives of the war had been fully accomplished. To keep U.S. forces in Iraq might well be the first step toward prolonged involvement of American forces in a highly unstable, volatile internal situation in Iraq. From this perspective, once the military objectives of the war were accomplished it was best to pull U.S. forces out of Iraq as soon as possible.

A Prospect Theory Explanation

Prospect theory is sensitive to the domain in which the decision maker operates and predicts (except for cases with very low probabilities) risk-averse behavior in the domain of gains and risk-acceptant behavior in the domain of loss. Rather than using monetary units to account for the decision as is common in prospect studies, we focus on risk aversion in the domain of gain seeking and risk seeking in the domain of loss as a function of changes in political capital (i.e., changes in public approval).

It is important to note that the war's objective was framed in such a way as to make the reference point not the ouster of Saddam Hussein but the expulsion of the Iraqis from Kuwait. This goal was formalized in a consensus agreement reached by the coalition partners and such key actors as the Soviet Union. Thus, the framing of the problem was not as a gamble involving two risky prospects but as one that compared a certain outcome ("stop the war") to a risky and uncertain prospect ("continue the march to Baghdad"). According to this frame, then, being able to force the Iraqis out of Kuwait put the president in the domain of gain.

Political leaders are risk averse with respect to changes in their political capital. The influences of the domain in which decision makers operate (gain vs. loss) on the risk propensity of national leaders is explored later in the context that the termination of hostilities, like other phases of interstate conflict, is the product of multiple factors. According to Janice Stein, the attempt to predict the likelihood of termination from exclusively military indicators misses the point. "The decision . . . also depends on political constraints" (1975, 20).

Loss aversion also constrains state leaders through public opinion. Stein (1975, 22) writes,

> often opinion has been aroused during the phase of hostilities and is resistant to a process of accommodation. . . . Policy-makers are constrained not only by the actions of their opponent, but also by the limits imposed by domestic audiences. The use of threat by the opponent reinforces those domestic groups who are most resistant to change and weakens those who are prepared to risk an innovative policy.

Negative mass opinion can thus serve as a major impediment to the process of conflict reduction.

Termination is surrounded by uncertainties and misperception. The continuation of a war is riskier than a negotiated settlement (the outcome of a war typically is more uncertain than the results of a particular settlement; see Stein 1975). The termination of a coalition war is even more difficult than that of a bilateral war because there are more players who must be consulted, and the players within a coalition often have varying if not conflicting agendas and goals (Wittman 1979; Kaplan 1980; Treverton 1987).

A Poliheuristic Explanation

Political leaders virtually always take into account (explicitly or implicitly) domestic political factors and consequences while making decisions. The non-compensatory principle of poliheuristic theory suggests that in a choice situation, if a certain alternative is unacceptable politically, then a high score on another dimension (for example, military) cannot compensate or counteract for it, and hence the alternative is discarded in the first stage of the decision-making process. Politicians will not shoot themselves in the foot by selecting alternatives that are likely to have a negative effect on them politically. The noncompensatory principle in foreign policy decisions suggests, then, that leaders will eliminate an option that is below the cutoff level on the political dimension. A necessary (although not sufficient) condition for most decisions by political leaders is that the decision will not damage them politically.

With regard to Iraq in 1991, public opinion was very important to key decision makers in Washington.[6] Given the history of Vietnam "and the fragility of the international coalition it is hard to say this concern was misplaced" (see George 1993, 95; see also Hybel and Kaufman 2006). The decision to continue the war was therefore discarded. In the second stage of the decision, as predicted by the theory, the administration focused on minimizing risks and maximizing benefits. Decisions on the termination of war are not always based on a comprehensive and comparative evaluation of all alternatives along all dimensions but, as suggested by poliheuristic theory, are often based on cognitive shortcuts and heuristics.

The predominant importance of domestic politics in foreign policy making by democratic leaders is well documented in the literature (see Russett 1990; Mintz and Russett 1992; Russett and Barzilai 1992; DeRouen Jr. 2001, 2003; Yetiv 2004). Taking it one step further, this phenomenon also implies that when information—processing heuristic models of decision making (elimination by aspects, prospect theory, preference reversal, etc.) are applied to political situations, gains or losses and risks or rewards, should be viewed in political (and not monetary) terms. Recall our previous mention of studies demonstrating that leaders use force in the international arena when their performance ratings are in the critical 40 to 60 percent range (Ostrom and Job 1986; Russett 1990; Mintz and Russett 1992; Brulé and Mintz 2006) and even

---

[6] Some White House officials "had been influenced in this direction by their memory of the Korean War, when the Truman administration, after achieving its objective of evicting North Korean forces from South Korea, escalated its war aim to unification of the two Koreas by force" George (1993, 95).

more often when their popularity decreases among their supporters (Morgan and Bickers 1992).

Poliheuristic theory thus differs considerably from theories of war termination, such as game-theoretical and rational actor models (see Zagare 1983; Brams 1985), because it emphasizes information-processing decision heuristics rather than rational calculations and integrates the "domestic politics as the essence of decision" argument with rational models of decision making.

For example, a leader may be seen as either too weak or too aggressive during peace negotiations and lose domestic support and subsequently power (Iklé 1971, ch. 4).[7] The public, in contrast, may demand that the leader terminate hostilities when war casualties are excessive or when the conflict has run on for too long – for example, French public opinion regarding the conflict in Indochina in the 1950s (Randle 1973, 432–433). When the public perceives the war to be immoral or illegal, the public mood may shift to one of cooperation. Finally, if the citizens of a nation sense that their country could eventually become the target of an invasion, the public mood is likely to swing to one of nonhostility (ibid.). In contrast, when such constraints are not present, a country's bargaining position is strengthened vis-à-vis an adversary that does suffer from such constraints. For example, during the Vietnam war, North Vietnam's position was strengthened because it did not suffer from the same constraints the United States did.

The termination of war is also a process in which political and military power merge so that a solution tolerable to all sides can be reached (Fabyanic 1987). Leaders are faced with the decision of whether to maintain the level of hostility, to escalate hostility, or to terminate involvement. According to Wittman (1979), a commitment to a current course of action (war) is a function of the comparison between the perceived utility of continuing the action and the perceived utility of terminating hostilities.

An Organizational Politics Explanation

The organizational politics model provides a partial explanation of the 1991 decision not to invade Iraq. If we treat members of the U.S. coalition as entities in an organizational politics model, it is clear that when the war ended, their SOP was not to invade Iraq in the absence of UN authority to go beyond driving Iraqi forces out of Kuwait. This decision was the result of fear that an invasion would play into Saddam's hands in characterizing the war as occupation and aggression by the United States (Schwarzkopf 1993). Whereas the use of SOPs in

---

[7] The termination of hostilities is a phase in a larger process (see Stein 1975, 7). Barringer (1972) establishes six phases of a conflict of which termination is only one. He recognizes however, "that any conflicts may move from phase to phase in a variety of sequences; conflicts do not progress in an orderly directional path from phase to phase" (quoted in Stein 1975, 13).

this case does fit the organizational politics model, other aspects of the model (such as the "within agency" dynamics) are less applicable to this example.

A Bureaucratic Politics Model

The bureaucratic politics model does not provide an adequate explanation of the decision not to invade Iraq in 1991. The U.S. decision exhibited a relatively high (and uncommon) consensus among various bureaucracies that make up the U.S. government. Reports indicated that Chairman of the Joint Chiefs General Colin Powell seemed wary of using force to remove Saddam from power. Powell did not want to cripple Iraq. He believed it was an important counterweight to Iran.

The State Department was likewise reluctant to recommend such a move, mainly because of the fear of dissolving the multicountry coalition, including Arab nations that participated in the broad coalition. Secretary of State James Baker thought that an invasion of Iraq would be difficult and dangerous and would create divisions with Arab allies, as well as go beyond the terms of the UN Security Council resolution. Additionally, Baker believed that Iraq was a useful counterbalance to Iran's Shiite fundamentalism (Baker 2006).

The National Security Council supported a limited war that would only remove Hussein from Kuwait. An invasion of Iraq would mean changing objectives in midstream and would be risky. Finally, the White House believed that the cost of the invasion would be too high, and choosing not to invade could be easily justified.

This consensus among U.S. entities, bureaucracies, and organizations does not therefore support the bureaucratic politics model, which would have predicted bargaining among bureaucracies over their role in the invasion. Whereas such a process characterized interagency bargaining in the decision to force Iraq out of Kuwait, it was considerably less evident in the decision not to continue to Baghdad in 1991.

APPLIED DECISION ANALYSIS

Applied Decision Analysis (ADA) is an analytic procedure aimed at recreating or "reverse engineering" decisions of leaders, groups, and coalitions using a decision matrix. ADA enters the minds of decision makers in an attempt to uncover their decision rules. The procedure has been used to explain and predict decisions of leaders such as Hassan Nasrallah of Hezbollah, Khaled Mashal of Hamas, Osama bin Laden of al-Qaeda, and others.

It is now clear that there are distinctions in how decision makers process information. Important insight can be gleaned from the way in which decision makers search through data to make a decision. Different decision models can

Alternatives

Dimensions		Do nothing	Diplomatic pressure	Approach Castro	Invasion	Air strike	Blockade
	Security						
	Economic						
	Political						

⇒ **intradimensional search**

⇓ **interdimensional search**

Figure 5.1. Decision Matrix for Cuban Missile Crisis. Adapted from Allison (1971, 56–62).

be linked to different search patterns. The rational model implies a maximizing decision rule and a holistic search pattern. The decision maker looks at all alternatives along all dimensions. In cognitive models, the decision maker economizes by taking mental shortcuts – heuristics.

We can use a simple matrix to outline the basics of information processing. The decision matrix (or table) is simply a chart that provides a useful visual reference. The rows and columns represent decision dimensions and alternatives respectively. With this simple matrix, we can explore the various search patterns of decisions makers. We can also compare the dynamics of the models. For instance, we can show how a rational process could lead to a different choice than would a cognitive process.

A Simple Example: The Cuban Missile Crisis and the Decision Matrix

Figure 5.1 is a matrix designed to illustrate the presidential decision during the Cuban Missile Crisis. President Kennedy told members of EXCOM during the crisis that he expected them to explore all possible options and weigh the costs and benefits of each (Allison 1971). The alternatives included do nothing, apply diplomatic pressure, approach Castro, invade, and conduct an air strike or blockade (Allison 1971).

The dimensions (security, economic, and political) represent the key realms in which the decision maker operates. Each of the empty cells represents an outcome with varying implications. For instance, the first cell will contain outcome information for the security implications of doing nothing. If the Kennedy administration chose not to take action, the Cold War security balance could have tilted in favor of the Soviets. There would also be a probability associated with such an eventuality. In this case, the probability would be fairly high that doing nothing during the crisis would have had negative repercussions for U.S. security.

The utility is simply a measure of how positive the outcome is. In the rational actor model decision makers compare all alternatives along all dimensions while trying to maximize positive and minimize the negative outcomes. In a practical sense, the decision maker would sum all of the columns in the matrix and choose the alternative with the highest score. Time constraints and incomplete information make such an extensive search more difficult.

The rational ideal is thus very demanding. It also becomes more complicated when probabilities are taken into account. There might be a very positive outcome with a very low probability of success. Prospect theory takes the risk domain of the actor into account. The poliheuristic model uses cognitive shortcuts in the first phase of the decision and rational calculations in the second phase of the process.

As we pointed out in Chapter 2, information searches can be intradimensional or interdimensional. In the latter case, the search proceeds by sequentially exploring each alternative. In Figure 5.1, this would mean taking up the "do nothing" option and then determining how it fares along each dimension. This would be followed by exploring the "diplomatic pressure" option and then proceeding similarly through all other options. This is how the rational process, described earlier, would proceed. In the intradimensional search, information is processed predominately by picking a dimension and then assessing how each alternative fares on this dimension.

For example, a decision maker could assess each alternative on the basis of how it fares along the political dimension. It is reported that even at the height of the Cold War in 1954 President Eisenhower weighed alternatives along the political dimension (DeRouen Jr. 2003). Public opposition to another land war in East Asia one year after the Korean War was a major reason the president refused to aid the French in Indochina directly. The president streamlined the decision process by focusing on the political dimension. This decision was reached despite his concern that a "row of dominos" could fall in East Asia. By using this type of search pattern, the decision maker need not explore the other dimensions. This is a simple example. Generally speaking, the rational model implies an interdimensional search, whereas cognitive models economize while searching intradimensionally.

ADA: A Closer Look

The ADA procedure consists of the following tasks:[8]

1. Identify the set of alternatives available to the leader – for example, use force, apply sanctions, or do nothing.
2. Identify the set of dimensions or decision criteria that may explain the decision – for example, a military dimension, an economic dimension, a political dimension, and a diplomatic dimension.

[8] This section is taken from Mintz, Chatagnier, and Brule (2006).

3. Assign weights (importance level) to dimensions (optional) – for example, rate the military dimension of the decision to use force as very important, the economic and political dimensions as important, and the diplomatic dimensions as somewhat important.
4. Identify implications – for example, the economic implications of the use of force alternative in the case of Iraq in 2003 were high, in the hundreds of billions of dollars.
5. Rate implications of each dimension on each alternative.
6. Identify decision rule(s) used by leaders – for example, determine whether the leader utilized a poliheuristic decision rule, a maximizing rule, or a satisficing model.

The tasks are carried out in these two main steps:

STEP 1: IDENTIFY THE DECISION MATRIX OF THE DECISION MAKER. A decision matrix consists of a set of alternatives, the dimensions (or criteria) for selecting among these alternatives, and an assessment of the implications of each alternative for each dimension. Weights (or level of importance) can be assigned to each dimension if the analyst observes that dimensions should receive unequal weight in the analysis. One can also use counterfactual scenarios to analyze potential actions and reactions of leaders of other countries.

The Decision Board software (http://www.decisionboard.org) has been used to develop and organize the information relevant to individuals' decisions through the construction of decision boards or matrices. After one chooses the number of dimensions and alternatives relevant to the decision, the Decision Board displays a generic matrix, which can be tailored to the specific policy problem.

Alternatives. The set of *alternatives* includes the likely courses of action a decision maker may reasonably consider when faced with some problem or decision scenario. For example, when involved in negotiations with a state, a terrorist organization's leader may consider the following: "continue with attacks," "temporarily halt attacks," "stop attacks," or "continue attacks while negotiating" (so-called "negotiation under fire"). In another example, applicable to state leaders when faced with an international crisis, a leader may consider the following alternatives: "do nothing," "apply sanctions," "contain the situation," or "use force."

Dimensions. A *dimension* is an organizing theme for related information and variables relevant in evaluating the alternatives. Thus, if the leader of a terrorist organization is concerned with the political consequences of a decision while in negotiations with a state, then public support, the flow of financial contributions, recruitment levels, and other variables related to this general organizing theme may be used to evaluate his alternatives. Among other reasons, organizations use terrorism to increase the market share of popular support. Examples of other dimensions that may influence the terrorist leader's decision are relations with other countries (e.g., Iran or Syria) and the likelihood of operational success.

Weights. *Weights* indicate the importance level of each dimension – for example, from 0 (not important at all) to 10 (very important). Thus, in the terrorist leader example, the analyst assigns different weights to the political, diplomatic, and operational dimensions, unless he or she considers each dimension to have equal weight in the decision. Patrick James and John Oneal (1991) have used the following decision criteria or dimensions in their analysis of decisions to use force: military, economic, political, and diplomatic. The Decision Board can be analyzed to uncover decision rules of leaders.

Implications. The *implications* consist of a description of the likely consequences of an alternative for a given dimension. Each alternative has implications corresponding to each dimension. For example, in the case of the terrorist leader, the "stop attacks" alternative has implications for the organization's political standing, relations with other countries, and operational success of the organization, which are all relevant dimensions.

Ratings. Implications can be rated by the analyst, for example, from −10 (very bad) to +10 (very good), although assigning numerical ratings to implications is optional. For example, if choosing the alternative "stop attacks" is likely to result in a loss of public sympathy or a decline in financial contributions, the analyst should assign a negative rating (very bad, −8 or −9) to the political implications of "stop attacks." In contrast, if "continue attacks" is likely to lead to an outpouring of public sympathy and increasing recruitment levels, then this alternative should receive a positive rating (e.g., very good, or +8).

STEP 2: UNCOVERING THE DECISION CODE OF LEADERS. It is possible to discern the decision rule used by an individual in making decisions. Leaders and other policy makers can choose either the alternative with the highest overall utility or the alternative that is good enough. The former is a maximizing strategy, which is generally associated with rational choice approaches, and the latter is a satisficing strategy generally associated with bounded rationality. Decision makers who use satisficing strategies can search alternatives until one meets or exceeds a preset threshold of utility (as in cybernetic theory), or sequentially eliminate alternatives that do not meet a preset threshold along certain key dimensions until one remains (as in the "elimination by aspect" strategy). Combining rational and cognitive elements of the decision process results in a two-stage poliheuristic decision process.

Application to Decisions of Leaders of Terrorist Organizations:
Bin Laden and al-Qaeda

If we apply the ADA procedure to a large number of decisions, we can uncover the "decision DNA" (or decision code) of leaders. Alex Mintz, John Tyson Chatagnier, and David Brulé (2006) analyzed several of Osama bin Laden's decisions. They looked at the choices he made regarding attacks on the World Trade Center (in 1993 and 2001), his decisions regarding the claim of responsibility for the 2001 attack, his decision to attack the USS *Cole* in 2000, the merger with Egyptian Islamic Jihad, and finally, the two more recent European attacks (in London and Madrid).

On the basis of their analysis, the authors conclude that bin Laden's decision code indicates that

1. Bin Laden is "more of a self-interested player than an organizational player (despite his rhetoric to the contrary)" (Mintz 2007b, 13; also see Mintz, Chatagnier and Brule 2006). Bin Laden is concerned with "accumulating and preserving political power, especially within the al-Qaeda organization. Though his interests are generally congruent with the organization's interests, when they diverge, the analysis shows that he has selected the option that is most beneficial to him politically"(ibid). This often means hindering a potential rival at the expense of additional quality leadership for the group.

2. Bin Laden's decision rule is not always linear (op cit. 13). This is often the case when rivalries appear in the organization. "Though bin Laden sees the personal political aspects as the most vital components of a decision, his identity is inextricably bound with al-Qaeda's. As such, organizational factors play secondary roles in his decisions. In cases in which he chooses his own personal interests over the good of the organization (e.g., the bombings in Europe) . . . he eliminates what would be the overall optimal choices in favor of an alternative that most benefits him alone" (ibid.).

3. It is because of this drive for power that bin Laden's decision code "is most vulnerable when a competing leader emerges. He is then willing to sacrifice to an extent the benefit to the organization in favor of his own political survival. By encouraging dissent in the al-Qaeda ranks, it seems possible that the organization could be made to destroy itself from within" (ibid., Mintz et al. 2006).

ADA is generic. It can be used to uncover any foreign or domestic policy decision made by world leaders. Examples include decisions by members of the United Nations Security Council, leaders of terrorist organizations, leaders of adversarial (and sympathetic) states, and President Ahmadinejad of Iran.

CONCLUSION

Though it has solid support in social science research, the rational model has been the target of criticisms and revisionism. The bounded rationality and cybernetic approaches discussed in this chapter highlight the rather excessive demands on the human brain that the rational decision model makes. The organizational and bureaucratic politics models, with their emphases on SOPs, political struggle, and coalition building, demonstrate that the rational model is not the final word in foreign policy decision making. Poliheuristic theory combines elements of the rational model and the cognitive school by adding a preliminary step to the rational process. Psychological factors are largely ignored in the rational model. This is the subject of Chapter 6.

PART FOUR

DETERMINANTS OF FOREIGN POLICY DECISION MAKING

6

Psychological Factors Affecting Foreign
Policy Decisions

Foreign policy decisions are shaped by many factors. The real world is complicated, and many variables are taken into account when decisions are made. The
role of information processing, framing, and cognitive biases in decision making points to the need for a psychological approach to FPDM. In this chapter,
we assess how factors such as the personality and beliefs of leaders, leadership
style, emotions, images, cognitive consistency, and the use of analogies influence and shape foreign policy decision making. Overall, these factors call into
question the explanatory power of the rational model. Decision makers are
not necessarily "irrational" but rather are limited in their ability to carry out
all the steps of the rational model. This section describes the forces that cause
decision makers to deviate away from the rational ideal and toward a more
cognitive-based model of decision making.

PSYCHOLOGICAL FACTORS

Decisions at the highest rungs of government are usually made by small groups
or powerful individuals. Psychological factors can potentially have great impact
on decisions made by these small units (Cashman 1993). The impact is even
greater if the decision making occurs during a crisis, the government is a
dictatorship, or the country is newly independent or experiencing regime
change.

Kennedy's decision during the Cuban Missile Crisis was influenced primarily by the relatively few members of EXCOM. Winston Churchill's dominance
as a decision maker during World War II is another example of crisis decision
making. If the government is a dictatorship, the personal characteristics of
the leader can be paramount. Thus, the personal idiosyncrasies of powerful
autocratic leaders such as Fidel Castro of Cuba, Mao Tse-tung of China, Kim
Jong-il of North Korea, Joseph Stalin of the Soviet Union, Hafez al-Assad of
Syria, or Saddam Hussein of Iraq become important. If a country is unstable,
small decision units or individuals can be important. If a country is newly

Table 6.1. *Psychological factors shaping
foreign policy decision making*

Cognitive consistency
Evoked set
Emotions
Images
Belief systems and schema
Analogies and learning
Leaders' personality
Leadership style

independent and institutions are not yet developed, leaders can be very influential. Examples here include Mahatma Gandhi of India, Mustafa Atatürk of Turkey, and Joseph Tito of Yugoslavia.

Leaders must "gather and process the information at hand to reach an appropriate decision or judgment – one that fits with both the facts and the circumstances – strategic and political" (Renshon and Renshon 2008, 510). There are numerous psychological factors that can shape decisions. As mentioned, most of these effects regard small decision units. We summarize some of the more well-known factors in Table 6.1.

Cognitive Consistency

Cognitive consistency is perhaps the most prominent theory of how perception influences decision making. Cognitive consistency means that decision makers downplay certain information that is inconsistent with prior **images** and **beliefs** or pay inordinate attention to information consistent with those images and beliefs. Whereas in groupthink, information that went against group consensus was ignored, here the tendency is to perceive incoming information in light of previously held expectations. In other words, incoming information is processed according to "pre-existing images" (Jervis 1976, 117), and decision makers "perceive what they expect to be there" (ibid., 143). The information that is consistent with prior images and expectations is therefore of paramount importance, whereas the search for other types of information is curtailed. In essence, we are talking here of closing off one's mind to anything not compatible with preexisting beliefs during a decision. Previous views and beliefs are not seriously questioned. For example, John Foster Dulles routinely downplayed information that contradicted his prior beliefs about the Soviet Union (ibid., 143).

Jervis notes that a pitfall of cognitive consistency is that the decision maker can become overconfident in his position and dismiss important alternative viewpoints. He also notes that cognitive consistency can hinder change and lead to rigid policies. The Falklands War of 1982 provides a classic case of misperception and overconfidence. In making the decision to invade the Islands, the leaders of Argentina's military junta did not expect Britain to respond so forcefully and quickly (Levy and Vakili 1992). Argentina expected a quick victory that could not be prevented by the British.

Evoked Set

Jervis notes another impact that perceptions can have on decision making. **Evoked set** refers to the "immediate concerns" that are foremost in the mind of a decision maker (Jervis 1976, 203). Decision makers can be influenced by concurrent events. In other words, the focus of the actor's attention can influence how new information is perceived. The implication is that knowing what is foremost in the decision maker's mind can help us predict and understand the decision. Jervis notes that it is difficult for decision makers to reorient their attention from this information. This is evidenced by an example he gives (ibid., 215–216). In 1973, Israeli jets shot down a Libyan airliner that was en route to Cairo. The foremost concern of the Libyan pilots was finding their way to the airport. In not responding appropriately to the Israeli fighter jets, they raised doubts in the minds of the pilots. For their part, the Israelis probably refused to believe that the Libyans did not know the identity of the jets in pursuit of the commercial airliner. In this situation, Jervis notes that each side overestimated the degree of the other side's understanding of the circumstances.

Greg Cashman (1993, 57) provides another example of evoked set from a similar international incident that was widely reported in the press. In this case, decision makers were predisposed to see incoming information in a certain way. In 1988, the USS *Vincennes* shot down an Iranian plane. The American crew was predisposed to perceive the Iranian plane as a hostile enemy because intelligence reports had predicted an Iranian attack and there were recent reports that Iran had F-14s stationed in the region. As Cashman notes, lacking verifiable information from other sources, the evoked set helped portray the plane as hostile when in fact it was a commercial plane.

Emotions

There is ample evidence that **emotions** play an important role in foreign policy decisions. Leaders are known to be influenced by mass opinion, which, in turn, is influenced by domestic and international events. Nations often retaliate against attacks and provocations on their citizens and territory – acts that evoke such emotions and feelings like hatred, fear, anger, desire for revenge, insecurity, and so on. Rose McDermott (2004b, 692) writes that emotion comprises thoughts, motivations, sense of experience, and physical sensations and is not quite the same as mood or feeling.

Specific emotions can exert specific effects. McDermott (ibid., 700–701) explains how emotion plays a role in decision making. For example, extreme emotions such as fear or anger can make it more difficult for decision makers to be objective. Emotions can also have a more positive role. Love, sympathy, and empathy are all important influences on decision making. The neural pathways in the brain that transmit emotion are rapid and can therefore increase speed and accuracy in decision making. Emotion can "arouse" a decision maker toward closure even in the face of uncertainty.

The role emotion plays in crises cannot be ignored (Maiese 2005). Maiese writes that because emotion is usually involved at the onset of the conflict, it is vital that third parties and disputants understand its impact when it comes time to, for example, end a conflict.

Emotions are known to influence how leaders process information and the importance they assign to various dimensions in emotionally loaded situations versus emotionally neutral situations. Consider the following example. In March 2002, more than 130 Israeli civilians were killed in terrorist attacks committed by Palestinian groups such as Hamas, Islamic Jihad, and the al-Aqsa Martyrs' Brigades (the military branch of Fatah). These attacks reached their peak on March 27, 2002, with the event known as the Passover Massacre, in which a Palestinian suicide bomber killed thirty people at the Park Hotel in Netanya, Israel. The symbolic nature of the attack – on a Jewish holiday, with people praying or sitting around the Passover dinner table – had evoked among many deep emotions of hatred and desire for revenge toward Palestinians and consequently prepared the ground and led to Israel's Operation Defensive Shield.

Nehemia Geva, Steven Redd, and Katrina Mosher (2004) have shown using experimental methods that emotions affect how people process information and make decisions. Hatred, love, fear, threat, and support all produce not only different choices from opposite emotions, but also variations in the way people arrive at a choice (spontaneous vs. calculated, maximizing vs. satisficing, intuitive vs. rational). According to these authors, terrorist events "trigger numerous emotions ranging from hate and revenge, despair and anger, to determination and resolve. . . . Emotions influence both the processes and outcomes of foreign policy decision making. Emotions can affect information processing in two distinct ways. First, we posit that emotions will affect the cognitive capacity of decision makers" (ibid., 1), primarily by narrowing their choice set, that is, the number and types of options that decision makers may consider en route to a foreign policy choice. In addition, emotions can lower the threshold for selecting a particular course of action by a priori reducing the amount of information to be processed per alternative. "Second, emotions may have a thematic effect on the process of foreign policy decision making" (ibid, 1). Emotions may alter or modify the relevancy of incoming information during the decision task, in a sense, coloring information and introducing a form of selective attention.

Images

The mental representations we use to frame and organize the complicated world around us are called **images** (Voss and Dorsey 1992, 8). Images are a sort of stereotype that the mind uses to categorize events and people. Thus images are formed by cognitive processes (Herrmann, et al. 1997). Images are useful to simplify the complicated world, but they put the decision maker at risk of overgeneralization and bias (Cashman 1993; R. Hermann 1985; R. Cottam 1977; Herrmann et al. 1997). Images are formed by an interplay of three assessments each state makes of the other: strategic balance, perceived opportunity or threat, and perceived culture (R. Herrmann et al. 1997, 407–408).

Early studies of images focused on how U.S. decision makers viewed Soviet leaders. For example, a study of 1970s-era Politburo speeches found that the Soviets categorized the Americans through an enemy stereotype image (R. Herrmann 1985). In turn, Soviet leaders who harbored the strongest image of the United States as enemy were more likely to express militaristic attitudes. This is consistent with a central concept of image theory that images are associated with an accompanying set of preferences (Cottam and Preston 2007, 26). Because images convey a qualitative assessment, the image that persisted during the Cold War was one that portrayed the Soviets as an enemy even when the Soviet Union was making cooperative moves. Images tend to persist.[1]

Images are an important input to other aspects of foreign policy decision making. For example, operational code and cognitive mapping each use images to explain decision making in foreign affairs (ibid.). Similarly, Cashman (1993) says images are used to create belief systems. These topics are covered below.

Beliefs, Belief Systems, and Schema

Do the beliefs of leaders influence foreign policy decision making? **Beliefs** provide powerful frames for interpreting and understanding the decision situation (Renshon and Renshon 2008, 512). Beliefs may block and shape incoming information (Walker 1983, Walker and Schafer 2004; Walker and Schafer, forthcoming). The influence of domestic and international factors on decision making is mediated by the beliefs of leaders.

A leader's **belief system** implies inferences about "the preferences of both Self and Other regarding policy outcomes" (Walker and Schafer, forthcoming, 31). The intersection of these two sets of preferences regarding policy outcomes influences a leader's strategies, tactics, moves, and decisions. Beliefs can also

[1] More recent studies reveal how the use of images can also assist in the analysis of leaders. For example, it is possible to combine image theory with Margaret Hermann's work on leadership traits to arrive at a means of predicting the type of policy responses certain images will evoke (Cottam and Preston 2007).

shape how leaders process information, whether they use holistic or nonholistic search, maximizing or satisficing strategies, or compensatory or noncompensatory calculations, as well as the sequence of the information search and how they weight that information.

Stephen Walker and Mark Schafer (forthcoming, 5), point out that beliefs as "internal dispositions located within the individual may affect foreign policy decisions in different ways. Herbert Simon (1985) refers to this possibility as the process of radical irrationality in which actions are based on feelings unmediated and uninfluenced by thought processes." A second possibility identified by Simon is "the process of substantive rationality in which actions are based solely on information about the environment internalized by thought processes. Cognitive processes are necessary for action, but they are endogenous to the situation to the extent that they simply mirror reality" (Walker and Schafer, forthcoming, 5).

According to Walker and Schafer (ibid., 5–6), a third possibility is "the process of bounded rationality in which actions are mediated by thought processes that contain a mixture of feelings, beliefs inferred from previous experiences (old information), and current perceptions of stimuli in the present environment (new information). Both the old and the new pieces of information are associated with the arousal of feelings of positive and negative affect as motivational biases, which help to specify preferences for different courses of action (Simon 1957, 1985). If these two kinds of information are at odds with one another and if decisions are based on the former, then beliefs become sufficient conditions for action."

Schema is "an individual's cognitions about some person, role, group, event or other object" (Kuklinski, Luskin, and Bolland 1991, 1341). Schema is an important concept in foreign policy analysis because it is known that the impact of prior information is profound and affects decisions at all levels of analysis. Schemas are time- and labor-saving tools that people store for use.

Operational Code Analysis

Operational Code Analysis (OCA) is an approach to the analysis of political leaders that "may focus narrowly on a set of political beliefs or more broadly on a set of beliefs embedded in the personality of a leader or originating from the cultural matrix of a society" (Walker and Schafer 2000b, 2–3). OCA uses content analysis and formal modeling methods in the analysis of how beliefs affect policies related to foreign policy, security policy and economic affairs (ibid.). The central puzzle of the "operational code analysis" program is "when and how do the beliefs of leaders act as pivotal causal mechanisms in explaining and anticipating the processes of strategic interaction between states at several levels of decision: moves, tactics, strategies, and policy preferences" (Walker and Schafer, forthcoming, 6). In other words, the main challenge of OCA is linking beliefs with foreign policy behavior at different levels of decision (Walker and Schafer, forthcoming).[2]

An analysis of Henry Kissinger's operational code (see Walker 1977, 1991) can serve as a case in point. Walker revealed that Kissinger's belief system resembled the logic of the Prisoner's Dilemma game. Analysis of U.S. bargaining moves and tactics toward North Vietnam

> showed constraints imposed by Kissinger's ranking of the outcomes of (1) domination, (2) settlement, (3) deadlock, and (4) submission, in the subjective game represented by his belief system. He attributed a similar ranking to North Vietnamese leaders and spent almost four years employing diplomatic and military tactics to persuade them that each side should risk moves toward settlement rather than domination in order to avoid a deadlock outcome. (Walker and Schafer, forthcoming, 15)

Walker and associates have also studied the operational code of U.S. presidents Woodrow Wilson, Lyndon Johnson, Jimmy Carter, Bill Clinton, and George W. Bush.

Analogies and Learning

As mentioned in Chapter 3, the "cognitive miser" models rely on shortcuts rather than consistency seeking. Sometimes information processing is affected by memories of previous experiences. **Analogies** represent a powerful cognitive shortcut. When leaders experience events that require a decision, there is a tendency to reflect back to past events that presented similar circumstances, alternatives, and potential outcomes. The past events are referred to as analogs. Analogies help us to make sense of the environment and new situations (Houghton 1996). If an alternative was selected and implemented to perfection, the decision maker might learn from this experience. Analogy and its counterpart, **learning**, can provide useful shortcuts. However, as we demonstrate later, they might just as easily lead to disastrous outcomes if the wrong lessons are learned or if the current situation is not an accurate reflection of reference events. Andrew Sage (1990) refers to the use of analogy in decision making as a skills method.

An understanding of how nations learn can help us to make sense of the *goals* states pursue, the *ways* they pursue them, and the way they make decisions (Goldsmith 2005, 1). Learning from the past "occur[s] when policymakers look to the past to help them deal with the present" (Khong 1992, 6). A more

---

[2] According to Walker and Schafer (forthcoming), OCA consists of an automated system of content analysis that retrieves the beliefs of each leader and a software program for parsing event data that uncovers the signals and strategies of each state during the crisis. Operational code analysis largely springs from the work of Alexander George (1969), who expanded on earlier work by Nathan Leites (1953).

complex definition is "a change of beliefs (or the degree of confidence in one's beliefs) or the development of new beliefs, skills or procedures as a result of the observation and interpretation of experience" (Levy 1994, 283). Many studies of foreign policy decision making attribute state behavior to distribution of resources, alliances, or regime type. However, a focus on learning can help account for choices even when these factors do not vary within a government (Goldsmith 2005). Leaders can learn from each other and from events in their own past. A few detailed examples of learning and analogy follow.

The "Munich Analogy" and Use of Analogies in U.S. Foreign Policy

Much has been written on the so-called Munich analogy in which Chamberlain gave in to Hitler during the Czechoslovakia affair. Since those events of the 1930s, leaders and pundits have interpreted current events in light of this failed historical example of appeasement. In other words, when faced with a decision over how to deal with a despot (or someone portrayed as a despot), the analogical lesson is that one should not to give in because dictators cannot be trusted to live up to bargains. The Munich analogy is thus a cognitive shortcut that informs leaders to deal with aggressors forcefully.

The Munich analogy has been used countless times in reference to the Korean War, the Vietnam War, and various Soviet actions during the Cold War (Neustadt and May 1986; Khong 1992; Levy 1994; S. Anderson 2007). The decision to escalate the Vietnam War in 1965 was also linked to the Korean analogy of 1950 (Khong 1992). During the war with Iraq that began in 2003, Vice President Dick Cheney and Secretary of Defense Donald Rumsfeld equated opponents of the war in Iraq to those who appeased Hitler in 1938.

When Americans were taken hostage in Iran in 1979, the Carter administration relied on the 1976 Israeli raid at Entebbe as an analogy (Houghton 1996). The conditions were quite different – Tehran is far inland and the hostages were in the middle of the city. The Israeli hostages at Entebbe were being held at the airport, so a surgical rescue operation was much more feasible. As it happened, the Entebbe analogy of a quick rescue mission to free hostages led to a disastrous outcome as the American helicopters crashed in the desert en route to rescue the hostages. As it turned out, the more circumspect secretary of state, Cyrus Vance, himself invoking analogies of prior hostage situations in China, Cambodia, and North Korea, was proven correct. After the hostages served their political purposes, the hostage takers released them (Houghton 1996).

There have been a series of hostage incidents that have provided the basis for analogical reasoning. In 1949, several American consular officials were taken hostage in Mukden, China. The incident was resolved peacefully. In 1968, North Korea captured the USS *Pueblo* and took its crew hostage. The hostages were released after several months of negotiations. Seven years later, the Pueblo incident became an analog when Cambodia captured the USS *Mayaguez* and held the crew hostage (Neustadt and May 1986, ch. 4). The Ford administration launched a failed rescue mission that resulted in the death of forty-one marines. Taken together, these analogies led Vance and (initially) Carter to favor a diplomatic solution to the crisis in Iran (Houghton 1996).

Analogies are especially likely to be invoked when the base events are recent (Maoz 1990). In 1983, the Reagan administration relied on the Iranian Hostage analogy, less than three years removed, in the Grenada situation. Secretary of State George Shultz revealed, albeit indirectly, that the Grenada venture was linked to the fallout of both the Beirut tragedy and the Iranian hostage taking as he responded to a question of a possible linkage:

> and the President had to weight this – with the violent and uncertain atmosphere that certainly was present in Grenada, the question is: Should he act to prevent Americans from being hurt or taken hostage? I think that if he waited and they were taken hostage or many were killed, then you would be asking that same question: Why didn't you in light of this clear, violent situation, take some action to protect American citizens there? I don't want to get into the position of second-guessing myself, but I'm trying to say one has to weight these considerations and be willing to take a decision in the light of all the circumstances, and that is what the president did. (Shultz 1983)

It is clear that the potential for a hostage situation was a major feature of the decision landscape. In his memoirs, Shultz (1993, 331) also revealed that the director of the State Department's political and military affairs bureau warned against repeating Carter's mistakes during the Iranian hostage crisis. The president himself told a group of military personnel a week after the invasion, "we weren't about to wait for the Iran crisis to repeat itself, only this time in our own neighborhood – the Caribbean" (Bostdorff 1991, 744). Shultz and Robert McFarlane were the earliest advocates of employing force based on the Iranian hostage crisis analogy (DeFrank and Walcott 1983, 75; see also Hooker 1991, 65; Hybel 1990, 270).

Analogies are also more likely when key decision makers are involved in both the current event and the historical basis for the analogy. For example, National Security Advisor Zbigniew Brzezinski was in Israel at the time of the hostage rescue from Entebbe in 1976. It was no surprise that he would oppose Secretary of State Vance and President Carter in his support for a similar operation three years later when Americans were taken hostage in Iran (Houghton 1996). As we describe in the next section in an extended discussion of analogical reasoning, Che Guevara's presence in Guatemala in 1954 during the U.S.-backed military coup would shape his behavior five years after he had come to power in revolutionary Cuba. Guevara's firsthand experience in all situations strengthened the analogical connections.

CASE STUDY: ANALOGIES IN U.S.-CUBAN RELATIONS, 1954–1967

U.S.-Cuban relations in the 1950s and 1960s provide interesting examples of decision making with the use of analogies. During this period, key individuals and agencies from each country were involved in fateful decisions. This case study highlights analogical reasoning and learning from the past. We see examples of analogies used both successfully and unsuccessfully in major episodes involving the U.S. and Cuba during this era. The Guatemalan coup of 1954 provided a basis for analogy for both Cuba and the United States. The lessons taken away by Cuba from the events of 1954 led to a successful defense of the islands during the Bay of Pigs invasion. The Cubans used their successful revolution as an analogy at least twice in the 1960s, but each case resulted in failure. The final analogy we explore is from the American perspective. In 1967, as the United States helped the Bolivians track Che Guevara's ragtag army, they applied analogies from the Vietnam War.

As discussed in Chapters 1–3, information processing is often affected by previous experiences of similar circumstances. Such analogies become cognitive shortcuts. Decision makers can learn from previous experiences. Jervis (1976) observed that analogies were most relevant when key decision makers personally experienced events that are the basis of the analogy. The individuals and organizations that we focus on in this extended case study are Fidel Castro, Che Guevara, presidents Eisenhower and Johnson, the State Department, and the CIA. Many of the same actors were involved in critical decisions that were made from the early 1950s through the late 1960s.

The Analogies Provided by Guatemala, 1954

We begin in 1954. It was that year that the Eisenhower administration carried out a CIA-led overthrow of the leftist regime of Jacobo Arbenz in Guatemala. As it happened, a young doctor from Argentina named Ernesto Guevara had drifted to Guatemala and become enamored with this first socialist government in the Western Hemisphere. It was here that Guevara began seriously to consolidate his Marxist leanings.

While Guevara was watching the United States overthrow a democratically elected government in Guatemala, Fidel Castro and others who took part in the ill-fated attack on Cuba's Moncada military barracks on July 26, 1953, were in Mexico City plotting their second attempt at a Cuban Revolution. The Cubans had been released from prison in Cuba and then exiled. Guevara and many other leftists fled Guatemala and ended up in Mexico City in the wake of the coup. While in Mexico City, it seemed inevitable that Guevara would cross paths with Castro and his colleagues. It was said that during their first meeting, the two spoke for hours. Castro, himself young, middle class, and educated, was taken with Guevara and soon invited him on their pending trip over the Gulf of Mexico back to Cuba.

The Guatemalan coup had been in large part a CIA-backed bluff. The coup plotters did not have an overwhelming military force. Some have observed that Arbenz could have armed the masses that were still loyal to him and won the day. Instead he fled the country, and the military dictator Castillo Armas took power. None of this was lost on Guevara. He witnessed first-hand that if the military turned against the government, all could easily be lost.

As soon as Castro came to power in Cuba, the regime held tribunals to root out potential counterrevolutionaries. Guevara himself presided over these early tribunals and many subsequent executions. Of course, many opponents of the revolution fled to the United States. The upshot was that the new Cuban government looked back on Guatemala, and the lesson learned was that the United States was likely to try an offensive strategy. To meet this head-on, Castro focused immediately on creating a loyal army with his younger brother Raul in charge.

It seems likely that Guevara discussed this with Castro during their lengthy conversations in Mexico leading up to the revolution. When Castro came to power in 1959, one of the first acts of the revolution was to purge the military of potential counterrevolutionaries. Although many who did not welcome the drastic change in regime began the exodus to South Florida, others were lined up and executed at La Cabaña Fortress. The man put in charge of these summary trials was none other than Che Guevara. The decision to purge the military and carry out a great number of executions provides a clear example of analogical reasoning. Guevara witnessed first-hand how Arbenz succumbed to a military that was unfriendly and could be influenced by the United States. The solution was to gain quick and complete control of the military. Military command was turned over to the one person whose loyalty to Fidel could not be questioned his younger brother Raul. This was accompanied by the creation of Committees for the Defense of the Revolution. These are equivalent to "neighborhood watch" groups, organized to keep an eye on those suspected of being disloyal to the revolution.

The United States seems to have looked back on Guatemala with rose-colored lenses. There is ample evidence that President Kennedy did not fully investigate the Bay of Pigs plan in great depth or with a critical eye (Neustadt and May 1986, ch. 8). Ironically, recently declassified documents reveal that the United States was already keeping tabs on Guevara as far back as 1956 when he was arrested with Castro in Mexico City (Ratner and Smith 1997, 15). At least three years before Guevara became an official figure in revolutionary Cuba the United States was aware that he had been in Guatemala during the coup of 1954.

We jump ahead to 1960. The Eisenhower administration and the new government of Cuba were at odds over the Cuban decision to take delivery of

Soviet crude oil. The American refineries refused to refine this oil, and a serious foreign policy impasse ensued. The Eisenhower government began looking at options that would result in the removal of Castro from power. It is here that we see our second use of analogy. This time analogy was used by American decision makers (see Etheredge 1985). The CIA quickly voiced support for a Guatemala-type operation. That is, the U.S. government would train and equip exiles in another country and then have this force launch an invasion that would trigger further opposition within the country. One of the central merits of this plan was that it did not involve the use of American soldiers.

Just as Guevara was involved in events in 1954 and 1959, key American players such as the CIA's Allen Dulles were involved in the Guatemalan and Bay of Pigs decisions.

The Bay of Pigs

The Cubans were ready for the American-backed invasion. Castro came off as a heroic figure directing the Cuban response from an open vehicle speeding to the scene of the action. From the Cuban perspective, the failed Bays of Pigs (known in Cuba as Playa Giron) invasion helped consolidate the revolution and more or less permanently vilify the United States. It did not help the American cause that late in the invasion President Kennedy withdrew part of the plan calling for American air-support. Castro hailed the victory as the first military defeat of the United States in Latin America.

A furious President Kennedy and his administration quickly went to work trying to learn from its mistakes. There is strong evidence to indicate that the analogies invoked in the planning stages of the Bay of Pigs invasion were overly optimistic (Ryan 1998). One of the major failings of the Bay of Pigs operation was related to intelligence. The Americans thought that popular uprisings in the wake of the exile invasion would lead to the overthrow of Castro. Nothing could have been further from the truth. The attack consolidated Castro's grip on power and gave his fledgling regime a victory over the United States that would be used to whip up nationalism for decades to come. The invasion gave Castro further opportunity to appear in charge. The United States either did not know or failed to consider that the revolution was popular and that Castro had purged the military of potential counterrevolutionary elements. The CIA's Bay of Pigs plan reflected a "wishful thinking" bias and the fiasco permanently altered the role of the CIA in directing military missions.

The main study of the Bay of Pigs (carried out by General Maxwell Taylor) revealed that American counterinsurgency policy should be thought of in political, economic, and social terms rather than merely military ones (Ryan 1998, 23–24). Low-intensity doctrine should be concerned with winning over the population, not just killing rebels. This lesson was ultimately not applied with any measure of success in Vietnam, but Henry Butterfield Ryan argues that it was used successfully in the Guevara-led Bolivian crisis a few years later.

The Cuban *Foco* and Africa, 1965

In the early years of the revolution, Guevara took several high-profile government positions. He was also a sort of roving ambassador for Cuba and traveled to China and many African and Warsaw Pact countries in the early 1960s. During this time Guevara became disenchanted with the Soviets. He had very high expectations of the communist superpower and began to criticize the Soviets publicly. Castro, who was more pragmatic because of his position as head of state, was much more circumspect in his dealings with the Soviets. Of course, this position was necessary if Cuba was going to continue to receive favorable economic aid and trade deals from the Soviets. Although we may not know the full story for some time, this may explain why at this time Guevara wrote a personal letter to Castro relinquishing his Cuban citizenship and declaring his desire to become involved in revolutionary struggles elsewhere. Guevara seems to have left Cuba on good terms, and it is well established that Guevara had always wanted to foment revolution in South America.

The Cuban Revolution was fought using a new strategy that came to be known as the *foco*. The French journalist Regis Debray popularized the *foco* in his 1967 book *Revolution in the Revolution?* Debray's book drew heavily on the writings of Guevara's earlier book *Guerrilla Warfare* (1961). The *foco* strategy went against the conventional, popular revolution theories of Marx, Lenin, and Mao that required large peasant uprisings. The Cubans insisted that a small group of armed and politically aware rebels could lead a guerrilla fight against a stronger government army. The rebels could use the rural terrain to their advantage and only strike at the army when conditions were favorable. The revolutionary *foco* is directed by the rural guerrillas fighting the government and recruiting peasants in the countryside. This was a unique way of conducting guerrilla warfare. Thus, the twelve to twenty Cubans that survived the original boat trip from Mexico and the disastrous landing were able to regroup and work their way westward in several small columns. As they went, they captured equipment from the army and recruited peasants from the mountains. The message of the *foco* is that revolution need not wait for peasant enlightenment. The revolution could take shortcuts. The implications of this new way of thinking made Western policy makers uneasy.

The decision to free himself from his Cuban role to take a more internationalist position was made using analogical reasoning. Guevara decided to apply the *foco* strategy in the civil war in the Democratic Republic of the Congo (DRC). The *foco* had proven successful in Cuba, and Guevara expected to achieve a similar outcome in Africa. To further ensure the mission's success, he took with him a group of elite Cubans, most of who had fought in the Cuban Revolution. This is a clear case of using analogy in a decision. The Cuban government wanted to help insurgents win a civil war in Africa so that Cuba could enhance his international reputation as a vanguard state in the fight against imperialism.

The biggest obstacle the *foco* faced in Africa was that the rebel leadership preferred to remain apart from the troops and relax and party in the safety of other African cities such as Dar es-Salaam, Tanzania. (Ironically, one of the absentee rebel leaders, Laurent Kabila, came to power in Zaire almost thirty years later but was assassinated shortly thereafter). This violated one of the cardinal rules of the *foco*: that the rebellion was to be directed from the bush by the guerrilla leadership. The lack of effective African leadership at the front constantly thwarted Guevara's attempts to galvanize the *foco* and was never resolved during his time there (Gálvez 1999). The lack of leadership was directly correlated with an overall lack of esprit de corps in the bush where the fighters demonstrated no real willingness to engage the enemy.

A month and a half into the campaign, Guevara ticked off other factors that were hampering the African *foco*: (1) lack of a central command, (2) overall lack of commitment to the revolution, (3) misuse of weapons, (4) lack of discipline and parochialism, (5) inability to coordinate large troop movements, and (6) lack of firearm training (Gálvez 1999, 92). The parochialism was a recurring problem because various tribal loyalties pulled fighters toward competing loyalties.

Rather than "Cubanize" the conflict in the DRC, Guevara wrote in his diary that the Cubans became "Congolized" (Gálvez 1999, 45–46). In other words, instead of imparting the Cuban *foco* to the Africans, the tribalism and lack of effective leadership in the conflict zones was having a negative impact on Cuban morale and ability to carry out the fight. Guevara was constantly being thwarted in his efforts to go to the front to be more directly involved in training the African fighters. The African leaders such as Kabila either were threatened by Guevara (because these leaders were enjoying a hedonistic lifestyle in the rear) or really did not want to see him in harm's way (Gálvez 1999, 113). Either way, they did not take full advantage of Guevara's ability to motivate and train fighters at the front in the *foco* style.

Summarizing, Guevara did not see a clear leader capable of turning the situation around. The fighters were not dedicated or serious about becoming politically aware. There was no systematic effort to work harmoniously with the small farmer sector that was crucial to food supplies (Gálvez 1999). Guevara lamented that the farmers were the only significant sector in that part of the country, and there was no effort made by the rebels to win them over. The peasant farmers had only the land needed to feed themselves, so this offered no vehicle for pushing them toward supporting the rebels (Gálvez 1999, 281–282). Although the government army often mistreated the farmers, the rebels lacked the capacity and willingness to exploit this to their benefit (Gálvez 1999, 282). In short, the conditions were not ripe for a Cuban-style *foco*.

Once again we see that analogical reasoning did not work. The African situation was quite different from conditions in Cuba during the 1956–1959 revolution. The charismatic Castro demonstrated a willingness to place himself at the front throughout the campaign. Other leaders such as Guevara, Raul Castro, and Camilo Cienfuegos also led from the battlefield. Unlike the situation in Africa, these men were able to inspire dedication and discipline in their charges. In Cuba, the rebels were able to exploit the grievances of the peasant farmer class. The rebels offered basic services and promised a better future with land reform and better access to health care and education. Thus, the Cubans won over the countryside population and were able to get food and recruits from these areas. The Cuban *foco* also did not suffer from the tribalism that confounded loyalty and discipline in Africa.

The African experience was more or less a disaster for Guevara. The lessons taken from the Cuban revolution did not apply very readily in Africa. The conditions were different and the analogy was too superficial to be useful. In carrying out Cuban foreign policy of exporting revolution, Guevara applied the Cuban methods of guerrilla warfare that he had written about and experienced firsthand, and it failed rather miserably.

Bolivia, 1966–1967

The next interesting analogy-based decision involves Guevara's ill-fated venture in Bolivia. Although all of the details may not be known for some time, after the African failure, Castro and Guevara made the decision that Guevara would lead a new rebel front in Bolivia. The goal was to begin in Bolivia and then spread the revolution to other parts of Latin America. There is much disagreement over whether Castro was looking to get rid of Guevara (perhaps because of Guevara's public criticisms of the USSR) or simply giving in to the Argentine's longstanding goals of returning to South America to foment revolution, but we need not go deeply into that debate here. Suffice it to say a preponderance of the evidence indicates that the Bolivian decision was probably made at the specific request of Guevara and that there was no irreparable, serious split between the two revolutionaries.

Ryan (1998) notes the similarities between the Cuban decision to go into Bolivia and the American decision to undertake the Bay of Pigs. Each decision was overly optimistic because they were based on recent analogy with key players on both sides involved in both decisions. Each regime used analogy selectively and ignored vital information that might have resulted in opting for other alternatives. The Americans were blind to the fact that Castro was popular with a large segment of the Cuban people. Furthermore, most of Castro's opposition had been either imprisoned or executed or had left the country. Castro had then armed the loyal masses – something that Arbenz had failed to do in 1954. These loyal masses, if anything, could be seen rushing to the site of the invasion in 1961, not rushing to help overthrow Castro.

The Cubans saw Bolivia as a soft target because its regime and its military were considered inept. Similar circumstances had made the *foco* possible in Cuba. Bolivia had a large number of miners and peasants who could form the basis of a popular revolution. The miners could become a politically aware opposition movement that made conditions even more favorable than Cuba in some ways. Guevara planned for the rebels to operate in a part of the country with dense vegetation (Ryan 1998, 71) as they had in Cuba. However, in applying the *foco* analogy the Cubans downplayed potential weak points in the plan. First, Guevara would be leading a rebel army that was, initially at least, dominated by Cubans. In other words, the rebels were outsiders. They were not fluent in the local Indian dialects. Thus, the bearded rebels were perceived as foreigners and they invoked fear in many of the peasants they encountered. During the Cuban *foco* the rebels swept through the countryside and easily recruited peasants willing to take up arms. During the Bolivian campaign, there was little to no success recruiting able-bodied, native peasants.

Second, the Cubans were not familiar with the terrain in the part of Bolivia where the rebellion was to begin (Ryan 1998). Third, the rebellion was undertaken before a clear and reliable link to the cities was in place. Fourth, the Communist Party of Bolivia officially disavowed the rebellion and thus offered no support. Finally, and perhaps most important, there had been a revolution of sorts in 1952 in Bolivia that had distributed land to peasants. Thus, in addition to being frightened by the unshaven foreigners encountered during the Bolivian campaign, the peasants were largely unconvinced by the Marxist dogma of Guevara and his men. Taken together, it is clear that the conditions in Bolivia in the late 1960s were quite different from those in Cuba a decade earlier. The rebels were attempting a rural *foco* when the miners and disenchanted urbanites probably represented more willing recruits.

Despite these facts, there are those who defend the suitability of Bolivia for Guevera's mission. A recent book by Bolivian rebel Rodolfo Sandaña (2001) defends the selection of Bolivia for the *foco*. Sandaña argues that tin miners in Bolivia were politicized and ready to support the armed struggle.

From the American perspective, the Bolivian operation reveals a case of successful learning and analogical reasoning. In his study of the downfall of Guevara, historian Henry Butterfield Ryan (1998) notes that the Cuban Revolution triggered a strong reaction to low-intensity warfare in the Western Hemisphere. As mentioned, Ryan notes it was U.S. failures in Vietnam that helped the United States learn how to deal properly with small-scale insurgencies. Ryan notes that the United States also studied and learned how better to fight low-intensity warfare by studying Guevara's *Guerrilla Warfare*.

Throughout Guevara's Bolivian campaign, the United States exercised great restraint. Bolivia repeatedly asked for more offensive weapons systems, and the United States turned down the requests. The United States also had a strict policy of not sending American troops into the combat zones. The U.S. Ambassador to Bolivia commented later that the State Department had very specifically issued an edict that no Americans should enter the conflict zones and that it wanted to avoid "another Vietnam" (Ryan 1998, 51). The Pentagon had also agreed to the policy. Further, the United States also fought the Bolivian attempt to obtain and use napalm. In short, Ryan notes that the mistakes made in Vietnam (and, to a lesser extent, the Bay of Pigs) were not repeated, and the crisis was not allowed to become "Americanized." The United States was leery of the Bolivians indiscriminately attacking rural villages trying to root out rebels and their sympathizers. An article in the *Times* of London quoted an American diplomat clearly applying a Vietnam analogy to Bolivia (Ryan 1998, 79). The diplomat noted that if civilians were harmed with napalm and other excessive uses of force, this would build greater sympathy for the rebel cause. This is what had happened in Vietnam.

Although these circumspect policies led to good results for the United States, the lack of a U.S. overreaction very likely hurt Guevara's recruiting and overall ability to win "the hearts and minds" of Bolivian peasants and miners. Ryan argues that Guevara wanted another Vietnam. The decision made by the Johnson administration to be careful and circumspect was based on learning and analogy. This is a clear example of how analogy can be beneficial if the "right" lessons are learned.

Again, the Bolivian uprising was based on the Cuban *foco*. In Cuba, a small group of rebels was able to mount a successful revolution by using the geography to their advantage and recruiting from the disenchanted rural peasantry. Bolivia also had a large, poor rural sector and was also led by a military government friendly to the United States. On the surface, conditions in the two countries seemed analogous. But these analogies were misleading and led Guevara down a disastrous path. There were important lessons to be learned from the Cuban *foco*, but a thorough and honest assessment of the situation in Bolivia would have revealed that conditions were not ripe there for this type of operation. Most notably, Guevara lacked popular support, knowledge of the region, urban support, and support of the Bolivian Communist Party (see Ryan 1998).

The United States, in contrast, successfully applied lessons recently learned from Vietnam. In applying lessons of moderation by not giving aggressive weapons systems and napalm to Bolivia and by keeping Americans out of the combat zones, the United States denied Guevara's apparent goal of creating another Vietnam (Ryan 1998).

Taken as a whole, it is clear that analogies played important roles in many of the key decisions made by Cuban and American leaders during the 1950s and 1960s. As Jervis notes, when decision makers experience prior events themselves, there is a greater chance these events will become used as analogies and shape decisions and outcomes.

Of course, analogies can lead to poor outcomes if they are not used appropriately (S. Anderson 2007; Khong 1992). Decision makers have a tendency to use analogies because of the complexities of the world and limitations of the brain to handle information. However, there is evidence that humans have a tendency to apply analogies in a superficial sense that can lead to oversimplification (Khong 1992). These pathologies are borne out in our case study of U.S.-Cuban relations in the 1950s and 1960s.

Although the use of analogies is fraught with pitfalls, "high-complexity" leaders – those who demonstrate a strong ability to articulate differences, for example, in policies, ideas, places, and people – apparently use more sophisticated analogical reasoning incorporating a diverse pool of analogs drawn from various points in history and regions of the world (Dyson and Preston 2006).

Leaders' Personality

Whereas cognitive theories that deal with perception and misperception focus on how information processing can shape decisions, affective theories explore how **personality** and emotions such as insecurity and fear can affect decisions (Mandel 1986, 253). David Winter (2003, 110) defines personality as the "individually patterned integration of processes of perception, memory, judgment, goal-seeking, and emotional expression and regulation." Studying the personality of leaders can help us understand why some leaders make certain decisions, whereas other leaders facing a similar situation make completely different decisions.

In terms of how it affects decision making, Winter (2003) writes that personality influences the weighting of preferences and how decision makers react to symbols and cues. He also notes that personality shapes how a person deals with emotion. Winter (2003, 115–117) breaks down personality into four elements: temperament, cognitions, motives, and the social context. Temperament refers to the observable components of behavior such as energy level and neuroses. The social context is observable and involves factors such as gender, class, race, culture, ethnicity, and generation. Cognitions are factors such as beliefs, values, and attitudes. Motives include goals and defense mechanisms. Cognitions and motives are less observable.

Margaret Hermann developed a technique to assess the personality of leaders without actually interviewing them known as Personality Assessment-at-a-Distance (1983; discussed in Preston 2001). The method works by using content analysis to analyze the transcripts from spontaneous interview responses. Using these data M. Hermann (1984, 1999) specifies a number of personality groupings that are relevant to FPDM. These are nationalism, belief in one's ability to control events, distrust of others, in-group bias, need for power, problem solving versus group maintenance and dealing with others, self-confidence, and conceptual complexity (see also Preston 2001, 12). Ronald Reagan is an example of a president low in conceptual complexity but high in nationalism and belief in one's ability to control events. These personality traits shaped his behavior – especially during his first term – as he dealt with the Soviet Union.

M. Hermann (1987; cited in Winter 2003) uncovers personality profiles of leaders based on the four elements of motivation, social context, cognitions, and temperament. She created a framework to compile a complete personality profile that can be used to understand foreign policy actions. The profile generates a number of "orientations": expansionist, active independent, influential, mediator, opportunist, and developmental. The orientations are derived from an analysis of the four elements. For example, leaders who demonstrate the elements of power motivation, belief in ability to control events, cognitive complexity, and self-confidence are regarded as "influential" and desire to impact foreign affairs through a leadership role. President Clinton would fit this categorization. Expansionist leaders desire more territory and power based on their levels of nationalism, self-confidence, power motivation, and distrust. This might characterize Saddam Hussein leading up to the invasion of Kuwait. Leaders' personalities affect decision strategy and choice. McCrae and Costa (2006) report that personality does not change much after age thirty.

Leadership Style

Powerful individuals have the authority to make important decisions. Analyzing **leadership style** helps us to understand why certain decisions are made by leaders and why alternative courses of action are not taken. It also helps us to understand the decision process itself.

In a fascinating study of leadership style, Margaret Hermann et al. (2001) introduce an elaborate framework for understanding the inner workings of leadership style. The authors draw a distinction of whether leaders are goal driven or context driven. In the former, leaders are driven to solve a problem. In other words, these leaders are "task-oriented." They are unlikely to change their position or ideology. Staff are appointed on the basis of loyalty and similarity of outlook. Task-motivated leaders are less likely to require broad international or domestic coalitions before taking action and in maintaining a policy. President George W. Bush, for example, did not allow the lack of UN approval to prevent the invasion of Iraq in 2003 and persisted in the Iraq War effort in the face of congressional and public discontent about the war's progression.

At the other end of the spectrum are leaders who are more circumspect and adaptable according to the context of a current situation. These leaders consult, discuss, and are open to flexible solutions to different problems. They adapt their behavior to fit particular situations and gauge the opinions of other groups. They appoint staff on the basis of political realities rather than loyalty or overlapping ideology. These leaders work to build coalitions at the international level.

The essential difference between these two types – task oriented versus context oriented – is the degree of sensitivity to the political context. Task-oriented leaders are not very sensitive to the political context, whereas context-oriented leaders are. This has great relevance for foreign policy decision making, for it tells us whether and the extent to which politics constrains leaders in their actions. Because they are less likely to consult and compromise because of their tendency to challenge political constraints, task-focused leaders are more likely, for example, to lead a country into armed conflict. However, because they are keenly sensitive to domestic politics, context-focused leaders are less likely to bring their nations into armed conflict.

How can we assess a leader according to this dichotomy? Margaret Hermann et al. (2001) provide the key dimensions that guide us in understanding whether a leader will be more task oriented or context oriented: (1) whether the leader accepts political constraints, (2) the leader's willingness to accept new information, and (3) whether the leader is problem focused or relationship focused.

Leaders respond differently to political constraints. For example, we would expect democratic leaders to be more structurally constrained by legislatures, the press, public opinion, and opposition parties, as predicted by poliheuristic theory. Authoritarian leaders face few such constraints. But even within democracies, there is variation. Essentially, goal-oriented leaders are more likely to challenge constraints, whereas those who are context oriented will work within the confines of constraints. Working within constraints entails coalition building, empathy, sensitivity to constituents, and compromise.

A willingness to accept new information is also important at the individual level. Goal-oriented leaders are less open to new information, whereas context-oriented leaders actively seek out information. Resistance to new information by the former resembles groupthink or cognitive consistency. Information that goal-oriented leaders do seek is assessed on the basis of whether it supports initial beliefs. In terms of political sensitivity, if the leader is not sensitive to the aforementioned political dimension, then information will be used as a tool to sway others. This behavior is referred to as *advocating*. More politically sensitive leaders approach information gathering as *cue takers*. They seek out the positions of others and generally cast a wide net for information.

Types of Leaders: Crusader, Strategic, Pragmatic, and Opportunistic

By cross-matching these two dimensions, M. Hermann et al. (2001, 95) produce a typology of leadership style with four categories: crusader, strategic, pragmatic, and opportunistic. The *crusader* challenges political constraints and is closed to new information. This type of leader is essentially unconstrained in pursuing his or her version of the world. The example the authors provide is that of Fidel Castro. The *opportunist*, in contrast, is mindful of political constraints and pursues information. Political bargaining is a key component of this style of leadership (thus, we see the similarity with the bureaucratic politics model). This type of leader will not risk alienating politically important actors – in stark contrast to leaders such as Hugo Chavez of Venezuela or Kim Jong-il of North Korea.

The *strategic* leader challenges constraints but is open to information (ibid.). This type of leader knows what she wants and will seek information pursuant to achieving goals. This type of leader is politically bold but circumspect when it comes to acting out these ambitious aspirations. Hafez al-Assad of Syria exemplified this category (ibid.). Assad wanted the Golan Heights back from Israel and to be a regional player in the Middle East. To some extent, Syria maintained influence in the region indirectly through its actions in Lebanon. These actions were often subtle and could not be easily traced back to Assad. His overall strategy for the Heights did not involve risky direct threats. Another type of leader, *pragmatic*, fills out the group. These leaders respect political constraints but are closed to information.

Political constraints and attitude toward information can then be supplemented with the third dimension, motivation for action. These two types of motivation for action alongside the four categories of crusader, strategic, pragmatic, and opportunistic provide another eight nuanced categories (ibid.). For example, crusaders (closed to information and not responsive to political constraints) can be expansionistic or evangelistic depending on whether their motivation is problem based or relationship based, respectively. Expansionist leaders are those with a motivation provided by a problem that needs solving. These leaders will expand their control over resources or territory. Looking across all three dimensions, an expansionist crusader is driven to solve a problem and in doing so is closed to information and is insensitive to political constraints. An evangelist is a crusader who is more comfortable with relationships and influences others toward their cause in a style not unlike an evangelist preacher.

An incremental leader faced with a problem challenges constraints, is open to information (and is therefore strategic), and, in terms of motivation, is focused on maneuverability. A charismatic leader craving relationships also challenges constraints and is open to information (also strategic), but in terms of motivation focuses on relationships by urging others to act.

The next types, directive and consultative, are subsets of the pragmatic category. Leaders of these types respect the constraints of politics but are closed to information. If problem focused, the actor is referred to as directive. These actors direct policy discussions consistent with their personal views.

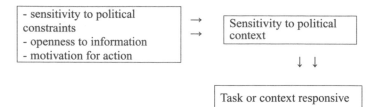

Figure 6.1. Leadership Style. Based on M. Hermann et al. 2001.

Consultative leaders, in contrast, tend to be relationship focused and thus will carefully track the positions of other elites.

The final two styles, reactive and accommodative, derive from the opportunistic category (respects constraints and is open to information). Those motivated to focus on a problem are termed reactive. These leaders determine the range of options and whether political constituencies will be receptive. This behavior is politically expedient. Each problem that arises is managed according to a consideration of options that meet a political threshold. Attentive readers will note the similarities between this type and both the rational actor and poliheuristic models. Those leaders motivated to focus on relationships are accommodative. These leaders are bridge builders. They seek to create consensus and increase accountability. The difference between the two is the motivation for action.

Summarizing, three dimensions – sensitivity to political constraints, openness to information, and motivation for action – help us to determine whether a leader will be goal or context oriented. Goal-oriented leaders are more likely to take forceful steps, whereas context-oriented leaders are more risk averse and take careful or incremental steps. Figure 6.1 depicts these relationships. The arrows represent the direction of causality. For example, the dimensions in the first box shape how politics will influence the decision, which in turn determines whether the actor is task- or context-responsive.

Margaret Hermann et al. (2001, 119) observe that as one moves away from a leadership style of constraint challenger/closed to information and toward one of constraints sensitive/open to information, the decisions become less definitive or clear-cut. The same is true as we move from expansionist to accommodative. Thus, the leadership-style framework can help predict relevant information on decisions.

It is possible to study the links between leadership style and advisory system structure. One such study analyzed this over time for several U.S. presidents (Preston 2001). The study develops a typology that explores how attentive a president is to the context of a decision. Presidents that are more attentive are said to be more cognitively complex. The decision context includes the policy environment and the position of his subordinates. The other axis of the typology is prior policy experience. Matching the two variables together in one table, there are four possible outcome categories: navigator, observer, sentinel, and maverick. Navigators are high on both variables, whereas mavericks are low on both. Navigators are vigilant, actively collect information, are engaged, and seek outside opinion, whereas mavericks are not as likely to seek outside information and can be disinterested, and their policy decisions can be ad hoc. The other two categories fall in between.

The typology is applied to Truman, Eisenhower, Kennedy, Johnson, George H. W. Bush, and Clinton. In terms of foreign policy, Kennedy, Eisenhower, Clinton, and Bush all displayed high attentiveness to the need for information and the decision context. Johnson and Truman displayed low complexity.

Leadership styles of vastly different individuals can also be studied using the comparative case study approach. In one important study of leadership style, Saddam Hussein and Bill Clinton are compared using case study evaluations, character analysis, and psycho-biographic analysis (Post 2003). The study compared the results from these analyses to the belief systems, personality, and cognitive and leadership styles of the two men.

COGNITIVE MAPPING

Robert Axelrod's (1976a) cognitive mapping technique takes a very different approach to the study of FPDM. A cognitive map is a graphical depiction of a belief system using either numbers or figures (Maoz 1990b, 116). In other words, cognitive mapping is a diagram of a particular decision maker's policy alternatives and causal assertions.

Arrows representing causal direction connect the points in the cognitive map. Zeev Maoz (1990b, 117) provides the example of Kissinger's cognitive map. Kissinger believed that Soviet foreign policy was driven by its conception of the balance of power. So this simple map contained two nodes: the first stated "Soviet conceptions of the balance of forces" and the second "the conduct of foreign policy." The causal arrow went from the first node to the second. This map was greatly influenced by Kissinger's beliefs about the Soviet Union.

The value of the cognitive mapping approach is that the overall image of the decision structure can be visualized. Cognitive mapping aids decision theory by exposing the nexus between what the decision maker asserts his choices are and his expected outcomes of those choices (Axelrod 1976a, 10).

Cognitive belief mapping is especially applicable to situations in which: (1) the decisions are vital to national security, such as those involving war; (2) decisions are made at the highest level by leaders unconstrained by bureaucracy; (3) long-range policy planning is performed – that is, policy with considerable uncertainty; (4) decisions are made regarding ambiguous or uncertain situations resulting from inadequate information; and (5) decision makers are constrained by stress (Holsti 1976, 30).

Axelrod (1976b) provides his own example of cognitive mapping. The subject of the study is the British Eastern Committee and British intervention in Persia in 1918. The committee was composed of five top-level decision makers and was in charge of British policy in the Middle East. Axelrod derives each committee member's cognitive maps on the basis of his verbal assertions, which had been transcribed verbatim. The actual transcripts are coded into two classes: causal assertions and concept variables. Causes and effects are linked by connectors, for example, the amount of money spent in Persia by Britain (cause) is not really justifiable (connector) for British utility (effect). This connector arrow would have a negative sign to reflect its connotation. Obviously, the reliability of the coding is of the utmost importance.

The results of the cognitive mapping process for the British Eastern Committee were promising. Each member's mapped causal beliefs corresponded to his eventual decision. The cognitive maps make it possible to determine whether the decision makers are using satisficing or other decision strategies. The greatest utility provided by the technique is a glimpse into the belief structure of the participants.

Leadership psychology refers to the "varied psychological elements and assumptions that every leader brings to the decision process" (Renshon and Renshon 2008, 510). In this chapter, we showed that a leader's personality, beliefs, images, emotions, and style all affect decision making. Both character psychology and motivation challenge the quality of decisions of leaders (ibid.).

CONCLUSION

This chapter reveals the psychological determinants of foreign policy decision making. Psychological factors refer to personal qualities such as emotion, personality, images, evoked set, and belief systems and how they influence the decision process and the actual outcome. Psychological factors such as evoked set can mean new information will typically be ignored. In this sense psychological factors can lead to processes akin to decision bias. The next chapter takes up other determinants of foreign policy decision making.

7

International, Domestic, and Cultural Factors
Influencing Foreign Policy Decision Making

INTERNATIONAL FACTORS

Foreign policy decisions are typically made in a strategic setting. Thus, behavior of adversaries and allies affects foreign policy decisions in an interactive sequential setting. For example, U.S. foreign policy during the Georgian crisis in the summer of 2008 was implemented in response to Russia's actions in Georgia. U.S. policy on missile defense in Europe affects Russia's decisions as well as Polish, Czech, and other European leaders' decisions. U.S. foreign policy goals and actions influence Israeli policies toward its enemies and friends. Factors such as the arms race, deterrence, the regime type of the adversary, strategic surprise, and of course alliances affect foreign policy decisions (see Table 7.1).

For example, it was empirically demonstrated that leaders of democratic states are much more likely to attack a nondemocratic adversary than they are another democracy. It is also clear that the mutual assured destruction (MAD) strategy affected superpower behavior during the Cold War and that the arms race between the United States and the USSR and between NATO and the Warsaw Treaty Organization (WTO) influenced many decisions not only of the actors directly involved in the race (the United States and the USSR) but also of third-party players such as China, India, South Korea, Israel, Japan, the Arab states, and, of course, European states. After considering the factors in Table 7.1, we turn to the analysis of domestic factors that shape foreign policy decisions, such as economic conditions (diversionary theory) and the role of public opinion.

Deterrence and Arms Races

Realists portray the international system as anarchic. To survive in a dangerous world with no overarching government, leaders must provide for the security of their states. Realism is built on the rational model. To survive in an

Table 7.1. *International determinants*
of foreign policy decisions

Deterrence
Arms races
Strategic surprise
Alliance formation
Regime type of the adversary

anarchic international system, states build up their defenses to the point that no rational state would invade. This is known as **general deterrence**. States also extend deterrence to other states. For example, Britain had a long-term military presence in Belize to deter Guatemala from carrying out its territorial claims and attacking. This type of deterrence is referred to as **extended immediate deterrence**. It is extended because Britain is extending its deterrent shield to a different region and immediate because there was an obvious and chronic threat posed by Guatemala.

Deterrence theory is usually understood through the rational lens. The rational school portrays deterrence in terms of cost-benefit analysis (Stein 1991, 9). Evidence from a broad range of cases of deterrence failure shows, however, that "political leaders depart in important ways from the norms of rational choice" (ibid., 20). In terms of extended deterrence, a potential attacker is not likely to advance against a protégé state (the state being protected) if the defender has credibly signaled that it will defend the protégé at any cost. Cognitive factors play a role because deterrence is as much a psychological phenomenon as it is a military one. As we will discuss, Argentina misperceived Britain's resolve to protect the Falkland Islands. Likewise, Saddam Hussein misperceived the U.S. commitment to defend Kuwait. U.S. leaders had not effectively communicated to Hussein that they would not accept an Iraqi invasion. Additionally, certain factors, such as level of trade between defender and protégé, are important determinants of successful deterrence (Huth and Russett 1990).

Bruce Russett (1963) found that the most important determinant of successful extended immediate deterrence were close economic, political, and military ties between the defender and the potential target. These ties are even more important than military superiority of the defender. The interdependence between the defender and its protégé can signal a strong commitment that can deter an attack on the protégé.

Although seemingly elegant in its simplicity, this relationship leads to a security dilemma. As states build their defenses to provide for their own survival, other states – particularly neighbors – perceive a threat, thus laying the groundwork for an arms race. **Arms races** are essentially competitive bouts of defense spending and military-capability building between two states or blocs of states (as during the Cold War). Many states are locked in long-term rivalries with other states. Examples of these enduring rivalries include India-Pakistan, Turkey-Greece, and North Korea–South Korea.

Arms races can influence foreign policy decision making. Michael Wallace (1982) argued that if two states become embroiled in a dispute that takes place in the context of an arms race, then escalation to violence is more likely. He refers to this as the "tinderbox hypothesis." His "preparedness hypothesis," on the other hand, suggests that if a state maintains a strong level of deterrence using high levels of defense spending, then a state unhappy with the status quo will not attack. Although somewhat contentious, the finding that arms races lead to war challenges the rational premise of realist thought. For example, the leading figure of post–World War II realist thinking, Hans Morgenthau, argued that the purpose of military preparations was to deter attack by presenting an unacceptable risk to potential aggressors. In other words, countries arm to prevent war. But Wallace asks whether competitive arms races can actually increase the chance of war. In an early statistical study, Wallace (1979) tested data from 1816 to 1965 to answer the following question: Are disputes between nations in arms races more likely to escalate? In other words, does the race create conditions that can quickly escalate to war with minimum provocation? This question reflects the tinderbox hypothesis. Wallace found that twenty-three of the twenty-six disputes that escalated to war were preceded by arms races. Only five of seventy-three that did not end in war were preceded by arms races. This finding is statistically significant and leads Wallace to conclude that arms races play a role in escalation. He does not argue that the races are direct causes (sufficient conditions) but rather that they are best conceived as necessary conditions.

The Wallace study drew some criticism. Responding to his critics, Wallace (1982) presented a second empirical look at arms races and war. In addition to testing the tinderbox hypothesis, Wallace cleverly specifies a "peace through preparedness hypothesis" that posits that "international conflict in which the distribution of military power favors the revisionist state are more likely to result in war than those in which the balance favors the status quo state" (ibid., 39). Additionally, "disputes accompanied by a shift in the distribution of relative power in the favor of a revisionist state, or to the detriment of status quo state, are more likely to escalate than those with no shift" (ibid., 40). In other words, if defense spending is intended to prevent war as Morgenthau claims, then when the revisionist or unhappy state, catches up there should be war because the status quo state had not armed itself sufficiently to prevent an attack. Wallace finds no evidence for the peace through preparedness model. So he again concludes that arms races are one of the factors that lead crises to escalate to war. Furthermore, he argues that if the preparedness argument does not hold, it becomes easier to accept and justify the pursuit of arms control and disarmament policies.

Paul Diehl (1983) refuted Wallace's findings and claims about arms races and war mainly on methodological grounds. He devised a new methodology to measure for arms races based on average rate of change in defense spending. Diehl's race measure required states to spend at least 8 percent per year for at least three years. He also allowed for multilateral races (e.g., NATO vs. WTO). Diehl argued that Wallace really only measured mutual buildups and had no way of knowing from aggregate data whether spending was directed toward a specific country. In other words, how can we really know that a country's defense budget is a direct result of its rival's spending? With these modifications in place, Diehl finds no link between arms races and war. Perhaps we can conclude that arms races are related to outbreak of war, but are probably not necessary or sufficient conditions. Nonetheless, the arms races between India and Pakistan; Israel, Syria and Lebanon; and China and Taiwan do give reason for concern.

As mentioned in Chapter 4, game theory can be used to understand arms races. Recall that game theory uses rational actor assumptions and logic to understand behavior and outcomes. We can again apply the Prisoner's Dilemma. In this case, the alternatives are to keep (arms) racing or to stop and cooperate. The payoffs are ranked in the following order: (1) arms superiority, (2) arms race, (3) cooperation, and (4) losing the arms race (Cashman 1993; Mingst 2002). Again, the dominant strategy in this one-shot interactive game is to keep racing. This alternative guarantees against receiving the worst outcome of losing the arms race. Because each player will choose to keep racing in this one-shot game with known payoffs, the Nash equilibrium is an arms race. If the two sides can open up lines of communication and negotiate, they might improve their payoff and attain the second-best outcome of an end to the arms race. This outcome is better in this game because each side can save resources that would otherwise go toward defense spending. This example can help us to understand why each superpower went for more and more advanced systems during the height of the Cold War. The arms race slowed somewhat with détente as then National Security Advisor Henry Kissinger recognized that superiority meant little in the face of MAD and second-strike capability.

Nuclear deterrence represents a different dynamic. It also hinges upon rational actor assumptions but in a slightly altered manner. If we use game theory, we can see that players are not always better off defecting. The payoffs in this noncrisis game are ranked as follows: (1) peace because neither side launches, (2) first strike, (3) nuclear exchange, and (4) being the target of a strike (Mingst 2002). If two states are roughly equal in their nuclear capabilities, it can be said that each possesses second-strike capability. That is, no matter how many nuclear warheads are directed at a state, the target state is guaranteed the opportunity for a retaliatory or second strike of comparable magnitude. The result is that neither state will rationally choose to launch a first strike. This framework came to be known as MAD, and several scholars, such as Kenneth

Waltz and John Lewis Gaddis, suggest that this system kept the Cold War from escalating. The stability of the system was fortified by agreements such as the 1963 Hot Line Agreement between the United States and Soviet Union. This post–Cuban Missile Crisis agreement was designed to prevent accidental or unintentional nuclear exchanges.

Later in the 1960s, the development of antiballistic missiles (ABMs) jeopardized this stable deterrence system. ABMs are designed to shoot down incoming missiles. The ability to eliminate a second strike might shift the payoff structure so that a leader might be tempted to launch a first strike. Subsequently, some fear that the National Missile Defense currently being developed in the United States will similarly undermine this stable deterrence.

Strategic Surprise

Military historian John Lewis Gaddis defines surprise strategy as one in which "force is used in an unexpected way at an unexpected time against an unexpected target, with a view to trying to achieve what more conventional methods of warfare cannot" (Gaddis 2002). Surprise affects foreign policy decisions. It can lead to biases and errors in decision making as a result of time pressure, stress, ambiguity of information, and lack of familiarity with the new challenge. The surprise itself can affect information processing during crises and ultimately the choices leaders make.

The U.S. retaliation in Afghanistan against the Taliban and al-Qaeda was a surprise to bin Laden (Gaddis 2002). Iraq's invasion of Kuwait in August 1990 took the United States – and most of the world – by surprise. The possibility that Soviet forces would have caught NATO forces by surprise while attacking in Central Europe characterized most of the Cold War era (Gray 2005).

The strategic surprise of 9/11 drastically shifted U.S. foreign policy to follow what President Bush defined as: "either you are with us or against us" (in the war on terrorism). Suddenly, Pakistan became key to U.S. foreign and security policy, and a regime such as the Taliban in Afghanistan became the enemy. Although bin Laden's record "was clear enough – the bombings of American embassies in Kenya and Tanzania in 1998, and the USS *Cole* in Yemen in 2000 – and there had already been an unsuccessful attempt on the World Trade Center itself, in 1993," these events were treated in isolation from each other and were not interpreted as a warning that an attack on U.S. soil was imminent (Gaddis 2002).

Foreign policy acts can also help avoid, prevent, or preempt strategic surprises. Fearing an attack by Syria in 2006 due to miscalculations and misinterpretation of Israeli intentions and moves, Israeli leaders went out of their way to send messages, signals, mediators, and messengers to Syria stating that Israel did not want war with Syria. During the war in Lebanon that summer, then Israeli Defense Minister Amir Peretz assured Syria that Israel did not plan on attacking Syria – a move that drew criticism from policy circles in Israel and abroad because it signalled to Syria that it could continue supplying Hezbollah with weapons and logistical support without being punished.

Geopolitical, cultural, and technological factors, as well as intelligence failures, can fuel strategic surprise (Gray 2005). Colin Gray has noted, however, that there are only a few historical cases in which strategic surprise helped make a decisive victory.

Alliances

One of the most important foreign policy decisions a leader will make relates to alliances. Military alliances, the most common form, are agreements between signatory states that spell out what each will do in the event of armed aggression. Decisions are made by leaders inviting new states to join a coalition and by leaders responding to invitations. The leaders of Turkey and Greece, for example, were faced with decisions when invited to join the NATO alliance. After joining alliances, states can sometimes decide to end their participation effectively. This was highlighted in Chapter 4 with the example of New Zealand and the Australia, New Zealand, United States Security Treaty alliance.

One means of dealing with the security dilemma is to form or join strategic alliances. Jack Levy (1975) outlines the means by which alliance formation can lead to stability. One school of thought holds that alliances reduce the uncertainty and misperception that can lead to war. The Falkland Islands War highlights the role that misperceptions can play. Alliance formation is also the core component of balance of power theory. Countries form alliances to counter a country that challenges the status quo. For example, coalitions were formed to defeat Hitler and Napoleon. A weaker state can enhance its domestic standing and thus avoid collapse by forming an alliance with a more powerful country.

Alliances can fuel arms races and lead to destabilizing counteralliances (ibid). Alliances can also become overly rigid. This is the common explanation given for the start of World War I as the Russian-Serbian and German–Austro-Hungarian pacts led the parties on a path to war that might have been avoided had the alliances not become so strong. Randolph Siverson and Joel King (1979) find that alliances help war spread and that nations that have alliances are therefore more war prone.

Bruce Bueno de Mesquita (2003, 489–490) describes three types of military alliances. The neutrality or nonaggression pact is a promise by signatories that each will not take part in any attack on the other. The next form, ententes, involves more of a commitment. In this case signatories promise to consult with each other in the event that one is attacked. Russia, Britain, France, and the United States signed such an agreement in World War I. Defense pacts contain language that specifies how each signatory will help any other signatory that is attacked. NATO is a classic example of a mutual defense pact. Alliance formation is an extension of foreign policy by other means. As such, it affects decision making in foreign affairs.

Regime Type of the Adversary

When a state faces a decision during an international crisis, the regime type of its adversary could be an influential factor. There is strong evidence that a democracy will not fight another democracy. There is something inherent in democracy that pushes disputants toward peaceful resolution rather than direct violent confrontation. If a democratic state is facing off against another democracy then violence might be automatically ruled out. Thus, regime type presents us with a heuristic that eliminates an alternative in a noncompensatory fashion.

Zeev Maoz and Bruce Russett (1993) outline two main explanations for the democratic peace phenomenon. The normative model holds that democracies externalize values of peaceful conflict resolution. Disputes in democracies are solved peacefully. In nondemocracies, leaders govern by coercion in winner-take-all systems. So democracies treat each other differently from the way they treat nondemocracies. If a democracy is in a dispute with a nondemocracy, then the democracy is more likely to resort to the more aggressive norms of the anarchic international system. This means that democracies are involved in many conflicts but not with each other. Survival is key in the anarchic system and democracies will be tough in dealing with nondemocracies. Democratic leaders will make the decision to shift to the norms of the anarchic system. The normative model implies that older democracies will be more peaceful because their peaceful norms of behavior are better established. There is a sense of stability and persistence of peaceful norms in older democracies. This is one reason building democracy in places such as Iraq is not easy.

The structural model also holds that democracies differ from nondemocracies. The "structures" are democratic institutions such as the legislative branch, opposition parties, courts, free press, interest groups, and so on. The institutions make it harder for executives to rush headlong into war. For instance, the U.S. Congress has the constitutional power to declare war and passed the War Powers Act over the veto of President Nixon. The media and the mass public scrutinize decisions to go to war in democratic states.

International challenges require democratic political leaders to mobilize domestic support for their policies. Support comes from groups that give legitimacy to the government. For example, legislatures, voters, the bureaucracy, and interest groups can give support. It is difficult to mobilize support from all of these diverse groups in a democracy. In a dispute involving two democracies, each country will face similar constraints on rushing headlong into war. There are two political processes at work (one in each country), so there is more time for diplomacy to work. In nondemocracies, the leader can start a war without gaining support from these groups. According to Maoz and Russett, democratic leaders can take shortcuts to war – thus avoiding the need to mobilize political support – only in times of emergency. For example, President Roosevelt did not have to wait to mobilize the public after Japan attacked Pearl Harbor in 1941.

Maoz and Russett hypothesize that the more democratic a dyad (pair of states) is, the lower the likelihood of a militarized dispute. This is known as the joint democracy hypothesis. They also expect dyads with more years of democratic rule to be more peaceful. This hypothesis tests the normative model. To get at the structural model, they compare presidential systems to parliamentary ones. The latter have more constraints on the executive. Looking at the years 1946 to 1986 they find strong support for the joint democracy hypothesis and slightly more support for the normative model. Structural constraints do not stop lower-level disputes like norms do. This implies that new democracies (e.g., former Soviet republics in Central Asia) may yet face disputes.

John Oneal, Bruce Russett, and Michael Berbaum (2003) look at the causes of peace using the framework provided by Immanuel Kant. The "Kantian triad" combines democratic government, free trade, and international law/organization. Realism contends that politics determines economics; or, put differently, trade follows the flag. From this perspective, security concerns could limit trade. For instance, toward the end of the Cold War, the U.S. government sanctioned the Toshiba Corporation for providing sensitive computer technology to the Soviet Union. Liberals, in contrast, suggest that free trade can have positive repercussions. The results of the study by Oneal et al. reveal that Kantian influences are more important determinants of conflict than are past conflict, contiguity, and distance between the countries. The policy implication is that the probability of a serious dispute between the United States and China goes down as China democratizes and bilateral trade increases. This finding has implications for the foreign policies of both countries.

There is a fair degree of contention over whether the democratic peace theory applies only to democratic dyads. In other words, do we expect the theory to hold only when it is two democracies that are involved in a dispute? Or is there something inherent in democracies that makes them more likely to negotiate rather than resort to violence in a dispute? The vast majority of democratic peace studies support only the dyadic variant of the theory.

Karl DeRouen Jr. and Shaun Goldfinch (2004) provide evidence of a monadic democratic peace. That is, democracies are inherently more peaceful than nondemocracies. Specifically, they show that democracies prefer to negotiate rather than use violence during international crises. They invoke the "new institutional" literature that suggests that democratic norms enhance the democratic character of institutions (see March and Olsen 1996). In addition to finding that democracies are more likely to be conciliatory in crises even if the adversary is nondemocratic, they show that democracy reduces the diversionary incentive. Their overarching conclusion is that democracy socially constructs a different type of human and that these humans prefer peaceful resolution.

For some scholars the democratic peace is hard to explain because one must examine reasons for something that did not happen (war among democracies). One study used the experimental method to shed light on the democratic peace. Alex Mintz and Nehemia Geva (1993) found that subjects approved the use of force significantly more when the adversary was nondemocratic than when the adversary was a democratic regime. They concluded that because attacking another democracy would be viewed as a failure of foreign policy, leaders of democracies eliminate the attack alternative when the adversary is a democracy.

A forceful challenge to the democratic peace is provided by Sebastian Rosato (2003), who argues that democracies are prone to surprise attack, do not always externalize peaceful norms, and do not credibly reveal private information about their willingness to fight. Notwithstanding these criticisms, the democratic peace is a useful theory of foreign policy decision making and international relations. It can explain both why states do not go to war and why they do.

DOMESTIC FACTORS

Domestic politics, economic conditions, and public opinion are among the most important domestic factors that shape foreign policy decision making.

Diversionary Tactics

International relations and domestic politics coalesce in the body of work known as **diversionary theory**. Scholars and pundits often question the motives of leaders who use military force. The notion that leaders use force at politically opportune times is known as diversionary theory. The "in group–out group hypothesis" developed by sociologists Georg Simmel (1898) and Lewis Coser (1956) states that conflict within a group can be diminished if the group is faced with a common external threat. This can be extended to foreign policy. The in group can be taken to mean the citizens of a country. Conflict within the group can be manifested as rioting, political scandal, or high unemployment. These examples of unrest could be proxied with measures of executive approval. Thus, a political leader who wants to survive in power might want to divert attention from domestic problems by using force against an external adversary.

Table 7.2. *Domestic determinants of foreign policy decisions*

Economic conditions (diversionary tactics)
Economic interests
Public opinion
Electoral cycles
Two-level games

DeRouen Jr. (2000) tested for potential diversionary dynamics in the United States. Because low public approval is said to be a cause for diversion and diversion is said to cause jumps in approval, DeRouen Jr. specifies a model that works in both directions. He finds that force is more likely when unemployment is high and that force leads to a jump in approval (the "rally 'round the flag" effect). A related study tests whether force actually diverts (DeRouen Jr. and Peake 2002). It shows that uses of force by American presidents reduces the percentage of the American public that views the economy as the most important problem. Thus, military force abroad diverts public attention away from a weak economy. A weak economy is one of the worst domestic political problems a president can face. If force is used abroad, it appears that public attention is diverted from the economy and toward other problems – even if only for a short time.

Alistair Smith (1996) adds a twist to the diversionary debate. Smith argues that small states can act strategically and avoid provocative behavior toward a stronger rival when the stronger state might have incentive to divert. In other words, if the stronger state has economic problems or the executive is experiencing declining popularity or suffering through a scandal, then potential targets with an eye on the stronger state will avoid providing a justification for an attack.

In a similar vein, leaders might want to appear to be strong and in charge at election time. To this end, they may take advantage of and seek out military opportunities just before an election. However, no conclusive evidence exists to demonstrate that leaders would be so irresponsible.

Economic Interests and Foreign Policy Decisions

Foreign policy decisions are often influenced by the state's economic interests. For example, the first Bush administration marketed the first Gulf War of 1991 to the public by stating that it was about jobs, about oil, and about economic security. Threatened access to valuable natural resources can shape U.S. foreign policy.

Expansionist policies of states are often viewed as stemming from pursuing their economic interests. Imperialistic motives are frequently attributed to foreign policies of states. Russia's policy vis-à-vis Ukraine is largely derived from the gas and oil interests of the former and the weakness of the latter.

Among the most important economic influences on foreign policy is the military-industrial complex. In January 1961, President Eisenhower warned in his farewell address, "against the acquisition of unwarranted influence, whether sought or unsought, by the military-industrial complex." Eisenhower's fear was that military-industrial interests would drive foreign policy in ways favorable to the military-industrial complex. The iron triangle consisting of Congress, the Pentagon, and defense industries is often viewed as a force pushing for costly weaponry and the sale of arms to other countries. Arms sales and transfers do serve as tools of foreign policy.

The Role of Public Opinion

Public opinion about a particular crisis may influence the use of force, escalation, termination, and other foreign policy decisions. David Brulé and Alex Mintz (2006) found that U.S. presidents refrain from using force when opposition to intervention is high and are likely to use force when public support for such actions is above 50 percent.

Certain internal pressures applied to national leaders in democracies sometimes compel them to seek peace. Randle (1973, ch. 10) observes that domestic politics – the public and the legislature – can act to force decision makers to move toward termination of hostilities. The public will demand peace in several related scenarios (ibid., 432–433). First, when public opinion reflects that battle deaths have been excessive or that the conflict has run on for too long – for example, French public opinion regarding the conflict in Indochina in the 1950s – the public will favor an end to hostilities. If the public perceives the war as immoral or illegal, the mood will shift to one of cooperation – for example, Italy in 1943. Finally, if the citizens of a nation sense that their country could actually become the target of an invasion, or if the country has in fact become the target of an invasion, the public mood is likely to swing to one of nonhostility (ibid.). When the constraints of public opinion are not present, as in authoritarian regimes, a country's bargaining position is strengthened vis-à-vis an adversary that has such constraints – for example, North Vietnam and North Korea (Handel 1978; 1989). When public opinion about the war is favorable, termination is unlikely.

Domestic political pressures are often related to international pressures (Randle 1973, 443). For example, a country might seek to stimulate public discontent toward the war in its adversary's country by capturing large cities, defeating elite combat units, and launching surprise attacks on sites previously considered impregnable. A country could also achieve the desired result by releasing "peace feelers" or propaganda in the adversary's country, thereby turning the public against the leader of that country. A final scenario, and one that approximates an option at the United States' disposal during the 1991 Persian Gulf War, is that a civil war can be incited in the adversary's country, thereby bringing about domestic instability and an end to the conflict.

War casualties also influence public support for the use of military force abroad. In an interesting experiment, Scott Gartner (2008) demonstrates that support for the war in Iraq declined when subjects were shown images of war casualties. This was especially true for images containing coffins covered by American flags. Images containing heroism had the opposite effect. Several quantitative studies of diversionary theory also find that presidential uses of force are less likely when the country is already in a major war such as Korea and Vietnam (see DeRouen Jr. 1995; 2001).

Electoral Cycles

Ample evidence suggests that electoral politics play an important role in the decision-making calculus of leaders. The timing of elections, leaders' quest for political survival, and political rivalry affect budgetary decisions on spending levels for "guns versus butter," the use of force, de-escalation, and the pursuit of peace agreements. Simply put, leaders whose political survival depends on voters' approval of their policies prefer to make voters happy rather than unhappy. When chances of reelection appear threatened or uncertain, leaders might decide to manipulate economic policy utilizing the advantages of office. Another option is the use of force or war.

One study looked at the relationship between war involvement and democratic electoral cycles from 1815 to 1980. The study suggested several ways in which elections could influence decisions to enter war (Gaubatz 1991). First, the public could demand peace, and there would be few war initiations by democracies at election time. Second, leaders might pursue "rally 'round the flag" effects, and there could be more wars at election time. Third, the decision may be tied to the mood of the public at that particular time (if the public demands hawkish, tough policies vis-à-vis international opponents, then leaders may resort to the use of force; however, if the public is in favor of dovish policies, leaders may refrain from using force). The findings indicate that just before elections, leaders seem to avoid major wars with high casualties (or wars that may appear that they will be major). Fourth, more wars are entered in later stages of the electoral cycle. On the whole, it appears that democracies are less warlike at election time.

Arguably, the electoral cycle can also influence the timing of defense contract awards and military spending (Mintz 1988; DeRouen Jr. and Heo 2000). Defense contracts represent large sums of money that can generate many jobs in a short time. Because contracts represent money already appropriated by Congress and they can be timed and geographically targeted, they seem to represent a prime tool for a president wanting to enhance his electoral fortunes (Mayer 1991). Because of the nature of the American presidential election system, it could present an incumbent with an advantage to release contracts in key parts of swing states before an election. In sum, there is a strong incentive for defense contracting decisions to be influenced by the electoral cycle. Such decisions, in turn, affect foreign policy decision making.

The Effect of Domestic and International Factors on Foreign Policy Decisions: Two-Level Games

The two-level game developed by Robert Putnam (1999) highlights the interactive process that occurs when a leader negotiates international agreements simultaneously at both the international level and the domestic level. Two-level games consist of international negotiation (Level I), in which the leader tries to reach an agreement with other leaders, and a domestic negotiation (Level II), "wherein the leader tries to get the agreement accepted by the legislature and his domestic constituencies." This simultaneous game at both levels "tends to slide the negotiators of both camps into an imbroglio where they have to conciliate intense domestic pressure with international pulls and pushes. The two types of pressure are fundamentally different, and the constraints imposed would not be encountered in the first place if the negotiations were held in a pure national or international game" (Boukhars 2001).

Consider the case of the Israeli-Syrian peace negotiations. Israeli prime ministers such as Rabin and Barak, among others, had to take into account in negotiating the terms of the potential agreement with Syria not only the international level (Israel vis-à-vis Syria) but also domestic constraints such as whether they had sufficient votes in the Israeli parliament (the Knesset), the opinion of their coalition partners (which was split in its support of such an agreement), and the domestic public's view. Allison Astorino-Courtois and Brittani Trusty (2000) claimed that several alternatives were eliminated from consideration by Rabin because of lack of support in the Knesset for the kind of territorial concessions in the Golan Heights required to reach a peace agreement. The authors have even speculated that President Hafez al-Assad of Syria did not want to pursue peace negotiations with Israel during the Rabin term as prime minister because he estimated that Rabin did not have the votes in the Knesset for an Israeli withdrawal from the Golan Heights.

Putnam's two-level game centers around the range of alternatives for Level I, the international set, that are acceptable to a majority at Level II, the domestic constituency. This range is known as the "win-set" for the country (Boukhars 2001). The win-set is defined as "the set of all possible Level I (international) agreements that would 'win' – that is, gain the necessary majority among the [domestic] constituents" (Putnam 1999, 439). By analyzing the international negotiations from the perspective of one country through win-sets, Putnam argued that it is possible to estimate the impact of domestic politics on the success of the international negotiation. From this model, then, Putnam hypothesized that "larger win-sets make Level I agreement more likely and, conversely, the smaller the win-set the more likely the negotiations will break down" (Boukhars 2001). Also, the relative size of the Level II win-sets "will affect the distribution of the joint gains at Level I. A smaller win-set at Level II can be a bargaining advantage for a country at Level I" (ibid). Along the same lines, the successful international agreement must fall inside the Level II win-set. The larger the Level II win-set, the more it is that a successful agreement will be reached. However, "the larger Level II win-set increases the likelihood that the Level I negotiator will be challenged by other countries" (ibid).

The domestic level comprises a number of actors, processes, and influences that have a strong impact on the final international agreement. Anouar Boukhars (2001) lists the mass public, the military, mass media, and political opposition as exerting pressure on leaders to accommodate their interests. Two-level games affect the choice set (which alternatives will be included and which will be excluded), the importance assigned by negotiators to each dimension (domestic, international), and the actual choice.

CASE STUDY: THE DOMESTIC AND INTERNATIONAL
UNDERPINNINGS OF DECISION MAKING — THE FALKLANDS
WAR, 1982

On April 2, 1982, the military junta that ruled Argentina invaded the Malvinas Islands. In the English language, the islands are known as the Falkland Islands. The British exercised sovereignty over the islands. The invasion is an important case study that highlights both domestic and international factors linked to foreign policy decision making. This case also cuts across and provides insights into all three levels of analysis: individual, small group, and coalition.

Diversionary Behavior

The **diversionary theory model** works at the state level. The in group–out group model of behavior has been adapted to explain foreign policy behavior. Turmoil within the state can be manifested as declining approval ratings for the leader, economic problems, strikes, riots, or even armed uprising. To divert attention from such problems, leaders can direct attention toward an external scapegoat. A savvy leader can whip up nationalistic tendencies and help frame the message that the "real problem" is the external foe.

Jack Levy and Lily Vakili (1992) provide compelling evidence that diversionary incentives were part of the decision process for both Argentina and Britain during the 1982 Falklands War. This is a particularly interesting case because it provides evidence that diversion is not confined to democracies. The authors demonstrate that domestic unrest brought on by serious economic woes and government human rights abuses led the military junta to launch a military campaign to take the British-held Falkland (Malvinas) Islands. Such a move turned Argentine attention away from the domestic shortcomings of the regime and soon there were mass nationalistic rallies supporting the regime and Argentine claims to the islands. This success was, however, short lived, and once Britain prevailed, the junta was quickly turned out.

For its part, Britain was also experiencing serious economic troubles in the months leading up to the invasion. A forceful response by the new Thatcher government in Britain diverted attention away from those domestic problems. The relatively quick victory was a huge success for Thatcher. However, Britain's forceful response was not driven by diversionary incentives; there was also a need to avoid political loss. The outgoing foreign secretary expressed a need to avoid "national humiliation" after the invasion (Freedman 1982, 200). Britain did not seriously consider a "no-action" alternative (ibid.).

Levy and Vakili (1992) claim that the military regime in Argentina was basically left with only one option – diversion. It had blown its chance at fixing the economy, and the defeat of the leftist rebels had eroded justification for authoritarianism. Public unrest was increasing because of the poor economy and lack of democratization. The Malvinas provided the perfect remedy. As a national symbol, the islands were a galvanizing force that could rally the public around the regime.

In the short term, the diversion was a success. Just after the invasion and occupation, the public rallied soundly behind the government. But the early success quickly faded. As it happened, Argentina had grossly misperceived Britain's commitment to the islands.

There is considerable evidence that protracted uses of force can actually hurt a leader's approval. This was the case for the United States during Korea and Vietnam and for several Israeli leaders during the prolonged occupation of Lebanon.

Deterrence and Misperception

The Britain, Falklands, and Argentina triad represented a classic example of extended immediate deterrence in the first section of this chapter. Recall that as a central plank of realist foreign policy doctrine, deterrence is built upon a foundation of rational decision making. Extended immediate deterrence is expected to work only when the protector clearly signals that it is willing to come to the aid of the protégé at all costs. The signaling becomes clearer when there are obvious economic and military ties between the protector and protégé. Deterrence and misperception are interrelated. For deterrence to work, power signals need to be credible.

Clearly these signals did not thwart Argentina from invading. Again, in pursuing its goal of diverting attention away from domestic problems, Argentina misperceived Britain's commitment to the Falklands. Levy and Vakili (1992) observe that Argentina did not expect Britain to respond militarily. The junta also expected the United States either to remain neutral or to support

Argentina's claim to the islands. Lawrence Freedman (1982) also notes that relations between the United States and Argentina were very good and that Britain had been sending mixed messages about its long-term plans for retaining the islands. The plan was for a lightning-fast invasion followed by negotiations with Britain from a position of strength. The invasion was indeed quick because the Falklands were only minimally defended. Three weeks after the invasion, the British were able to reach the islands, and the war began. As Freedman (ibid., 199) notes, Argentina had been overly optimistic.

Electoral Impact

The Falklands War had electoral implications. Just after it ended, Prime Minister Margaret Thatcher called for early elections and rode the popularity of the war to victory in British elections the next year. In fact, had the election been held just before the war, the Tories might have lost because her approval ratings were very low (Gaubatz 1999). As for the party of the military junta in Argentina, it was defeated and Argentina embarked on a more democratic path from that point. Its decision for war was fatal. So although the Falklands War might not have been motivated by diversionary tactics from the British perspective, it is linked to the postwar electoral cycle.

Similar linkages between foreign policy choices and elections can be seen in the 2008 U.S. presidential campaign. One of key questions asked of candidates was whether they would negotiate with leaders of rogue states. During the campaign Senator Barack Obama said that he would, and Senator John McCain has said he would not. The issue was even raised in the debate between these candidates and may have affected some voters' decisions. For example, some Christian Conservatives and Jewish voters may not like the idea of the United States talking directly to the President of Iran with no preconditions.

There are several important policy areas that can be better understood by using FPDM theories and insights. These include decisions on the use of economic instruments of foreign policy, international negotiation and bargaining, and foreign policy substitutability.

DECISIONS ON THE USE OF ECONOMIC INSTRUMENTS OF FOREIGN POLICY

In addition to questions of war and peace, leaders make decisions on a host of foreign economic matters. There are various forms of coercive economic policy at the disposal of leaders such as sanctions, embargos, or boycotts. The bargaining model of international relations holds that dominant states are able to bargain to their advantage. The dominant state can influence the foreign policy preferences of the weaker state by either rewarding or punishing past behavior or inducing future behavior (Richardson and Kegley 1980). Sanctions are generally considered a form of compellence intended to stop undesired behavior. For example, there were widespread sanctions levied against Rhodesia's (now Zimbabwe) white minority government.

The Decision to Use Sanctions as an Instrument of Foreign Policy

Countries apply sanctions against other countries to compel them to do something that they otherwise would have refrained from doing or to prevent them from doing things that they would have otherwise done. Sanctions are an important tool of foreign policy. They are a form of statecraft that is not as peaceful as negotiation but that is less aggressive than the use of armed violence.

The United States and its allies imposed sanctions on Iraq in hopes of compelling Iraq to abandon its nonconventional weapons programs. The UN Security Council approved the sanctions on August 6, 1990, after the Iraqi invasion of Kuwait. The council did not lift the sanctions after the war, but kept them in place "as leverage to press for Iraqi disarmament and other goals" (Global Policy Forum 2007). An "oil-for-food" program, which started in late 1997, helped alleviate some of the economic misery of the Iraqi people. The United States and United Kingdom announced that they would continue the sanctions as long as Saddam Hussein was in power. The sanctions were lifted by the UN soon after the invasion of Iraq in May 2003.

The UN Security Council imposed sanctions on Libya (in 1992) "to press it to hand over two suspects wanted for the 1988 bombing of a U.S. Pan-American Airways airliner over Lockerbie, Scotland" (ibid.). The UN suspended (but did not lift) the sanctions in April 1999 after Libya handed over the suspects for trial. In August 2003, Libya accepted responsibility for the bombing and agreed to a \$2.7 billion settlement. In return, "London and Washington immediately began to push the Security Council to lift all UN sanctions against Tripoli" (ibid.). The UN Security Council lifted the sanctions on Qaddafi's Libya on September 12, 2003, although the United States continued its sanctions until September 2004. In December 2003, Muammar Qaddafi granted permission to the UN weapons inspectors to check for weapons of mass destruction.

Sanctions do not always work. Richard Haass (1998) notes that sanctions designed to compel or coerce put the decision in the hands of the target. The target can decide how long to hold out. When sanctions are designed to punish past behavior, the sanctioning state can decide when to stop. Unilateral sanctions are difficult because the target state can turn to other countries to compensate for sanctioned items. Regime type is also a factor. Authoritarian regimes (e.g., Iraq under Hussein) are likely to allow their people to suffer hardship brought on by coercive sanctions. Finally, Haass notes that over time "sanction fatigue" can set in as the original impetus for the sanction loses its resonance.

Sometimes it is unclear whether sanctions are designed to compel or punish. The case of Castro's Cuba might fit into this category. In any case, the U.S.

embargo against Cuba basically left the decision in the hands of Castro, who not only refused to bow to the sanctions but also has used them to his political advantage over the past four decades.

Embargos and boycotts are other types of economic statecraft that are similar to sanctions. OPEC countries put an embargo on crude oil exports to the West during the Yom Kippur War of 1973. The embargo caused shortages that sent prices skyrocketing. This is an interesting case because, in contrast to the bargaining model that describes hegemonic strategies, the OPEC embargo demonstrated that developing countries could band together and wield influence at the international level. A boycott means that a country or group of people refuses to buy certain goods that are associated with a company or a state. For example, South African goods and sports teams were often boycotted during apartheid.

The Decision to Use Aid in Foreign Policy

Aid comes in two general forms: economic and military. It might be used as reward, punishment, or inducement. After a leader decides to deal with a situation using economic statecraft, several other decisions must be made. Two of these decisions are: (1) should economic or military aid be used? and (2) will aid be given as an inducement or reward?

Aid can reward past behavior; for example, it can be given by the United States to countries who supported the war in Iraq. It can be given to punish past behavior, for example, nonsupport for the U.S. position on UN votes. In fact, since the 1980s, the United States officially tracks UN voting behavior on key votes and links – or threatens to link – voting records to aid decisions. This is a clear indication that aid can be political. The United States signals to other states that it expects a certain level of acceptable behavior in return for aid. Countries might also give aid to induce future behavior. All of these factors are included in the multiple and often sequential decisions leaders make on whether to supply aid, the type of aid, and the amount of aid.

Taking into account the nature of the aid-behavior relationship, Karl De-Rouen Jr. and Uk Heo (2004) found that the United States tended to give military aid to Latin American countries and economic aid to African countries. In each case, aid was given as a reward for past behavior. Aid increased as a function of foreign policy similarity and compliance.

Nations provide military aid and supply arms to other nations. They do so for economic reasons (selling arms is a multibillion dollar business annually), for political reasons, as part of a commitment to an ally, and in an attempt to strengthen strategic ties with the recipient nation(s). Developing nations are the primary focus of foreign arms sales activity by weapons suppliers. During the past decade, the value of arms transfer agreements with developing nations made up roughly 60 percent of all such agreements worldwide. The United

States ranked first in arms transfers, followed by Russia and France (Grimmett 2005).

According to David Kinsella (1998), arms transfers exist not only in the security or economic realms. There is also a strong political current running through such policies. Arms transfers can help allies enhance their security. In terms of economics, a country with a significant military production capacity can make money selling weapons abroad. A poor country with small domestic industry might suffer from excessive defense spending if it overly relies on expensive defense technology from abroad. This is often the case for developing countries that are in conflict-prone areas or in which an authoritarian leader uses the military to stay in power. It is these cases in which we expect to find the classic "guns versus growth" or "guns versus butter" budgetary trade-offs occurring. The government spends so much on defense that budget items such as education, health care, and domestic investment suffer.

Politically, some countries become dependent on arms transfers from one or two suppliers. International politics plays out in the arms transfers decision when the exporting country uses the transfers for political leverage. Keith Krause (1991) observes that the United States and the USSR used military aid as a foreign policy tool during the Cold War and were more likely to decide on reward strategies when giving military aid. What this means is that the superpowers were more generous when the recipient countries complied with their foreign policies. The superpower policy of rewarding past behavior was an expression of power. Krause concludes that the use of superpower threats would not have worked as well because such behavior undermines the well-being of the relationship by, among other things, jeopardizing the political standing of leaders in recipient countries. Indeed, DeRouen Jr. and Heo (2004) find that for a majority of Latin American states foreign policy similarity leads to greater military aid from the United States.

In a related study of arms dependence, David Kinsella (1998) showed that arms transfers to a country increased the likelihood of conflict, but if the country was dependent on a supplier or two, the likelihood of conflict was muted. This is further evidence of the expression of supplier power. The exporting states can threaten to withhold, or actually can withhold, transfers in the face of an impending conflict that is opposed by the exporter. The U.S. role in the Yom Kippur War provides a good example of this. The administration threatened to withhold needed supplies if Israel defied U.S. demands by continuing offensive missions in Egypt.

NEGOTIATION AND MEDIATION DECISIONS

Foreign policy decision makers are often faced with incompatibilities between themselves and other actors. Managing conflict – either internal or external – typically involves the most important decisions a leader will have to make.

Public support for a leader usually declines if a conflict persists. Conflict also has a negative effect on development and often leads to human displacement. For these reasons, it is in the best interest of leaders to seek solutions to conflict. The parties might try to reach a bargain. **Bargaining** is a process of interdependent decision making in which the goal of each party is to get the best outcome in a situation for which the outcome depends on the choices made by all actors (Maoz 1990b, 378). Failing a satisfactorily bargained solution, policy makers might turn to two other means of resolving conflict: **negotiation** or **mediation**.

Three hallmarks of negotiation are: (1) it is a form of bargaining in which the parties coordinate their choices to form a collective outcome that is mutually acceptable as part of a joint decision process; (2) an actor is more likely to prefer negotiation over bargaining only if the most sought-after outcome is contingent on the other actor's agreement; and (3) negotiation takes place within a zone of agreement (ibid., 378–382). Negotiation is a form of bargaining with a slight twist. Michelle Maiese (2005) points out that negotiation is more likely to succeed in an environment that is conducive to positive emotional validation. Only then do the parties buy into the process. Positive emotions include respect and recognition.

If direct negotiation does not yield a mutually agreeable outcome, a mediator may be called on to be an intermediary between the parties. If the parties do not trust each other, a third party might be able to establish a credible framework for resolution. Here the parties talk to the mediator, and the mediator presents the position of each side to the other. Mediation is nonbinding. Decision makers involved in disputes will often voluntarily enter into a mediation process because it is relatively low in cost and nonbinding. In many cases, a leader has little to lose by agreeing to allow a third-party to mediate the dispute.

Jacob Bercovitch and Karl DeRouen Jr. (2004) identify a range of mediation actions from more passive to more active. **Communication-facilitation** strategies are those in which the mediator is a passive communicator passing on information. The mediator will build trust, arrange for interactions between the parties, identify issues and interests, supply missing information, develop a framework for understanding, and allow the interests of the parties to be discussed. **Procedural-formulative** strategies are those in which the mediator is granted a greater level of control over the mediation process. For example, a mediator may determine structural aspects of meetings such as the agenda and control the level of media publicity. **Directive strategies** are the most powerful form of mediation. The third party controls content and substance of the bargaining process by providing incentives for the parties. Tactics include changing expectations, inducing and rewarding concessions, warning of the costs of nonagreement, changing perceptions, and offering to verify compliance. Directive strategies lead parties to reevaluate the costs and benefits of cooperation and defection. Bercovitch and DeRouen Jr. find that experienced mediators using these proactive directive strategies are more likely to succeed in resolving internationalized ethnic conflict.

Ronald Fisher and Loraleigh Keashly (1991) list a set of third-party intervention types ranging from least to most proactive. Third parties play a **conciliatory** role when they act as information conduits so that tensions can be reduced. **Problem solving** involves third party conflict analysis and subsequent development of alternatives. In **arbitration** and **adjudication**, the third party assumes much more responsibility. In these cases, the third party is tasked with generating binding judgments. **Peacekeeping** is the most assertive form of intervention. Here the third party (typically a state or intergovernmental organization) deploys soldiers and civilian personnel to maintain a ceasefire, which involves the provision of military personnel by a third party (or parties) to supervise and monitor a cease-fire or develop democratic institutions and provide humanitarian relief. Mediation is an intermediate expression of third-party influence. It is more proactive than conciliation but much less imposing than peacekeeping (Kelman and Fisher 2003).

Many disputes are protracted and seemingly impossible to resolve. Some of the civil wars in Burma began in the 1940s and are still ongoing. Conflict between Israel and the Palestinians has endured for decades. Lee Ross (2008) of Stanford University identifies three significant barriers to successful negotiations: structural, strategic, and psychological. Structural barriers include domestic audience costs and spoilers. **Audience costs** are those an actor "pays" when displeasing some of its constituents. For example, the government of Sri Lanka would upset many of the Sinhalese majority if it ever granted an amnesty to Tamil rebels. **Spoilers** are actors who disrupt the peace process among negotiators. Strategic barriers include negotiating tactics such as bluffing and secrecy. In other words, private information the actors possess. Finally, psychological barriers include differing conceptions of the past and **reactive devaluation**. The latter concept means that actors will devalue proposals simply because they were offered by an adversary that is not trusted.

DECISIONS ON FOREIGN POLICY SUBSTITUTABILITY

Thus far, we have touched on a variety of foreign policy decisions and actions that are tied to international and domestic considerations. Leaders might sometimes decide to shift between these policy options. For example, responding to a dangerous international environment a leader might decide to shift to a policy of seeking more powerful allies rather than one of higher defense spending (Most and Starr 1989). Scholars have carved out a literature on foreign policy substitutability that suggests that individuals, leaders, and states substitute between different foreign policy instruments depending on the particular context (e.g., Morgan and Palmer 2000, 2003). In practical terms, this means that "through time and across space, similar factors could plausibly be expected to trigger different foreign policy acts" (Most and Starr 1989, 98).

Policy substitution models typically rely on rational explanations of foreign policy decision making (see Regan 2000). However, and as noted in Chapters 4 and 5, the rational assumptions are somewhat demanding and often unrealistic. If in fact, leaders are not the rational, optimizing individuals of rational choice but instead take cognitive shortcuts and select from a limited range of options, then the policy substitutability literature has greater theoretical value (DeRouen Jr. and Goldfinch 2007). Drawing on the new institutional literature, DeRouen Jr. and Goldfinch argue that individuals are largely socially constructed and are not the rational optimizers found in many substitutability studies or a simple realist model of foreign policy. Such individuals choose policy solutions and make policy decisions from a toolbox that is itself constrained and provided by the institutions within a particular society.

DeRouen Jr. and Goldfinch (2007) argue that the institutions of democracy socially construct individuals and constrain the set of foreign policy alternatives. This range of options in international crises reflects a preference for nonviolent methods of dispute resolution. Thus, they link a foreign policy substitutability model with the democratic peace literature and study foreign policy substitution during international crises. The main hypothesis is that to the extent that policies are substituted, democracies will substitute toward more peaceful alternatives. One of the hallmarks of a foreign policy crisis is that leaders have to react quickly to unfolding events. These reactions can range from cooperative outreach to direct use of violence. There can also be substitution among these policies over time. The policy options are characterized in the literature as cooperation, nonviolent coercion, and violence. The first option entails negotiation, mediation, arbitration, or adjudication. The second option includes sanctions, withholding aid, and threats of violence. Aid can be used as a form of statecraft by donor countries. For example, the United States monitors how regularly aid-recipient countries vote with them in the UN. The third option is the use of armed force.

DeRouen Jr. and Goldfinch find that both monadic and joint democracy enhance the likelihood that an actor will pursue a negotiated settlement to a crisis. They further show that when initial crisis management techniques are violent, democracies will eventually shift toward the use negotiation as the main crisis-management technique. In other words, democracies substitute toward cooperative behavior.

Benjamin Most and Harvey Starr (1989, 99) argue that since many different foreign policy decisions can result from a stimulus, we should not focus on these options in isolation. The challenge for those who study foreign policy decision making is to design studies that treat various behaviors as "component parts" of a larger puzzle (ibid., 99). The DeRouen Jr. and Goldfinch study of crisis behavior (2007) combines various behaviors such as use of violence, sanctions, and negotiation into a single, overarching framework of crisis management.

GENDER DIFFERENCES IN DECISION MAKING

Women have been heads of state in various countries. Here is a partial list of past and present examples: Margaret Thatcher, United Kingdom; Golda Meir, Israel; Indira Gandhi, India; Benazir Bhutto, Pakistan; Sirimavo Bandaranaike, Sri Lanka; Elisabeth Domitien, Central African Republic; Milka Planinc, Yugoslavia; Kim Campbell, Canada; and Agathe Uwilingiyimana, Rwanda.[1] Women have also held key influential positions in foreign policy making. In the United States, for example, Condoleeza Rice served as national security advisor and secretary of state, Madeline Albright as UN ambassador and secretary of state, Margaret Tutwiler as undersecretary of state, and Jeane Kirkpatrick as U.S. ambassador to the UN.

Evidence about gender differences in decision making comes from many sources and fields. It is well known, for example, that men and women have different shopping strategies and different ways of communicating and place emphasis on different things in relationships (Tannen 1990). Political scientist Richard C. Eichenberg (2007) pointed out that there is ample empirical evidence from the American context that women are less supportive of the use of military force than men. According to Eichenberg, women respond more positively to humanitarian interventions and to interventions involving UN troops (which men do not respond to at all). In contrast, Eichenberg found (ibid., 6) that "men respond more strongly to questions that mention 'terror' or 'terrorism' (usually phrased as part of the 'war against terror'). Men also increase their support more strongly when the question mentions military actions involving the NATO Alliance. Whereas women likewise respond positively to such actions, the magnitude of their reaction is simply less." The author speculates that this may be because "these two actions do not involve an international mandate, which does evoke more positive reactions from women." Eichenberg (ibid., 6) also claimed that this also may be due to "a more general aversion of women to more violent actions (at the margins)."

According to the Eichenberg, "gender differences vary substantially across societies and within a number of international conflicts. The data therefore cast doubt on any theory that would predict constant gender differences, most importantly any biological explanation" (ibid., 6). Pamela Conover and Virginia Sapiro's (1993) study analyzed gender differences in public reactions to the 1990–1991 Persian Gulf War. They found that when questions moved

---

[1] See "Women State Leaders" on Martin K. I. Christensen's Web site Worldwide Guide to Women in Leadership," http://www.guide2womenleaders.com/women_state_leaders.htm.

"from hypothetical wars to the Gulf War – the distance separating women and men grew, and on every measure, women reacted more negatively" (quoted in Eichenberg, 2003, 110).

Mary Caprioli (2000, 2003) examined the effect of gender inequality on state behavior in international relations. Specifically, Caprioli looked at the percent of women in parliaments, duration of female suffrage, percent of women in the labor force, and fertility rate on support for the use of military force. Her study substantiates the thesis that domestic gender equality has a pacifying effect on state behavior on the international level. Caprioli also examined the impact of gender inequality on the likelihood of intrastate violence from 1960 to 1997. She concludes that gender inequality not only undermines the status of women, it also actually makes internal conflict more likely (Caprioli 2003). Because gender inequality increases the likelihood of conflict, achieving gender equality is essential for achieving peace (ibid.).

Gender has also been explored as it relates to war across societies (Goldstein 2001). The fighting of wars spans most civilizations over time and space. Goldstein (410) argues that war making creates a gender identity for men and women and that the war's impact on the socialization of young males and females into their respective roles in turn perpetuates such gendered war roles.

Rose McDermott, J. Cowden, and S. Rosen (forthcoming) have conducted a series of experiments on sex differences in aggression, looking primarily at hormonal factors such as testosterone. They found that men were much more likely to engage in unprovoked attacks (in which they had not been attacked before by the other player) than were women.

CULTURAL DIFFERENCES IN DECISION MAKING

Research has shown that there are significant cross-cultural differences in decision making across societies. Maris Martinsons (2001) found, for example, that American, Chinese, and Japanese business leaders each exhibit a distinctive national style of decision making. Other scholars have identified cross-cultural differences in consumer behavior and decision-making styles. With respect to foreign policy decision making, Yi Yang (2004) examined the effect of a leader being in the gain versus loss domain on foreign policy processes and choices. He found that when confronted with a foreign policy crisis, Chinese students examined significantly more information than their American counterparts. The study, which used the Decision Board computerized platform in an experimental setting, concluded that the Chinese are more holistic in their information search than are North Americans.

In another study, Yi Yang, Nehemia Geva and Jiu Chang (2003) showed that American decision makers are more risk prone than are Chinese decision makers. The study also showed that cultural contexts affect the expected utility of the choice: Chinese students require a significantly higher expected utility score than American counterparts given the same choice" (ibid 18-19). There is ample evidence that cultural differences affect not only the actual choice but also the decision-making process.

In another study, researchers examined the effect of threat perceptions in three countries – New Zealand (low threat), the United States (medium threat), and Israel (high threat) – on the likelihood that the countries would violate the democratic peace assertion that democracies do not fight each other. The study showed that subjects in Israel were most likely to approve use of force against another democracy when proliferation of weapons of mass destruction was contemplated. Subjects in the United States were also likely to approve the use of force under such circumstances, whereas those in New Zealand were likely oppose such a policy (Mintz et al. 1995).

Because few, if any, nations in the Third World "became or are becoming First World states... the social, economic, political and cultural differences of Third World states are not easily adapting" to those of First World states (Weber 2001, 156). Leaders who make foreign policy decisions should take into account not only how their policies will be viewed at home but how their signals of action and inaction, peace overtures, threats to use force, and attempts at reconciliation will be interpreted by their opponents and other states. Analysts often think in Western terms when interpreting decisions of non-Western actors and attempt to apply Western norms to international affairs. As an example, for Westerners, the idea of a suicide bomber is unthinkable. However, in a community that is being bombarded with messages that suicide bombing is of enormous significance and that there are great benefits for being a *Shaheed* (martyr), acts of suicide terrorism are not uncommon.

The late Samuel Huntington (1993), coined the term "clash of civilizations." According to Huntington, wars will be fought across civilizations separated by religion and tradition. These conflicts will overshadow economic and ideological ones. Divisions are deep and naturally influence FPDM. With the end of the Cold War, international politics moves into a new era in which Western and non-Western civilizations will experience conflict (Huntington 1993), such as conflict between Muslim and non-Muslim civilizations.

Many scholars have criticized the clash of civilizations thesis, arguing that there are as many wars within civilizations as among civilizations. In 2008 alone, the Arab world experienced serious fights between, among others, Sunni and Shiites in Iraq, the Fatah and Hamas in the Palestinian community, and Hezbollah and various groups in Lebanon, as well as conflicts in Pakistan, Afghanistan, Yemen, and other places.

CONCLUSION

This chapter introduced a number of international and domestic determinants of foreign policy decision making. Leaders often make foreign policy decisions in a strategic setting. That is, the actor must also take into account what the adversary is doing. Domestic factors such as public opinion also may act as constraints on certain actions. For example, use of force and defense spending are arguably tied to public opinion. However, low approval or a pending election could also provide incentives for a timely and quick military action. Gender and culture also shape foreign policy making.

PART FIVE

MARKETING FOREIGN POLICY

8

Framing, Marketing, and Media Effects on Foreign Policy Decision Making

To garner public support for their foreign and security policies, state leaders need to market their policies to the public, the opposition, and their constituencies, allies, and adversaries. This chapter introduces several marketing and framing "tactics" that leaders use to promote their foreign policies.

The discipline of **marketing** primarily deals with the marketing of products and services to consumers and **customer relationship management** (CRM). **Political marketing** focuses on the marketing of political candidates, political platforms, and political parties. **International relations marketing** deals with the marketing of foreign policy and national security policies, including peace and war marketing (Mintz 2006). As we have shown in previous chapters, psychological factors contribute greatly to our understanding of foreign policy decision making. Psychological theories also draw our attention to the important role of framing and marketing foreign policy decisions. In this chapter, we show that marketing and framing exist and matter in foreign policy making.

MARKETING EFFECTS

Just as marketers promote their products to generate sales, it is crucial for state leaders to market their policies to different constituencies. Leaders can market war (including war initiation, escalation, and termination), peace, international agreements, and many other foreign policy decisions. One **marketing tactic** often used by leaders is **framing**. Framing, as previously explained, refers to the manner in which an issue is presented (see, e.g., Tversky and Kahneman 1981; Frisch 1993). Leaders try to impose or introduce and promote frames that affect how the public views a particular situation. For example, President Bush famously framed the sides in the global war on terror by declaring, "either you are with us, or you are with the terrorists." The president referred to the conflict as one "between good and evil" and as "us versus them" and declared, "if anybody harbors a terrorist, they're a terrorist. If they fund a terrorist, they're

149

terrorists. If they house terrorists, they're terrorists" (Mintz and Redd 2003, 205).

To enhance public support for their policies, leaders typically frame the situation to the public. The leader is not a passive observer of his or her political capital trying merely to avoid losses by fulfilling public expectations (see DeRouen Jr. 2001). Political leaders and their advisors actively frame and spin information. The **frame** "is that portion of his or her store of knowledge that the decision maker brings to bear on a particular context in order to endow that context with meaning" (Beach 1990, 51). The goal of spinning is to make the public evaluate favorably the policies advocated or enacted by the leader.

FRAMING EFFECTS

The frame operates as a lens through which the public looks at and examines the situation. In this regard, political leaders play the role of the optometrist who is providing or fitting glasses to consumers (Geva, Driggers, and Mintz 1996). The desire of politicians is to put on the public lenses that will make their policies and actions look good and, through negative framing and marketing, those of their opponents look bad. Naturally, the political "trick" is to identify these lenses or frames that will do the job. This identification may sometimes require our political optometrist to throw at the "consumer" (the public) more than one lens and monitor the consumer's reaction.

Information is never neutral in the policy process (Jones 1994). Leaders attempt to set a **reference point** so that it will benefit their position. **Gain framing** may lead to risk-averse behavior, whereas **loss framing** may trigger risky choices. In this chapter, we introduce various framing tactics and methods that affect foreign policy (see Table 8.1; see also Mintz and Redd 2003).

Frames are often effective when leaders highlight the **salience** of certain themes (e.g., terrorist attacks, nuclear threats, aggression) and discount other dimensions (e.g., the economic costs associated with the pursuit of the policy, the potential negative reaction of allies, etc.). This is known as **priming.** President Bush framed Senator John Kerry's votes in favor of the war in Iraq but against the allocation of $87 billion to the Department of Defense to support the war effort as examples of Kerry's flip-flops.

Because crisis situations often occur in an **interactive setting** (e.g., involving more than one actor), leaders typically attempt to frame the situation not only to their constituencies but also to their adversaries. In this chapter, we convey the notion that leaders are also vulnerable to **counterframing** by the opposition and the media and to framing by their own inner circles, advisors, and consultants. Finally, the chapter refers to decision makers being affected by their own frames, which they bring to the situation (e.g., relying on historical analogies, beliefs, and so on).

Table 8.1. *Framing tactics in foreign policy*

Thematic framing
Evaluative framing
Reference point
Symbolic framing
Threat framing
Emotional framing
Revolving framing
Counterframing
Counterproductive framing
Noncompensatory framing
Contrasting framing
Gain and loss framing
Framing by a third party
Contrasting framing
Salami tactic
Spinning

Source: Mintz (2006); Mintz and Redd (2003). Threat framing is mentioned in Hochberg-Marom (2008).

The Frame as a Political Lens

The accumulated findings in the field of social cognition highlight the effects of previous knowledge or experiences of the individual on how new information is interpreted, understood, and incorporated. The active frame during information processing was found to affect which parts of the reality are perceived (i.e., which information is relevant or irrelevant for further processing), how the information is interpreted and valued, and, finally, the choice among competing policy options.

When one explores the effects of the frame on the perception and interpretation of complex political environments one can identify two functions of a frame. The first is a **thematic** function that involves the introduction of a content dimension or organizing theme to the perception, assessment, and interpretation of the situation. In this context, the frame serves as a prism or lens, sensitizing the decision maker to specific contents in the environment (Geva et al. 1996). For instance, applying a frame that a target nation is democratic may lead the leader to perceive and interpret events in that country differently than when a nondemocratic frame is introduced. Such framing effects were observed by Alex Mintz and Nehemia Geva (1993) who found, using experimental settings, that a regime-type frame was sufficient to affect public approval of or opposition to the use of force. The frame in such cases affects the salience of the dimensions decision makers use in evaluating options. Moreover, a given frame may affect the nature of the alternatives that are included in the choice set. Hence, the thematic function of the frame can influence the choices of decision makers by prioritizing the contents of the decision matrix.

The second function of the frame is expressed along an **evaluative framing**. The frame can tint the evaluative meaning – the valence – of the situation in which the decision maker operates (Geva et al. 1996). In this sense, a frame can serve as the benchmark to which the external environment is compared. In other words, the frame operates as an evaluative anchor in the assessment of the environment. In this function, the frame operates the tint of the lens, affecting the "color perception" of the environment. Hence, a certain frame can make us perceive reality as rosier or grimmer and darker than is actually warranted by a particular situation (e.g., two contradicting frames of the domestic economy were thrown at the public during the 2004 presidential election – one that portrayed job losses, outsourcing, and the overall economy as a disaster and another that implied that things were moving forward).

For example, a thematic frame can sensitize a political leader to the economic costs of the war, as opposed to highlighting military or diplomatic dimensions. However, the frame can introduce a valence benchmark that is used in the assessment of how good or bad a situation is. The economic ramifications of a crisis can be evaluated in terms of decrease in unemployment versus an increase in employment. For example, during the presidential campaign of 2004, Senator Kerry often talked about the outsourcing of American jobs overseas as an example of the president's failed leadership. President Bush countered by claiming that the senator from Massachusetts was a big "tax-and-spend liberal." These frames evoked emotional reactions from respective constituencies and motivated the candidates' political base.

Who is Framing Whom? Framing the Public

One of the important roles of a leader as a foreign policy marketer is to **set the agenda** and the **reference point** for the public. Framing and marketing of foreign and national security policies are clearly important. Bruce Jentleson (1992) discusses public expectations for presidential leadership in foreign affairs. Framing and marketing is feasible in foreign policy (and mainly in crisis-ambiguous situations) because the public typically has limited knowledge and information about the crisis (Kegley and Wittkopf 1991, 300; Norris, Kern, and Just 2003). Karl DeRouen Jr. (2001) and Douglas Van Belle (2003) suggest that the media is a major channel through which leaders can interpret foreign policy events to educate or manipulate the public by carefully managing and selectively controlling the flow of information (see also Page and Shapiro 1989; Mintz and Redd 2003; Wolfsfeld 2004). Although some argue that the media has its independent role in interpreting world affairs to the public, particularly when the situations become complex (for example, crises) and the information sources are not easily accessible, the media often relies on information disseminated by the government.

Framing national security and foreign policy decisions for public consumption is an art performed by politically savvy presidents (Ostrom and Simon 1985; Aldrich, Sullivan, and Borgida 1989; Marra, Ostrom, and Simon 1990; Bostdorff 1991; Norris et al. 2003; Wolfsfeld 2004). Framing "can have significant political consequences for the entire social group" (Quattrone and Tversky 1988, 729–730). The public's perception of a problem can be changed by the framing of a given choice problem in a different way, without even distorting or suppressing information, merely by the framing of outcomes and contingencies.

Using the evaluative function of the frame, leaders can manipulate the salience of risks and pitfalls or the performance criteria (Ostrom and Simon 1984, 85; Richards et al. 1993; DeRouen Jr. 2001; Norris et al. 2003). For example, if the leader has convinced the public that the "surprisingly easy victory was due to his superior managerial skills," then the leader obtains higher public support (Richards et al. 1993).

Another framing tactic that helps tint the public lens is **symbolic framing**. The use of symbols typically evokes emotion and patriotic pride – which in turn increases public approval. For instance, Truman's decision to send military aid to Greece and Turkey after World War II was driven by fear of communism among the public (Rosati 1993, 395). Reagan justified the Grenada invasion by referring to the American medical students who were said to be in danger (ibid.). G. H. W. Bush marketed the Panama invasion to the public by referring to Manuel Noriega as a narco-trafficker (Rosati 1993, 395, 524–525). President Reagan called the Soviet Union the Evil Empire. G. W. Bush labeled Iran, Iraq, and North Korea the Axis of Evil.

Elizabeth Drew (1991, 181) claimed that the Bush administration "has told us that the war [in the Gulf 1991] is about oil, about Iraq's possession of chemical weapons and effort to achieve a nuclear weapon, about the threat Hussein poses to his other neighbors, and about the need to establish a new world order in the wake of the Cold War." One of the themes emphasized in the framing of the Iraqi threat in both 1990–1991 and 2003 was Iraq's unconventional weapons arsenal: during the Gulf Crisis, the president said to the U.S. troops in Saudi Arabia that Iraq might produce a nuclear weapon within six months to a year. "Every day that passes brings Saddam Hussein one step closer to realizing his goal of a nuclear weapons arsenal – and that's another reason, frankly, why our mission is marked by a real sense of urgency" (ibid., 243). G. H. W. Bush's National Security Advisor Brent Scowcroft said that letting the international embargo against Iraq run its course "raises the possibility that we could face an Iraq armed with nuclear weapons." Defense Secretary Cheney was more direct, saying, "It's only a matter of time until he acquires nuclear weapons and the capability to deliver them" (ibid., 312). The statement, "We are determined to knock out Saddam Hussein's nuclear bomb potential. We will also destroy his chemical weapons facilities" corresponds to this frame and to its tinting with a certain degree of fear – associating unconventional weapons with a ruthless dictator. Such **threat frames** (Hochberg-Marom 2008) were also very common in the months before the United States invaded Iraq in 2003.

In addition to frames that emphasized "rational" strategic U.S. interests abroad (e.g., oil), several additional **emotionally saturated frames** were raised by the Bush administration in 1990–1991; for example, fighting a just war against a ruthless dictator who possesses weapons of mass destruction.[1] President Bush likewise used these frames repeatedly in the 2003 crisis.

The multiplicity of frames used for the Gulf crises of 1990–1991 and 2003 illustrates the **revolving frames** concept. Different frames were introduced to the public in a process resembling an optometrist trying to find the appropriate lenses for the public, or a fisherman casting many baits with the hope that one will bring the big prize – strong public support.

It seems, however, that the multiple lenses that were offered to the public in the Gulf war of 1991 made the picture fuzzy. A *New York Times*–CBS poll from November 13–15, 1991, indicated that 51 percent of respondents thought that the president had not explained clearly enough why American troops were in the Gulf. This fuzziness is also reported by Bob Woodward (1991, 315):

> Several times in October, Robert Teeter, Bush's chief pollster, talked with the President about the Gulf policy. Teeter said he thought the administration had too many messages flying around. There was a lack of focus. He suggested that Bush return to the fundamentals that he had stated in August. The two with the strongest appeal were fighting aggression and protecting the lives of Americans, including the more than 900 Americans being held hostage in Iraq and Kuwait. About 100 had been moved to Iraqi military and industrial installations to serve as "human shields" to deter an American attack.

The choice of the "right" spin was not simple according to Woodward: "Scowcroft thought a new emphasis on the hostages would be changing horses in the middle of the stream, but he saw that public opinion polls were showing increasing doubts about the military deployment. Baker wanted to play the hostage card himself in a strong speech. Scowcroft was willing to go along" (Woodward 1991, 316). And the public liked what they saw through these frames. Rarely had a president such high rates of approval (Jentleson 1992).

In contrast, President George W. Bush focused on a smaller number of frames during the 2003 crisis. To deal with **counterframing** by the opposition, the administration was careful to mute a hazardous emotional frame associated with the use of force. Frequently, it was stated that in the Gulf crisis, use of force would not replicate the Vietnam quagmire.

---

[1] President Bush repeatedly compared Saddam Hussein to Hitler and constantly referred to Chamberlain's appeasement at Munich.

However, framing the public may at times be **counterproductive** because frames create certain expectations to be fulfilled by the leader. For instance, G. H. W. Bush's portrayal of Saddam as Hitler led the American people to expect his removal from power and hence evaluate any consequences short of that as not a full-fledged victory.

Framing beyond the Borders

The interactive nature of international conflicts or crises and the immediacy with which information about preferred policies is disseminated around the globe through the electronic media enables leaders to attempt to throw a few lenses across the national borders. These frames may be directed at real and potential allies (as part of coalition building) or toward adversaries to affect their decisions.

Throughout the Persian Gulf crises of 1990–1991 and 2003, Saddam Hussein had tried to frame western public opinion (as he successfully did prior to the invasion of Kuwait) by communicating a desire to work toward a peaceful solution while at the same time provoking rather than alleviating tensions with actions incongruent with his expression of a sincere desire for peace. For example, Iraq announced on August 3, 1990, that it would begin withdrawing troops from Kuwait in two days. At the same time, however, it became apparent that Iraqi forces were being reinforced rather than withdrawn. During the rest of August 1990, Saddam worked to solidify his hold over Kuwait and took western hostages to use as "human shields" to deter any attack.

When the conflict escalated and American soldiers were facing the Iraqi troops, Saddam tried to hit the American public with another frame. This time he took into account Americans' Vietnam Syndrome – aversion to military casualties in wars away from home. This was the premise underlying Saddam's promise for the "Mother of all battles." However, this frame played into the hands of the U.S. military leadership. It justified a larger deployment of American forces to the region and eventually tinted the military success as greater than it would have seemed on the basis of a simple evaluation of balance of power.

The administration was also busy during the conflict generating frames to establish and then solidify its coalition against Saddam. For instance, there are several accounts on the preliminary difficulties the administration had in convincing the Saudis to ask for American military help against Iraq (Woodward 1991). Furthermore, Secretary of State Baker was accumulating frequent flyer miles traveling from one capital to another trying to make leaders in the region see the conflict through the U.S. frames. Moreover, the administration tried to create a frame for the Iraqis and parts of the Arab world in which Saddam personally was the main cause of war so that the Iraqi people would get rid of their leader.

Advisory Group Framing and Manipulating

The complexity of foreign policy decision making involves a cast of various individuals in supporting roles to the president. During the decision-making process, the political leader may look for or be offered advice (and frames) from other individuals. This inclination is partly triggered by the human tendency to get validation for one beliefs and knowledge from others. This act of social validation of a social reality is delineated in the **social comparison theory** presented by Leon Festinger (1954). The impact of members of the presidential inner circle on the decision-making process was already addressed in Graham Allison's seminal work (1971) as he analyzed the bureaucratic decision model. Various findings in social psychology can add to this interpretation that the roles people play within an organization affect the frames they impose on situations. Role-induced frames thereby introduce a certain bias in the interpretation of a situation (independent from, or on top of, the organizational agenda a person has).

The advisory role of such persons may formalize the introduction of their frame to the situation. Furthermore, the complexity of the international environment fosters the tendency of decision makers to assess and validate their frames with others. This, in turn, provides ample opportunities for advisors and others to introduce their interpretations and thereby influence the dominant frame. For instance, a military advisor can frame a situation in such a way as to emphasize the strategic benefits of the use of force, whereas an economic advisor can frame it to exaggerate the economic costs of the operation. It should be noted that these frames must not be manipulative in nature because these advisors are affected by the role they are in. An example in this case is General Norman Schwarzkopf's framing of the risks involved in the 1991 attack. This frame affected the size of the deployed force. The frame can also be interpreted as an attempt to market the eventual interpretation of the success, because this frame led people to expect a difficult military clash.

Sources for framing of options available to the president include various individuals who participate in the decision process. These include members of the cabinet, heads of pertinent branches of the bureaucracy (CIA, Defense Intelligence Agency, Pentagon) and other consultants/advisors as part of structured (e.g., NSC) or semistructured inner circles of the president. They may also include sporadic contacts with other heads of nations and organizations. In the context of the Gulf crisis of 1991, these were British Prime Minister Margaret Thatcher, King Fahd of Saudi Arabia, and President Hosni Mubarak of Egypt. The main point here is that all these individuals could and did introduce their frames during the decision process.

Several sources attribute G. H. W. Bush's shift to a firmer stand against Saddam's aggression to his meetings with British Prime Minister Thatcher (Woodward 1991, 182). According to these sources, Thatcher was able to frame the situation as a chance for the United States to express its supremacy. This frame was quite different from the initial framing of the situation offered by Egypt's President Mubarak or Jordan's King Hussein. The latter tried to frame the Iraqi invasion as an Arab dispute that had to be solved locally.

Another attempt to affect the president's framing of the decision was evident in the different portrayal of the U.S. military options in the crisis. Within the military, the task was colored according to the specific military branch. For example, the ground forces depicted the use of force options as more difficult than did the air forces (this was also evident in the 2003 crisis). This was also clear from the military leadership's (generals Powell and Schwarzkopf) requests for an abundance of forces during the military buildup (the so-called Powell Doctrine) and in their estimates of casualties.

The effects of framing on decisions can be intentional or inadvertent (Quattrone and Tversky 1988). Were all the frames offered by others an honest advisory attempt to offer support to deal with an ambiguous situation or were they manipulative means? This is a question that is not easily answered. According to Zeev Maoz (1990a, 77), "manipulation of decisions differ from persuasion and other direct attempts to influence choice outcomes. Whereas manipulation focuses on structuring the group decision-making situation in a manner that assures success, persuasion entails direct attempts to influence or (pressure) individual decision makers into changing their preferences" (see also Mintz and Redd 2003). Within the operation of group decision making, it is difficult to differentiate between the direct and indirect attempts of framing.

The frame that is superimposed on the situation affects the type of details the leader sees and evaluates in the environment. The frame serves as the anchor or baseline against which all situational changes are evaluated. The effects of the frame on the nature of what is perceived and how it is evaluated shape the meaning that is assigned to the situation. The interpretation of the situation, then, triggers the decision process, because the assigned meaning determines whether there is a problem that requires some action. Lee Roy Beach (1990) concludes that frames that are imposed on a context have a powerful effect on the decision maker's reasoning about the context.

Leaders also try to frame their opponents in noncompensatory terms (Mintz 2006). During the 2004 presidential campaign Senator Kerry frequently talked about the potential for a dramatic shift in the composition and policies of the Supreme Court should the president be reelected. Ads sponsored by Swift Boat Veterans portrayed Senator Kerry as someone who "betrayed" them in Vietnam – enough for many voters to pursue a noncompensatory strategy on this one dimension (issue) alone, while deciding not to vote for the senator.

The effects of framing on decision making during the Gulf crises of 1990–1991 and 2003 are evident along the entire sequence of events. First, the framing of Iraq as the moderate force in the Gulf region during its war with Iran can account for the misinterpretation of the military information concerning the offensive implications of the Iraqi forces on the border of Kuwait. Subsequent decisions were influenced by the perception that Iraq was operating under a different frame. This change in frame is compatible with Beach's image theory (1990, 59) in which he suggests, "contextual evolution requires the frame to be changed. Often the necessity is signaled by the failure of some action that is predicated upon the inadequate frame." The failure, due to framing Iraq as the moderate force in the region, led to an adoption of a **contrasting frame** – Iraq as a menace to the region. As this frame was employed, Iraqi military cues were interpreted as a threat for attacking Saudi Arabia. This interpretation differs from the one raised by the Saudis themselves, who did not feel threatened by an immediate Iraqi attack. According to Woodward (1991), the United States had to convince the Saudis with quite a bit of information (e.g., aerial photos) before the Saudis were ready to invite American military protection.

Saddam's schematic perception of the situation was that the United States would not intervene. Moreover, his framing of U.S. foreign policy using the Vietnam analogy influenced his initial assessment that Bush would not play hardball. We shall return to this point later.

Whereas the previous analysis illuminated the effects of the frame on the interpretation of the situation, the next examples will deal with another aspect of framing and decision making, the determination of the frame employed in particular situations.

The frame is a prototypical representation of previous knowledge that is applied on a current target situation. In various situations, more than one frame can relate to a current situation. Within the context of foreign policy decision making, it seems that the first principle to operate in the selection of a frame is the search for similarity. Hence, the decision maker attempts to identify previous experiences to which the new events have resemblance (Klein 1989).

Naturally, the more expert the decision maker is, the more frames are available. This effect of expertise is evident in the posture G. H. W. Bush took during the Gulf crisis: "Bush seemed confident. The President said that he felt he knew more than anyone about the region, and also about the diplomacy, the military, the economics and the oil. I have been dealing with these issues for 25 years. . . . Those experiences allowed him to see all the pieces" (Woodward 1991, 315). For the president, the question was mainly on of which of the multiple frames that could be used for the Gulf crisis would be dominant.

A factor affecting the prevalence of a dominant frame is its accessibility. The frame comes from the decision maker's past experience with similar decisions (Beach 1990). Beer et al. (1987) pointed out that historical analogies are cognitive primers that tune the decision maker's mind toward a certain band wave. In the case of G. H. W. Bush, various accounts suggest that his concurrent reading of the situation relied on his experience in World War II, which also shaped the way he framed Saddam's activities. The comparison of Saddam to Hitler and Iraqi aggression toward Kuwait to Nazi activities was a central theme in the justification of Bush's decisions. This is evident in the president's address on August 8, 1990. The speech drew on some World War II analogies: Iraq had "stormed in blitzkrieg fashion through Kuwait . . . [and] appeasement does not work as was the case in the 1930s." The deployment was cast in terms of a "principled moral crusade, and the speech explicitly said that the mission was defensive" (Woodward 1991, 276–277). Identifying or interpreting the similarity of current events to previous situations facilitates the adoption of plans that worked successfully in the past. The labeling of the Iraqi invasion of Kuwait as parallel to Nazi Germany heightened the salience of the military option.

Another implication of framing the decisions on the use of force concerns the effects of the frame on the evaluation of the consequences and the utilities of the decision alternatives. Amos Tversky and Daniel Kahneman (1981) demonstrated that whether the situation is framed as a loss or as a gain affects the risk propensity of the decision maker. Framing the context of the decision making as a loss increases risk-prone behavior and the choice of risky alternatives. In contrast, framing the situation as a gain context increases the likelihood of risk-aversive behavior (i.e., going for a safe alternative).

Summary

International crises are attended to, assessed, and reacted to in correspondence to dominant frames such as the war on terrorism, the war in Iraq, threats from the Axis of Evil, and so on. This is true both for those involved in the decision and for those who evaluate the decision (i.e., the public). The frames that are imposed on the new situation are the catalyst for the policy options that are raised. In the case of foreign affairs in general and international crises in particular, the level of experience and expertise of the national leadership and their advisory groups is usually superior to that of the public. This expertise and easy access to media give the political leadership the ability to frame situations for the public.

The analysis of the Gulf crisis of 1990–1991 and the invasion of Iraq in 2003 exemplifies the foregoing propositions and the importance of the psychological approach to understanding decision making. Bush's experience in foreign affairs led to the rise of several variations on how to frame the invasion of Kuwait by Iraqi forces and the potential U.S. response. The available and accessible historical analog of the invasion to the Nazi regime was one of these salient frames. The multiple frames communicated to the public can be perceived as an attempt at political manipulation. Yet the multiplicity of frames also perplexed public opinion, to the point that fewer and more emotionally laden frames were used (e.g., the hostages and the annulment of the Nazi-like aggression).

David Brulé and Alex Mintz (2006) have shown, using a dataset of public opinion polls on the use of force in by the United States from 1949 to 2001, that presidents reject passive foreign policy options when public opinion strongly favors use of force and reject proforce options when the public opposes the use of force. Presidents receive marching orders from the public, not blank checks to do whatever they wants (ibid.). In line with the diversionary theories of the use of force, the framing, priming, and spinning of a given situation can help politicians to ascertain a favorable reaction to the use of force (Bostdorff 1991; DeRouen Jr. 2001).

MEDIA EFFECTS

Can the news media influence foreign policy decisions? Two theories have been offered to address this question: the so-called *CNN effect* and the *manufacturing consent* thesis (Peña 2003).

The "CNN effect" is a product of the Vietnam War and the widespread belief that the media was a factor in dwindling American support for the war (Gilboa 2005). CNN became a household name in 1991 during the Gulf War. In its most basic form, the effect is said to constrain the foreign policy decision making latitude of governments. The "CNN curve" describes the range of media influence from urging foreign policy action in a desperate situation to urging a retreat when a when a foreign policy leads to casualties (ibid.). From this perspective, the media got the United States into Somalia in 1992 with graphic depictions of starvation and then got it out with images of a U.S. soldier being drug through the streets.

In contrast, the manufacturing consent theory argues that elites control media and government and use media to create support for certain policies (ibid.). There are two ways in which manufacturing consent may take place: "the executive version, in which there is framing that conforms to the official agenda; and the elite version, in which news coverage is critical of executive policy as a consequence of elite dissensus" (Peña 2003).

Because of technological advancements, real-time news coverage allows information to be broadcast twenty-four hours a day from anywhere in the world, without regard for diplomatic secrecy. However, the ability of foreign policy makers to keep a situation secret often keeps them from dealing with "public hysteria" or media pressures (ibid.).

Monica Peña (2003) has noted that foreign news is focused on conflicts and that only a few conflicts are covered. Such coverage is determined by a variety of factors such as routine news making and newsworthiness considerations. However, what drives the attention of journalists in the first place toward a specific conflict?

Livingston (1997, 2–4) suggests a three-way typology of likely CNN effects (summarized by Peña 2003 as follows):

First effect is media as accelerants, in this modality, media are presumed to shorten the time of decision-making response. Yet, the media can also become a 'force multiplier,' a 'method of sending signals' to the opponent (1997, 2–4). This effect is most plausible to appear in conventional warfare, strategic deterrence, and tactical deterrence (ibid., 11). The second effect is media as impediment, this takes two forms, as an emotional inhibitor, and as a threat to operational security. One likely manifestation of the emotional inhibitor effect is the 'Vietnam syndrome' (Livingston 1997, 4), in which, it is presumed, public support is undermined by the media coverage of casualties. As a threat to operational security, the media are said to compromise the success of an operation by broadcasting it and, thus, revealing strategic information to the enemy, frustrating the success of the operation. This kind of effect ... is likely to appear during conventional warfare, tactical deterrence ... peace making and peace keeping operations. The third likely effect of the media on foreign policy making the Livingston (1997) mentions is that of agenda setting agent. It is presumed that the coverage of humanitarian crises puts the issue in the foreign policy agenda and drives intervention. (Peña 2003)

Nik Gowing (1996) finds that the relationship between policy makers and the media is not a "one-way" relationship. Rather it is "one of reciprocal influence" (Peña 2003). Despite the influence of media over policy makers, Gowing notes that media reports "shape the policy agenda, but do not dictate responses. They highlight policy dilemmas, but do not resolve them" (ibid.). Scholars have also noted,

the ability of the media to impact foreign policy is inextricably related to coverage, thus, the greater the coverage, the more direct the impact, however, the indirect impact of the media is also relevant for foreign strategy, since it could deviate efforts from the long-term, cost-effective, high priority concerns towards the short-term, cost-ineffective, low priority contingencies. Finally, humanitarian intervention is decided by a multiplicity of factors, out of which the CNN effect may be but one. (ibid.)

Gowing, Peña, and others have concluded that news media and foreign policy making processes "influence one another, sometimes directly, others indirectly. The degrees of their mutual influence are proportional to other circumstances, such as newsworthiness from the media point of view, and policy uncertainty, from the foreign policy making perspective" (Peña 2003). However, these conclusions may not be accurate in the context of non-Western, developing societies.

CASE STUDY: THE MARKETING OF THE U.S. INVASION
OF GRENADA, 1983[2]

Presidential decisions to use military force can provide one of the clearest examples of foreign policy marketing. These decisions entail high stakes and the risk of loss of human life. If uses of force become prolonged, it typically means bad political news for the president (e.g., Vietnam, Iraq War by 2006). Subsequently there are incentives for presidents (and other executives) to try to manage major events proactively. The invasion of Grenada in 1983 involved two of the factors discussed in this chapter. The administration effectively used political marketing and media manipulation and garnered political windfall in spite of serious operational shortcomings.

Background

On October 25, 1983, two days after a truck loaded with explosives killed more than two hundred United States Marines in Beirut, the United States invaded Grenada. The justification for the invasion was the need to restore order and protect American lives after the assassination of Prime Minister Maurice Bishop and several other leading members of the leftist New Jewel Movement government.

The invasion had been formally requested by the Governor General Paul Scoon of Grenada and the Organization of Eastern Caribbean States (OECS). Even had it not been for this formal request, it is likely that the United States would have resorted to the use of force considering the degree of military preparedness in the region. In this case study, we trace the decision-making process that led to the use of force on the island.

The primary justification for the invasion was to rescue approximately one thousand U.S. citizens, many of them medical students, and it is probable that the administration truly believed the students to be in danger. In retrospect, however, this argument turned out to be largely inaccurate. The chief administrator of the medical school, Charles Modica, emphasized that the invasion was "totally unnecessary" and had in fact been making plans to evacuate about 10 percent of the students who wanted to go (Kenworthy 1984, 637). The infamous "shoot-to-kill" curfew had also been lifted the day before the invasion. The most compelling evidence that the invasion should not have been justified as a rescue mission was that foreigners were free to leave the country at all times, and according to Carter's former National Security Council advisor on Latin American affairs, the invasion precluded an orderly evacuation of Americans (Kenworthy 1984, 638).

---

[2] This section is a revised and summarized version of material appearing in DeRouen Jr. (2001).

The Key Decision Makers

The alternatives for dealing with the crisis can be reduced to: do nothing; use covert/psychological operations (as in Guatemala in 1954 or Chile in 1973); and use full-scale force (see Andriole 1985, 80, 82; Hybel 1990, 270). The formal decision to execute Operation Urgent Fury, as it came to be called, came on Sunday, October 23 after two security council meetings in which the decision makers were reassured that casualties were expected to be light (DeFrank and Walcott 1983, 75). Then President Ronald Reagan, Vice President George H. W. Bush, Secretary of State George Shultz, National Security Advisor Robert McFarlane, and Secretary of Defense Caspar Weinberger were the central players. The overarching atmosphere surrounding the decision-making environment was one of consensus – that is, there was not much debate within the inner circle (Shapiro et al. 1983, 82; Hooker 1991).

The drive for consensus became evident because Defense Secretary Weinberger's preference for restraint in the use of force was strongly overshadowed by the State Department's advocacy of an all-out use of force (Hooker 1991, 67). From the outset, it appeared that the Grenada venture was a State Department project and that the input of the various agencies was not equally weighted as in a multiple advocacy setting (Hooker 1991). Bona fide multiple advocacy had very little room to obtain in an atmosphere in which aides told the president only what they knew he wanted to hear and feared giving the president bad news (Church 1982, 15).

The Marketing of the Decision

The barracks bombing in Lebanon led to an immediate and troubling drop in approval for President Reagan (Cannon 1991, 445). In Congress, many members began seriously questioning the president's plan for the U.S. military presence in Lebanon (Bostdorff 1994, 181). However, in the wake of the invasion of Grenada, presidential approval began to climb, and congressional pressure was alleviated. In a poll taken October 7–10, 1983, approval stood at 45 percent. It climbed to 49 percent during a poll taken October 21–24, and to 53 percent by the time of a poll taken November 18–21 (Edwards 1990).

The administration carefully managed the politics of the invasion (Bostdorff 1991). It meticulously tracked public opinion during the crisis and, as a reward, received a boost in ratings after the president's speech on television (Isaacson 1983, 37). The boost in public opinion numbers translated into Congressional support for the decision as open criticism of the invasion quickly died down (Isaacson 1983, 39).

The evidence gathered by Connell-Smith (1984), Isaak Dore (1984), Michael Rubner (1985–1986), Michael Levitin (1986), and Denise Bostdorff (1991) leads to a conclusion that the decision to intervene in Grenada was not based solely on realist factors such as the Soviet-Cuban threat and the cache of largely outdated weapons stockpiled in Grenada. Several studies, arguing from a realist perspective, assert that the U.S. intervention was fully justified in light of the nation's need to maintain international economic power and influence (Coll 1987) or simply because the United States, because it had "effective and determined leadership," deserved to use force as a "valid tenet of international politics (Motley 1983–84, 226).

The decision makers recognized Grenada as the type of low-risk venture that would rally domestic support (Thorndike 1989, 256) and, to the surprise of no one, Reagan used the invasion as a rallying point days later at a Reagan-Bush campaign reunion (Bostdorff 1991, 744). According to Bostdorff (1991), the Grenada venture was a promoted crisis that was managed closely by the president. The promotion occurred as the president fostered the notion that a state of urgency existed in Grenada; management took place as Reagan began to persuade the public to accept his solution as the most appropriate one (Bostdorff 1991, 737). After the president went on television to discuss the invasion, his critics became silent in the wake of the rally effect (Hinckley 1992).

As a result of the president's handling of the crisis, he garnered symbolic political resources and subsequently was able to withstand the resource deficit precipitated by the Marine barracks bombing. Symbolic resources are particularly valuable in cases, such this one, when the president has no one from whom to exact revenge (Bostdorff 1991, 745). Bostdorff (1991, 739) terms such symbols in which victory progresses into the future and distributes "needed symbolic reassurance," **condensation symbols**.

The Decision Process

The use of analogy is a useful heuristic in the face of time constraints. Many contingencies were not even considered primarily because the decision makers often lacked detailed or verifiable information and were operating under severe time constraints (Hooker 1991, 68). Secretary Weinberger was convinced, for example, that the administration did not know enough to act (Shultz 1993, 329). By "insulating" the president from the Pentagon's desire for more time, Shultz and McFarlane facilitated a noncompensatory decision process (Shultz 1993, 344).

The decision to use force appears to fit a noncompensatory decision structure. Recall that noncompensatory strategies can require the identification of one dimension as paramount (elimination by aspect [EBA], lexicographic decision rule [LEX]), or there can be multiple dimension thresholds (conjunctive decision rule [CON]). We have argued in this book that the political dimension is the most important to the decision makers, as evidenced by the way the president managed the issue with the public, the press ban, and the wariness of the decline in approval that would be precipitated by an American hostage situation. We can then rule out the CON strategy because it does not appear that all three dimensions warranted thresholds from the decision makers. The domestic dimension did not present an acute situation because the economy was on the road to recovery and unemployment had just dropped substantially (Hugick and Gallup 1991, 22).[3]

The president only resorted to an international explanation for the use of force (i.e., the threat framing of the Soviets using the new runway as a refueling depot, or Cuban-style exportation of revolution in the smaller islands of the Caribbean) after the fact. Then it was used to market the decision. Earlier the president had been careful to label the venture a rescue mission. Interestingly, President Johnson had similarly presented the situation in the Dominican Republic in 1965, in which he first said he sent in the Marines as a rescue mission, and after the fact said it was a move to thwart "another Cuba" in the region (Kegley and Wittkopf 1987, 118). Perhaps the Soviet/Cuban threats, and indeed the entire international dimension, were subordinate to the political dimension. After all, the United States had little international support even from its closest allies (Cohen 1984).[4] In the UN, only El Salvador, Israel, and the participating Caribbean states supported the invasion. Consequently, the international dimension largely proved to be a restraint to the use of force; the United States was unable to win the diplomatic skirmishes in Europe as Britain did during the Falklands War (Cohen 1984, 163).

The sequence of events indicates that the first, and likely only, alternative considered was the use of force. The administration did not appear to consider seriously the covert alternative (see, e.g., Shultz 1993), perhaps because of the time constraints and the need quickly to shift the focus away from Beirut. Furthermore, when officials at the invasion-day briefing were asked where CIA chief William Casey was, they responded that they did not know, further leading to the conclusion that a covert/psychological operation was not being considered (Clines 1983). It also seems unlikely, although it is difficult to verify, that the decision makers ever seriously contemplated doing nothing. Reagan ran on a strong platform in 1980 that promised to return America to international (military) preeminence, and a failure to act so close to home would be interpreted as reneging. The choice of an alternative before considering others is of course consistent with the bounded rationality/satisficing principles. Time constraints and situational pressure apparently forced the decision makers to take "cognitive shortcuts" (see Einhorn and Hogarth 1981; Holsti 1990; Shultz 1993). Larry Speakes, the president's spokesman, commented that it was "a very narrow planning operation," which even excluded him (Clines 1983).

---

[3] See also, "A Rose-Colored Recovery," *New York Times*, 14 November 1983.
[4] See also, B. Feder, "U.S. Warned by Mrs. Thatcher," *New York Times*, 26 October 1983.

Judging from the evidence that covert operations and the possibility of doing nothing were probably never considered, and that the use of force was proactive in terms of creating a diversion from the tragedy in Beirut, the LEX model seems the best way to describe the decision modus vivendi in the case of Grenada. Recall that the LEX strategy identifies the most important dimension, and then the alternative with the highest utility along this dimension is selected. Bostdorff's (1991) argument that the affair was politically managed dovetails neatly with the conception of the LEX model as proactive (i.e., the executive "creates" situations in which the use of force brings political windfall). In this case, the windfall circumvented the unpopular policies in Lebanon, avoided a potential hostage crisis that would be politically damaging, and gave the president a significant boost just months before his campaign for reelection.

Could the Process Actually Have Been a Compensatory One?

The weight of the evidence seems to indicate that a compensatory process was not carried out. First of all, the speed in which the decision had to be made makes it more likely that the decision involved the cognitive shortcuts embedded within the noncompensatory approach (see Payne, Bettman, and Johnson 1988). When time is limited, as it was in this case because of the overlap of events in Beirut and Grenada, it has been shown that a noncompensatory process is more efficient. Second, and as already mentioned, it does not appear that all alternatives were compared, or even entertained (Hooker 1991, 67–68). According to Richard Hooker (1991, 68, n. 46), the reason an exhaustive search was not carried out was that information regarding the military capabilities of the opponent was incomplete. Subsequently, the decision process "degraded" and the State Department was able to monopolize all information reaching the president.

CONCLUSION

Leaders sell their decisions to the public in order to enhance their standing. Leaders typically want to make decisions that are supported more than they are opposed. This chapter outlined marketing and framing strategies that decision makers use to garner support for their foreign policy choices. Leaders are not totally at the mercy of public opinion. To some extent, savvy marketing can win support that otherwise would not have been there.

PART SIX

CONCLUSION

9

Conclusion

Foreign policy problems are inherently complex (Steinbruner 1974, 2002).
Consequently, making foreign policy decisions is a complicated task with wide-
ranging ramifications. Foreign policy decisions are made by a single leader (e.g.,
the president), a group (e.g., Congress), or a coalition (e.g., in parliamentary
democracy). There are several types of decisions: one-shot single decisions,
interactive decisions, sequential decisions, and sequential interactive decisions. Foreign policy decisions are influenced by the personality of leaders,
the foreign policy environment, international and domestic factors, decision
setting, and decision dynamics. Decisions affect subsequent decisions and often
set a "path" for new decisions.

Foreign policy decisions are typically made in an interactive setting (i.e.,
involving an opponent, an ally, or both) and under dynamic conditions (in
which new information enters the decision situation during crisis). The foreign
policy environment is typically characterized by a high level of uncertainty,
considerable risk, and incomplete information, and decisions often have to be
made in unfamiliar settings.

Foreign policy decisions are often made under time and information constraints; involve value-tradeoffs and sunk costs; are influenced by perceptions
and misperceptions, images and belief systems, emotions, and *internal* political and economic calculations; and are shaped by the personality of leaders,
miscalculations, agendas, and interests.

Foreign policy decisions are also affected by a series of *international* influences such as deterrence, the arms race, strategic surprise, the regime type of
the adversary, alliances, and so on. Leaders are susceptible to cognitive biases
and errors in making foreign policy decisions.

Examples of such biases and errors include the shooting from the hip bias,
the wishful thinking bias, the plunging in bias, the preference over preference
bias, the overconfidence bias, the poliheuristic bias, and the bias of underestimating of opponents' capabilities and intentions while overestimating one's

169

own capabilities. Such biases often lead to suboptimal and even bad decisions. Many decisions are also susceptible to the groupthink syndrome. A psychological approach to decision making highlights the fact that cognitive biases affect information processing and ultimately the choice that is made.

Despite these challenges to optimal decision making in the foreign policy arena, state leaders are expected to make good decisions and to be responsible and accountable for the choices they make. Leaders also attempt to market their foreign policy in peacetime and wartime. They do so to garner public support for their policies. Leaders often frame information about the foreign policy event, their good intentions, their opponents' bad behavior and intentions to the mass public, their constituencies, and their opponents. For example, during the second war in Lebanon in July 2006, Hezbollah's leader Hassan Nasrallah pointed out that Hezbollah's missiles could target Israeli cities even south of Haifa. This "threat framing" tactic (Hochberg-Marom 2008) was aimed at rallying domestic audiences and the masses in the Arab world, mobilizing recruits, satisfying Nasrallah's allies (Iran and Syria), threatening Israeli leaders and citizens, and demonstrating to his supporters and others that Hezbollah was winning the war.

Six models of decision making can explain foreign policy decisions. At the core of the rational actor model is cost-benefit evaluation of alternative courses of action used in an attempt to select the "best" alternative (the one with the highest net gain) according to the "maximizing" principle. The bounded rationality, cybernetic model assumes that the alternative that is "good enough" or "satisfices" will be selected, without necessarily engaging in an exhaustive search of information along all alternatives and all dimensions.

The poliheuristic model combines rational and cognitive elements of decision making in a two-stage decision process. The first step represents the cognitive model and the second a rational model. Domestic politics is the "essence of decision" in the poliheuristic model of foreign policy decision making. Alternatives that threaten the political survival of the leader are eliminated from consideration outright (the first stage). "Surviving" alternatives are then evaluated on the basis of analytic, rational calculations.

According to prospect theory, people are sensitive to the domain in which they operate. Leaders are risk averse with respect to gains and risk acceptant with respect to losses. Decisions are made with respect to the reference point. Losses loom larger than gains.

In the bureaucratic politics model, bureaucracies pull and haul and advance their goals and agendas. On the basis of this model, decisions are the outcome of compromises among bureaucracies. "Where you stand on the issue depends on where you sit" in the bureaucracy (Allison 1969, 771). Finally, the organizational politics model highlights the use of standard operating procedures (SOPs) in decision making within agencies and organizations.

WHAT DOES IT ALL MEAN?: A CASE STUDY OF THE U.S. DECISION
TO INVADE IRAQ IN 2003

The U.S. decision in 2003 to invade and conquer Iraq consisted of a series of **sequential decisions**: whether to attack, and if so, whether to attack from the air, the ground, or both; whether to conquer Iraq; whether to abolish its army; whom to put in power; how long to stay; and, of course, multiple decisions on force level, troop reduction and withdrawal, and so forth.

Because no weapons of mass destruction were found in Iraq, the administration probably overreacted to the Iraqi threat. This overreaction was largely based on the **belief** among the White House, the National Security Council, and the intelligence community that Iraq possessed WMD and that these WMD constituted an immediate and growing threat to the United States and its allies in the Middle East and elsewhere. Members of the **decision unit** in this case were President George W. Bush, Vice President Dick Cheney, Secretary of Defense Donald Rumsfeld, Secretary of State Colin Powell, Deputy Secretary of Defense Paul Wolfowitz, Director of the CIA George Tenet, Chief of Staff Andrew Card, and National Security Advisor Condoleezza Rice. With the exception of Secretary of State Powell, members of the decision unit were very supportive of the decision to invade Iraq (Woodward 2004).

A key **advisory group** to the administration were members of the so-called neoconservative movement (known informally as "neocons") who share more or less the same background, worldview, **belief system**, and orientation. Their think tank, headed by Bill Kristol is called the Project for a New American Century (PNAC). Many officials and supporters of regime change in Iraq took part in PNAC's policy formulation. PNAC wrote an open letter to President Clinton in 1998 in which it urged regime change in Iraq as official policy.[1] The letter was signed by several individuals who would be in positions of prominence in the Bush administration. Donald Rumsfeld and Paul Wolfowitz, two key future members of the Bush Defense Department, signed the letter. John Bolton, Undersecretary of State for Arms Control and later ambassador to the UN, also signed the letter. Richard Perle, the chairman of the Defense Policy Advisory Committee from 2001 to 2003, was a signatory.

Because there was no real challenge to the views that the neocon group presented to the president and vice president, conditions were prime for a **groupthink syndrome**, which indeed occurred. Specifically, with the exception of Colin Powell, there was no opposition within the decision unit to the invasion, and expert advice on threats to U.S. postinvasion forces were largely ignored in favor of more "supportive" information about the invasion and the promising prospect of turning Iraq into a democracy.

---

[1] See the open letter at http://www.newamericancentury.org/iraqclintonletter.htm.

In lieu of the Shock and Awe campaign, serious **miscalculations** by the administration were evident. The president bet on the quality and supremacy of the U.S. military vis-à-vis its adversary (Iraq). Iraq was **perceived** as militarily weak, within the context of the **historical analogy** of 1991 and the sanctions of the 1990s. The architects of the war were **overconfident** in the ability of the United States to turn Iraq into a democracy. Instead of looking at the Lebanese model of a multiethnic society with conflicting political interests, agendas, and religious factions, as well as competing ideologies, they believed that Iraqis would greet the United States and its partners with open arms as liberators and quickly adopt the democratic values and system of the West. In retrospect, this was **wishful thinking** on the part of the administration, at least in the short term.

There was clearly an **underestimation** of the capabilities of the Iraqi insurgency to inflict harm on the United States and coalition forces. There was also a **miscalculation** of the will of the Iraqis to challenge the new status quo and **misperception** of the **risks** involved to U.S. ground forces occupying Iraq. A few months after the U.S. invasion of Iraq, Senator Ted Kennedy (D-MA) compared the U.S. involvement in Iraq to the quagmire in Vietnam. His analogy did not receive much weight and was even ridiculed.

Historical analogies of Iraqis fleeing Kuwait and images of Iraqis being almost destroyed at the end of the war provoked the general **belief** about the weakness of the Iraqi army. Because of the 1990–1991 experience, the belief within the administration was that it was a **familiar** situation. Coming right after the successful invasion of Afghanistan, there was a belief that the U.S. armed forces were invulnerable. However, generalizations from one theater to another were another **bias** exhibited by decision makers in the crisis.

If U.S. military planners **learned** something from the first Gulf War (of 1991), it was that the Iraqi military is no match for U.S. and coalition forces (Yetiv 2004, 222). The Gulf War ended with roughly two hundred dead U.S. soldiers – a small number by any count, although it constitutes a serious loss for every family hurt. Indeed, the military invasion of Iraq was successful in the **short run** but ignored potential problems in the **long run**. The administration's reluctance to deal with contradictory information that came from UN weapons inspectors about the lack of WMD in Iraq and information from intelligence agencies that Iraq did not have ties to al-Qaeda showed how the **bias** of ignoring critical contradictory information that is not supportive of your interests and goals can influence a critical decision.

President Saddam Hussein of Iraq was **framed** as posing a major threat to the United States, its allies, and its interests in the Middle East. The framing also involved portraying his regime as having ties to al-Qaeda and other Jihadist terrorist organizations. The media used these **thematic and threat framing tactics**. **Public opinion** supported an invasion of Iraq – with 60 to 70 percent approval – especially if such an invasion was authorized by the United Nations.

Economic interests (vast reserves of oil in Iraq, the importance of Iraq to the oil market), threats to U.S. interests in the region, the **nondemocratic regime of the adversary** (Iraq), and the **economic conditions** in the United States all influenced the decision to invade Iraq. It is hard to believe that if Iraq had been a democracy, the United States and its coalition partners would have invaded it. Moreover, the end of the Cold War and the breakup of the Soviet Union enabled the invasion of Iraq (and Kuwait) because no **deterrence** from the Soviet Union was present to prevent it. It is hard to imagine that the United States would have attacked Iraq, a country with economic, strategic, and political ties with the Soviet Union, during the Cold War.

The United States and its **coalition** partners did not take into account **cultural and political factors** in the makeup of Iraqi society and its polity – specifically, the tribal and ethnic composition of the Iraqi society and the threat the invasion posed to Sunni political control of Iraq. President George W. Bush may have wanted to prove wrong his dad's critics, who viewed the decision not to march to Baghdad in 1991 as a colossal mistake. However, little preparation for postwar Iraq was in place (known in the military as Phase IV planning).

The decision to invade Iraq was made in a **dynamic setting**, with new information introduced by UN inspectors during the crisis; this information did not alter the U.S. position, although there were no special stress or time constraints on the administration that would have made it a must-do decision. Serious **information problems** were evident as contradictory views such as those of Colin Powell were largely ignored (Woodward. 2004). Studies have shown that the personality of leaders such as UK Prime Minister Tony Blair (Dyson 2007) also had a strong influence on the decision.

Substantial **sunk costs** in terms of force levels deployed, the financial cost of the war, mounting casualties, prestige to the United States and the West, and economic interest in the Middle East made it extremely difficult for President Bush to reverse himself and withdraw from Iraq given the perception that the United States had not won the war. However, staying in Iraq is also problematic due to the mounting human toll, the **perception** of lack of progress there, and the fear of "the day after" the withdrawal. The decision to stop the war would have to have been made in an **interactive setting** vis-à-vis what the government of Iraq could and was willing to do to stop the daily bloodshed in Iraq. As the Bush presidency came to an end, the United States was emotionally and physically tired of the war.

The **applied decision analysis** procedure helps us simplify decision tasks, such as President George W. Bush's decision to invade Iraq in 2003. A **decision problem** consists of a **set of alternatives** (continue the war on terrorism, stop the war, pursue terrorists without large-scale uses of force) and a **set of decision criteria**, such as geostrategic, political, military, economic, and diplomatic considerations. After alternatives and dimensions are identified, weights can be assigned to different dimensions based on their importance to the decision, and ratings are assessed for the implications of each alternative on every dimension. This allows for the creation of a **decision matrix**, which can be analyzed on the basis of the **decision models** described in Chapters 4 and 5.

In terms of the **two-level game** construct, both domestic and international dimensions are important when analyzing the decision. **Domestic audience costs** should not be underestimated in the decisions to invade and especially to withdraw from Iraq.

Following the invasion of Afghanistan by the United States and its NATO allies, President Bush faced the following options with regard to the invasion of Iraq:

1. stop the war on terrorism,
2. pursue terrorists without large-scale uses of force, or
3. continue the war on terrorism.

There were several decision criteria for the administration to consider – specifically,

1. geostrategic considerations,
2. economic considerations (oil),
3. political calculations (primarily public opinion),
4. military factors (clear military advantage over Iraq, the perception of which was based on the Gulf War of 1991, compared with the risk of attacking Iran or even North Korea),
5. the belief (expressed on numerous occasions by administration officials) that Iraq possessed WMD, and
6. the claim that Iraq had links to al-Qaeda.

How would the different decision models explain President Bush's 2003 decision? Using the **rational actor model**, the decision to invade Iraq in 2003 consists of an evaluation of the alternative courses of action across dimensions. Cost-benefit assessment of each of the alternatives is performed and the alternative with the highest net gain is selected. The administration evaluated the alternatives of continuing the war on terrorism, pursuing terrorists without full-scale campaign, and stopping the war on multiple dimensions, such as the global war on terrorism, the economic consequences of the invasion, its political ramifications, the implication for the potential use and proliferation of WMD, projected U.S. and coalition casualties, and the potential for turning Iraq into a democracy. If the rational actor model was employed, this evaluation apparently led the administration to believe that the invasion was the optimal choice.

Using a **bounded rationality cybernetic approach**, the administration might have selected the alternative of pursuing terrorists without full-scale use of force – that is, using heavy air strikes or a brief invasion removing Saddam Hussein from power and then turning Iraq over to the Iraqi people. This would have been perceived as a "good enough" option for at least some in the administration.

A **poliheuristic** account of the U.S. decision to invade Iraq in 2003 would have explained the president's rejection of the "stop the war on terrorism" alternative primarily on the basis of political calculations. Public opinion (running between 60 and 70 percent) was solidly behind the president on the invasion, and also seemed to reject the alternative of pursuing terrorists without full-scale war (Mintz 2006). The president could have selected this second alternative (as had been done in the Philippines against Abu Sayyaf), but rejected it in the initial stage because it was not "visible" enough for Bush's domestic audience and failed to satisfy the public's desire for a continuation of the war on terrorism in the wake of 9/11.[2] According to poliheuristic theory, the option of continuing the war would have been selected, in the second stage of the decision process, on the basis of the overall, multidimensional assessment of the geostrategic, economic, military, diplomatic, and political dimensions of the alternatives.[3]

A **prospect theory** explanation of the U.S. decision to invade Iraq would predict that the president was in the domain of gains following the invasion of Afghanistan and that, consequently, would not attack Iraq. However, if the administration's reference point was the 9/11 attack, which resulted in thousands of civilian casualties, then the administration was in the domain of loss and would seek to continue the war on terrorism.

According to the **bureaucratic politics** model, various agencies and groups within the administration – the Department of Defense, the Department of State, the National Security Council, the Central Intelligence Agency, the armed forces, and the neoconservative groups – have each tried to advance their agendas and goals. Consequently, with the exception of the U.S. Department of State, they all would have supported invading Iraq and removing Saddam Hussein from power.

As is evident from the foregoing analysis, although most decision models would have predicted the invasion of Iraq by the Bush administration, some decision rules (i.e., the bounded-rationality model) would have predicted a different outcome.

CONCLUSION

In this introduction to FPDM we sliced the topic along four main dimensions: the decision environment (types, levels, and biases), models of FPDM

---

[2] D. Brule, personal communication to Alex Mintz, 2005. Also see Yetiv (2004).
[3] This case is analyzed using poliheuristic theory in Mintz (2006).

(rational and alternatives), determinants of FPDM (psychological, international, and domestic factors), and the marketing of decisions. FPDM is a rich and diverse subfield of international relations. There is no single means of assessing and understanding FPDM. This overview will help set the stage for further integration of the different approaches to FPDM.

APPENDIX

Foreign Policy Simulation and Exercise

KEY BENEFITS

- Students are exposed to policy scenarios that simulate decision-making processes.
- Students play the role of leaders.
- Students make "actual" foreign policy decisions.
- Students apply decision-making concepts, theories and models to real world situations and scenarios.
- Students improve their decision-making skills through the use of a unified, systematic methodology for organizing information about a foreign policy event and analyzing policy options.
- Students gain insight into the actual decision-making processes of political leaders.

CLICK ON http://www.decisionboard.org to access simulations, examples and exercises.

References

Aldrich, John, John Sullivan, and Eugene Borgida. 1989. "Foreign Affairs and Issue Voting: Do Presidential Candidates 'Waltz Before a Blind Audience?'" *American Political Science Review* 83: 123–141.

Allison, Graham. 1969. "Conceptual Models and the Cuban Missile Crisis." *American Political Science Review* 63(3): 689–718.

Allison, Graham. 1971. *Essence of Decision: Explaining the Cuban Missile Crisis.* Boston: Little, Brown.

Anderson, Paul. 1983. "Decision Making By Objection in the Cuban Missile Crisis." *Administrative Science Quarterly* 28: 201–222.

Anderson, Sheldon. 2007. "Condemned to Repeat It: The Misuse of Historical Analogy in U.S. Foreign Policymaking." Paper presented at the annual meeting of the International Studies Association, Chicago.

Andriole, Stephen. 1985. "A Decision Theoretic Analysis of the Reagan Administration's Decision to Invade Grenada." In *American Intervention in Grenada*, ed. Peter Dunn and Bruce Watson. Boulder: Westview.

Arrow, Kenneth. 2007. http://www.epsusa.org (accessed Dec. 18, 2007).

Astorino-Courtois, Allison and Brittani Trusty. 2000. "Degrees of Difficulty: The Effect of Israeli Policy Shifts on Syrian Peace Decisions." *Journal of Conflict Resolution* 44(3): 359–377.

Axelrod, Robert. 1976a. "The Cognitive Mapping Approach to Decision Making." In *Structure of Decision*, ed. Robert Axelrod. Princeton, NJ: Princeton University Press.

Axelrod, Robert. 1976b. "Decision for Nonimperialism: The Deliberations of the British East India Company in 1918." In *Structure of Decision*, ed. Robert Axelrod. Princeton, NJ: Princeton University Press.

Axelrod, Robert. 1984. *The Evolution of Cooperation.* New York: Basic Books.

Baker, James. 2006. "The Gulf War: An Oral History." *Frontline*, PBS, http://www.pbs.org/wgbh/pages/frontline/gulf/oral/gates/1.html (accessed Oct. 5, 2009).

Balz, Dan. 1991. "Bush, Major Talk Tough on Iraq." *Buffalo News*, March 17.

Bar-Joseph, Uri and Rose McDermott. 2008. "Personal Functioning Under Stress: Accountability and Social Support of Israeli Leaders in the Yom Kippur War." *Journal of Conflict Resolution* 52(1): 144–170.

Bazerman, Max. 2006. *Judgment in Managerial Decision Making*, 6th ed. Hoboken, NJ: John Wiley & Sons, Inc.

Beach, Lee Roy. 1990. *Image Theory: Decision Making in Personal and Organizational Contexts*. Chichester, UK: Wiley.

Bedard, Paul. 1991. "Did U.S. Blow Chance to Knock Out Saddam?" *Washington Times*, March 28.

Beer, Francis, Alice Healy, Grant Sinclair, and Lyle Bourne Jr. 1987. "War Cues and Foreign Policy Acts." *American Political Science Review* 81: 701–715.

Bendor, Jonathan and Thomas Hammond. 1992. "Rethinking Allison's Models." *American Political Science Review* 86(2): 301–322.

Bercovitch, Jacob and Karl DeRouen Jr. 2004. "Mediation in Internationalized Ethnic Conflicts: Assessing the Determinants of a Successful Process" *Armed Forces and Society* 30(2): 147–170.

Berger, Marilyn. 2002. "Cyrus R. Vance, a Confidant of Presidents, Is Dead at 84." *New York Times*, January 13.

Biglaiser, Glen and Karl DeRouen Jr. 2004. "The Expansion of Neoliberal Economic Reforms in Latin America." *International Studies Quarterly* 48(3): 561–578.

Billings, Robert and Stephen Marcus. 1983. "Measures of Compensatory and Noncompensatory Models of Decision Behavior: Process Tracing versus Policy Capturing." *Organizational Behavior and Human Performance* 31: 331–352.

Bostdorff, Denise. 1991. "The Presidency and Promoted Crisis: Reagan, Grenada, and Issue Management." *Presidential Studies Quarterly* 21: 737–750.

Bostdorff, Denise. 1994. *The Presidency and the Rhetoric of Foreign Crisis*. Columbia, SC: University of South Carolina Press.

Boukhars, Anouar. 2001. "A Two-level Game Analysis of the Complexities of Interstate Rivalries in the Maghreb." Columbia International Affairs Online Working Papers, May, http://www.ciaonet.org/access/boa02/index.html (accessed Sept. 3, 2009).

Brams, Steven. 1985. *Superpower Games*. New Haven, CT: Yale University Press.

Brannick, Michael and Joan Brannick. 1989. "Nonlinear and Noncompensatory Processes in Performance Evaluation." *Organizational Behavior and Human Decision Processes* 44: 97–122.

Braybrooke, David and Charles E. Lindblom. 1963. *A Strategy of Decision: Policy Evaluation as Social Process*. New York: Free Press of Glencoe.

Brule, David and Alex Mintz. 2006. "Blank Check or Marching Orders? Public Opinion and Presidential Use of Force." In *Approaches, Levels and Methods of Analysis in International Politics: Crossing Boundaries*, ed. Harvey Starr. New York: Palgrave, Macmillan.

Bueno de Mesquita, Bruce. n.d. "The Game of Conflict Interactions: A Research Program." University of Rochester, Rochester, NY.

Bueno de Mesquita, Bruce. 1981. *The War Trap*. New Haven, CT: Yale University Press.

Bueno de Mesquita, Bruce. 2003. *Principles of International Politics: People's Power, Preferences, and Perceptions*, 2nd ed. Washington, DC: CQ Press.

Bueno de Mesquita, Bruce, Alastair Smith, Randolph M. Siverson, and James D. Morrow. 2003. *The Logic of Political Survival*. Cambridge, MA: MIT Press.

Bueno de Mesquita, Ethan. 2005. "The Quality of Terror." *American Journal of Political Science* 49(3): 515–530.

Cannon, Lou. 1991. *President Reagan: The Role of a Lifetime.* New York: Simon and Schuster.

Cannon-Bowers, Janis, Eduardo Salas, and Sharolyn Converse. 1993. "Shared Mental Models in Expert Team Decision Making." In *Individual and Group Decision Making: Current Issues*, ed. N. John Castellan Jr. Hillsdale, NJ: Lawrence Earlbaum, Associates.

Caprioli, Mary. 2000. "Gendered Conflict." *Journal of Peace Research* 37(1): 51–68.

Caprioli, Mary. 2003. "Gender Equality and Civil Wars." World Bank CPR Working Paper no. 8. Washington, DC: World Bank.

Cashman, Greg. 1993. *What Causes War? An Introduction to Theories of International Conflict.* New York: Lexington Books.

Church, George. 1982. "How Reagan Decides." *Time*, December 13.

Clines, Frances. 1983. "Days of Crisis for President: Golf, a Tragedy and Secrets." *New York Times*, October 26.

Cohen, Eliot. 1984. "Constraints on America's Conduct of Small Wars." *International Security* 9: 151–181.

Coll, Alberto. 1987. "Why Grenada was Important." *Naval War College Review* 40: 4–18.

Connell-Smith, Gordon. 1984. "The Grenada Invasion in Historical Perspective: From Monroe to Reagan." *Third World Quarterly* 6: 432–445.

Conover, Pamela and Virginia Sapiro. 1993. "Gender, Feminist Consciousness and War." *American Journal of Political Science* 37(4): 1079–1099.

Coser, Lewis. 1956. *The Function of Social Conflict.* New York: Free Press.

Cottam, Martha. 1977. *Foreign Policy Motivation: A General Theory and a Case Study.* Pittsburgh, PA: University of Pittsburgh Press.

Cottam, Martha. 1994. *Images and Intervention: U.S. Policies in Latin America.* Pittsburgh, PA: University of Pittsburgh Press.

Cottam, Martha and Thomas Preston. 2007. "Building Stronger Images of Leadership: A Framework for Integrating Image Theory and Leadership Trait Analysis (LTA) into a More Powerful Tool for Analyzing Leaders-at-a-Distance." Paper presented at the annual meeting of the International Studies Association, Chicago.

Dawes, Robyn. 1964. "Social Selection Based on Multidimensional Criteria." *Journal of Abnormal and Social Psychology* 68: 104–109.

Debray, Regis. 1967. *Revolution in the Revolution? Armed Struggle and Political Struggle in Latin America.* Trans. Bobbye Ortiz. New York: MR Press.

Decision Board 4.0. Software developed by Alex Mintz, programmed by Eyal Mintz. http://www.decisionboard.org.

DeFrank, T. and J. Walcott. 1983. "The Invasion Countdown." *Newsweek*, November 7.

De Groot, Hans. 1988. "Decentralization Decisions in Bureaucracies as a Principal-Agent Problem." *Journal of Public Economics* 36(3): 323–337.

DeRouen Jr., Karl. 1995. "The Indirect Link: Politics, Economics and U.S. Use of Force." *Journal of Conflict Resolution* 39(4): 671–695.

DeRouen Jr., Karl. 2000. "Presidents and the Diversionary Use of Force." *International Studies Quarterly* 44(2): 317–338.

DeRouen Jr., Karl. 2001. *Politics, Economics and Presidential Use of Force Decision Making.* Lewiston, NY: Edwin, Mellen.

DeRouen Jr., Karl. 2003. "The Decision Not To Use Force At Dien Bien Phu: A Poliheuristic Perspective." In *Integrating Cognitive and Rational Theories of Foreign Policy Decision Making*, ed. Alex Mintz. New York: Palgrave Macmillan.

DeRouen Jr., Karl and Shaun Goldfinch. 2004. "Democracies Prefer to Negotiate: Institutionalized Democracy, Diversion and Statecraft during Internationalized Crises." In *New Directions in the Study of International Relations*, ed. Alex Mintz and Bruce Russett. Lexington, MA: Lexington.

DeRouen Jr., Karl and Shaun Goldfinch. 2007. "The Democratic Peace and Substitutability during International Crises: Institutionalised Democracy and Foreign Policy Choices." In *Institutions and Market Economies: The Political Economy of Growth and Development*, ed. Rik, Garside. London: Palgrave MacMillan.

DeRouen Jr., Karl and Uk Heo. 2000. "Defense Contracting and Domestic Politics." *Political Research Quarterly* 53(4): 753–770.

DeRouen Jr., Karl and Uk Heo. 2004. "Reward, Punishment or Inducement? U.S. Economic and Military Aid, 1946–1996." *Defence and Peace Economics* 15(5): 453–470.

DeRouen Jr., Karl and Jeffrey Peake. 2002. "The Dynamics of Diversion: The Domestic Implications of Presidential Use of Force." *International Interactions* 28(2): 191–211.

Diamond, John. "CIA Review Faults Prewar Plans." *USA Today*, October 12, 2005. http://www.usatoday.com/news/washington/2005-10-11-cia-iraq-report_x.htm (accessed Sept. 3, 2009).

Diehl, Paul. 1983. "Arms Races and Escalation: A Closer Look." *Journal of Peace Research* 20(3): 205–212.

Dore, Isaak. 1984. "The U.S. Invasion of Grenada: Resurrection of the 'Johnson, Doctrine.'" *Stanford Journal of International Law* 20: 173–189.

Dougherty, James and Robert Pfaltzgraff. 1990. *Contending Theories of International Relations*. New York: Harper and Row.

Drew, Elizabeth. 1991. "Washington Prepares for War." In *The Gulf War Reader: History, Documents, Opinions*, ed. Micah L. Sifry and Christopher Cerf. New York: Random House.

Dyson, Stephen. 2007. "Alliances, Domestic Politics and Leader Psychology: Why Did Britain Stay Out of Vietnam and Go Into Iraq?" *Political Psychology* 28(6): 647–666.

Dyson, Stephen and Thomas Preston. 2006. "Individual Characteristics of Political Leaders and the Use of Analogy in Foreign Policy Decision Making." *Political Psychology* 27(2): 265–288.

Edwards, George with Alec Gallup. 1990. *Presidential Approval: A Sourcebook*. Baltimore, MD: Johns Hopkins Press.

Eichenberg, Richard C. 2003. "Gender Differences in Public Attitudes toward the Use of Force by the United States, 1990–2003." *International Security* 28(1): 110–141.

Eichenberg, Richard C. 2007. "Gender Differences in Support for the Use of Military Force in Cross-National Perspective: The War System, Modernization, and the Universal Logics of Military Action." Paper presented at the annual meeting of the Midwest Political Science Association, Chicago, April 2007.

Einhorn, Hillel. 1970. "The Use of Nonlinear, Noncompensatory Models in Decision Making." *Psychological Bulletin* 73: 221–230.

Einhorn, Hillel. 1971. "Use of Nonlinear, Noncompensatory Models as a Function of Task and Amount of Information." *Organizational Behavior and Human Performance* 6: 1–27.

Einhorn, Hillel and Robin Hogarth. 1981. "Behavioral Decision Theory: Processes of Judgment and Choice." *Annual Review of Psychology* 32: 53–88.

Eisenband, Dori. 2003. "Application of the Poliheuristic Theory of Decision to the Political Process." Paper presented at the Conference on the Nexus between Domestic and International Relations, March Texas A&M University, College Station, TX.

Etheredge, Lloyd. 1985. *Can Governments Learn? American Foreign Policy and Central American Revolutions.* Elmsford, NY: Pergamon Press.

Fabyanic, Thomas. 1987. "Air Power and Conflict Termination." In *Conflict Termination and Military Strategy,* ed. Stephen J. Cimbala and Keith Dunn. Colorado: Westview Press.

Fearon, James. 1994a. "Domestic Political Audiences and the Escalation of International Disputes." *American Political Science Review* 88(3): 577–592.

Fearon, James. 1994b. "Signalling versus the Balance of Power and Interests: An Empirical Test of a Crisis Bargaining Model." *Journal of Conflict Resolution* 38(2): 236–269.

Feder, Barnaby. 1983. "U.S. Warned by Mrs. Thatcher." *New York Times,* 26 October.

Feith, Douglas. 2008. *War and Decision: Inside the Pentagon at the Dawn of the War on Terrorism.* New York: HarperCollins.

Ferejohn, John. 1991. *Rationality and Interpretation: Parliamentary Elections in Early Stuart England.* In *The Economic Approach to Politics,* ed. Kristen Renwick Monroe. New York: HarperCollins.

Festinger, Leon. 1954. "A Theory of Social Comparison Processes." *Human Relations* 7: 117–140.

Filson, Darren and Suzanne Werner. 2002. "A Bargaining Model of War and Peace: Anticipating the Onset, Duration and Outcome of War." *American Journal of Political Science* 46(4): 819–838.

Filson, Darren and Suzanne Werner. 2004. "Bargaining and Fighting: The Impact of Regime Type on War Onset, Duration, and Outcomes." *American Journal of Political Science* 48(2): 296–313.

Fisher, Ronald and Loraleigh Keashly. 1991. "The Potential Complementarity of Mediation and Consultation within a Contingency Model of Third Party Intervention." *Journal of Peace Research* 28(1): 29–42.

Fiske, Susan and Shelly Taylor. 1991. *Social Cognition,* 2nd ed. New York: McGraw-Hill.

Forman, Ernest and Mary Ann Selly. 2001. *Decision by Objectives.* New York: World Scientific.

Freedman, Lawrence. 1982. "The War of the Falkland Islands, 1982." *Foreign Affairs* (Fall): 196–210.

Frisch, Deborah. 1993. "Reasons for Framing Effects." *Organizational Behavior and Human Decision Processes* 54: 399–429.

Gaddis, John Lewis. 2002. "On Strategic Surprise." *Hoover Digest* (2)(Spring). http://www.hoover.org/publications/digest/3437371.html (accessed Sept. 3, 2009).

Gálvez, William. 1999. *Che in Africa: Che Guevara's Congo Diary.* Melbourne, Australia: Ocean Press.

Gartner, Scott. 2008. "Deadly Pictures: An Experimental Analysis of Images of Death and the Casualty-Opinion Nexus." Paper presented at the annual meeting of the American Political Science Association conference, Boston.

Gaubatz, Kurt Taylor. 1991. "Election Cycles and War." *Journal of Conflict Resolution* 35(2): 212–244.

Gaubatz, Kurt Taylor. 1999. *Elections and War: The Electoral Incentive in the Democratic Politics of War and Peace.* Stanford, CA: Stanford University Press.

George, Alexander L. 1969. "The 'Operational Code': A Neglected Approach to the Study of Political Leaders and Decision-Making." *International Studies Quarterly* 13(2): 190–222.

George, Alexander L. 1972. "The Case for Multiple Advocacy in Making Foreign Policy." *American Political Science Review* 66: 751–785.

George, Alexander. 1980a. *Presidential Decisionmaking in Foreign Policy.* Boulder, CO: Westview Press.

George, Alexander. 1980b. "Domestic Constraints on Regime Change in U.S. Foreign Policy: The Need for Policy Legitimacy." In *Change in the International System,* ed. Ole Holsti, Alexander George, and Randolph Siverson. Boulder, CO: Westview Press.

George, Alexander. 1993. *Bridging the Gap: Theory and Practice in Foreign Policy.* Washington, DC: United States Institute of Peace.

Geva, Nehemia, Russell Driggers, and Alex Mintz. 1996. "Effects of Ambiguity on Strategy and Choice in Foreign Policy Decision Making: An Analysis Using Computerized Process Tracing." Paper presented at the annual meeting of the American Political Science Association, August 29–September 1, San Francisco.

Geva, Nehemia, Steven Redd, and Katrina Mosher. 2004. "International Terror, Emotions and Foreign Policy Decision Making." Paper presented at the annual meeting of the International Studies Association, Montreal, March 17.

Gilboa, Eytan. 2005. "The CNN Effect: The Search for a Communication Theory of International Relations." *Political Communication* 22: 27–44.

Global Policy Forum. 2007. "Sanctions Against Iraq." http://www.globalpolicy.org/security/sanction/indexone.htm (accessed Sept. 3, 2009).

Goemans, Heins. 2000. *War and Punishment.* Princeton, NJ: Princeton University Press.

Goertz, Gary. 2004. "Constraints, Compromises and Decision Making." *Journal of Conflict Resolution* 48(1): 14–37.

Goldsmith, Benjamin. 2005. *Imitation in International Relations: Observational Learning, Analogies and Foreign Policy in Russia and Ukraine.* New York: Palgrave MacMillan.

Goldstein, Joshua. 2001. *War and Gender: How Gender Shapes the War System and Vice Versa.* Cambridge: Cambridge University Press.

Gowing, Nik. 1996. "Real-time TV Coverage from War, Does it Make or Break Government Policy?" In *Bosnia by Television,* ed. James Gow, Richard Paterson, and Alison Preston. London: British Film Institute.

Gray, Colin. 2005. *Transformation and Strategic Surprise.* Carlisle Barracks, PA: Strategic Studies Institute, U.S. Army War College.

Grimmett, Richard. 2005. *Conventional Arms Transfers to Developing Nations, 1997–2004.* Congressional Research Service Report no. 33051. Washington, DC: Congressional Research Service.

Guevara, Che. 1961. *Che Guevara on Guerrilla Warfare.* New York: Praeger.

Haass, Richard N. 1998. *Economic Sanctions and American Diplomacy.* Washington, DC: Council on Foreign Relations.

Hagan, Joe. 2001. "Does Decision Making Matter?" *International Studies Review* 3(2): 5–47.

Hagan, Joe, Philip Everts, Haruhiro Fukui, and John Stempel. 2001. "Foreign Policy by Coalition: Deadlock, Compromise, and Anarchy." *International Studies Review* 3(2): 169–217.

Halperin, Morton. 1974. *Bureaucratic Politics and Foreign Policy.* Washington, DC: Brookings Institution Press.

Handel, Michael. 1978. "The Study of War Termination." *Journal of Strategic Studies* 1: 51–75.

Handel, Michael. 1989. *War, Strategy and Intelligence.* London: Routledge.

Hermann, Charles, Janice Gross Stein, Bengt Sundelius, and Stephen Walker. 2001. "Resolve, Accept, or Avoid: Effects of Group Conflict on Foreign Policy Decisions." *International Studies Review* 3(2): 133–169.

Hermann, Margaret. 1983. *Handbook for Assessing Personal Characteristics and Foreign Policy Orientations of Political Leaders.* Columbus, OH: Mershon Center Occasional Papers.

Hermann, Margaret. 1984. "Personality and Foreign Policy Decision Making: A Study of 53 Heads of Government." In *Foreign Policy Decision-Making: Perceptions, Cognition, and Artificial Intelligence,* ed. David Sylvan and Steve Chan. New York Praeger.

Hermann, Margaret. 1999. *Assessing Leadership Style: A Trait Analysis.* Columbus, OH: Social Science Automation, Inc. http://www.socialscienceautomation.com/Docs/LTA.pdf (accessed Sept. 3, 2009).

Hermann, Margaret. 2001. "How Decision Units Shape Foreign Policy: A Theoretical Framework." *International Studies Review* 3(2): 47–82.

Hermann, Margaret, Thomas Preston, Baghat Korany, and Timothy Shaw. 2001. "Who Leads Matters: The Effects of Powerful Individuals." *International Studies Review* 3(2): 83–132.

Herrmann, Richard. 1985. "Analyzing Soviet Images of the United States: A Psychological Theory and Empirical Study." *Journal of Conflict Resolution* 29(4): 665–697.

Herrmann, Richard, James F. Voss, Tonya Y. E. Schooler, and Joseph Ciarrochi. 1997. "Images in International Relations: An Experimental Test of Cognitive Schemata." *International Studies Quarterly* 41(3): 403–433.

Hinckley, Ronald. 1992. *People, Polls and Policymakers.* New York: Lexington, Books.

Hirshberg, Matthew S. 1993. *Perpetuating Patriotic Perceptions: The Cognitive Function of the Cold War.* Westport, CT: Praeger.

Hochberg-Marom, Anat. 2008. "Global Marketing of Terror Organization: Al Qaeda." Ph.D. dissertation, in progress, Department of Political Science, Tel Aviv University.

Holsti, Ole. 1972. *Crisis, Escalation, War.* Montreal: McGill-Queens University Press.

Holsti, Ole. 1976. "Foreign Policy Formation Viewed Cognitively." In *Structure of Decision,* ed. Robert Axelrod. Princeton, NJ: Princeton University Press.

Holsti, Ole. 1989. "Crisis Decision-Making." In *Behavior, Society, and Nuclear War,* ed. Philip Tetlock, Jo Husbands, Robert Jervis, Paul Stern, and Charles Tilly. New York: Oxford University Press.

Holsti, Ole. 1990. "Crisis Management." In *Psychological Dimensions of War,* ed. Betty Glad. Newbury Park, CA: Sage.

Hooker, Richard. 1991. "Presidential Decisionmaking and Use of Force: Case Study of Grenada." *Parameters* 21: 61–72.

Houghton, David. 1996. "The Role of Analogical Reasoning in Novel Foreign-Policy Situations." *British Journal of Political Science* 26(4): 523–553.

Huber, Evelyne and Michelle Dion. 2002. "Revolution or Contribution? Rational Choice Approaches in the Study of Latin American Politics." *Latin American Politics and Society* 44: 1–28.

Hudson, Valerie M. 2005. "Foreign Policy Analysis: Actor-Specific Theory and the Ground of IR." *Foreign Policy Analysis* 1(1): 1–30.

Hugick, Larry and Alec Gallup. 1991. " 'Rally Events' and Presidential Approval." *Gallup Poll Monthly* (309): 15–27.

Huntington, Samuel P. 1993. "The Clash of Civilizations?" *Foreign Affairs* 72(3): 22–49.

Huth, Paul and Bruce Russett. 1990. "Testing Deterrence Theory: Rigor Makes a Difference." *World Politics* 42(4): 466–501.

Hybel, Alex. 1990. *How Leaders Reason.* Oxford: Basil Blackwell.

Hybel, Alex and Justin Kaufman. 2006. *The Bush Administrations and Saddam Hussein: Deciding on Conflict.* New York: Palgrave Macmillan.

Iklé, Fred. 1971. *Every War Must End.* New York: Columbia University Press.

Ingimundarson, Valur. 2003. "A Western Cold War: The Crisis in Iceland's Relations with Britain, The United States, and NATO, 1971–74." *Diplomacy and Statecraft* 14(4): 94–136.

Ireland Michael, and Scott Gartner. 2001. "Time to Fight: Government Type and Conflict Initiation in Parliamentary Systems." *Journal of Conflict Resolution* 45: 547–568.

Isaacson, Walter. 1983. "A Rallying Round for Reagan." *Time,* November 14.

Jakobsen, Peter Viggo. 2000 "Focus on the CNN Effect Misses the Point: The Real Media Impact on Conflict Management is Invisible and Indirect." *Journal of Peace Research* 37(2): 131–143.

James, Patrick and John Oneal. 1991. "The Influence of Domestic and International Politics on the President's Use of Force." *Journal of Conflict Resolution* 35(2): 307–332.

James, Patrick and Enyu Zhang. 2004. "Chinese Choices: A Poliheuristic Analysis of Foreign Policy Crises: 1950–1996." Paper presented at the annual meeting of the International Studies Association, Montreal, March.

Janis, Irving. 1982. *Groupthink,* 2nd ed. New York: Houghton, Mifflin.

Janis, Irving and Leon Mann. 1977. *Decision Making: A Psychological Analysis of Conflict, Choice, and Commitment.* New York: Free Press.

Jentleson, Bruce. 1992. "The Pretty Prudent Public: Post Post-Vietnam American Opinion on the Use of Military Force." *International Studies Quarterly* 36: 49–74.

Jervis, Robert. 1976. *Perception and Misperception in International Politics.* Princeton, NJ: Princeton University Press.

Jervis, Robert. 2006. "Understanding Beliefs." *Political Psychology* 27(5): 641–663.

Jervis, Robert, Richard N. Lebow, and Janice G. Stein, eds. 1985. *Psychology and Deterrence.* Baltimore, MD: Johns Hopkins University Press.

Johnson, Dominic, Rose McDermott, Emily Barrett, Jonathan Cowden, Richard Wrangham, Matthew MacIntyre, and Stephen Peter Rosen. 2006. "Overconfidence in War Games: Experimental Evidence on Expectations, Aggression, Gender and Testosterone." *Proceedings of the Royal Society of Biological Sciences* 273: 2513–2520.

Johnson, Eric and Robert Meyer. 1984. "Compensatory Choice Models of Noncompensatory Processes: The Effect of Varying Context." *Journal of Consumer Research* 11: 528–541.

Jones, Bryan D. 1994. *Reconceiving Decision-making in Democratic Politics: Attention, Choice, and Public Policy.* Chicago: University of Chicago Press.

Kahneman, Daniel and Amos Tversky. 1979. "Prospect Theory: An Analysis of Decision under Risk." *Econometrica* 47(2): 263–291.

Kahneman, Daniel and Amos Tversky. 1982. "The Simulation Heuristic." In *Judgment Under Uncertainty: Heuristics and Biases*, ed. Daniel Kahneman, Paul Slovic and Amos Tversky. New York: Cambridge University Press.

Kaplan, Jay. 1980. "Victor and Vanquished." In *On the Ending of Wars*, ed. Stuart Albert and Edward Luck. New York: Kennikat Press.

Kegley, Charles and Eugene Wittkopf. 1987. *American Foreign Policy: Pattern and Process*, 3rd ed. New York: St. Martin's Press.

Kegley, Charles and Eugene Wittkopf. 1991. *American Foreign Policy: Pattern and Process*, 4th ed. New York: St. Martin's Press.

Kelman, Herbert and Ronald Fisher. 2003. "Conflict Analysis and Resolution." In *Oxford Handbook of Political Psychology*, ed. David Sears, Leonie Huddy, and Robert Jervis. New York: Oxford University Press.

Kenworthy, Eldon. 1984. "Grenada as Theater." *World Policy Journal* 1: 635–667.

Khong, Yuen Foong. 1992. *Analogies at War: Korea, Munich, Dien Bien Phu, and the Vietnam Decisions of 1965*. Princeton, NJ: Princeton University Press.

Kinne, Brandon J. 2005. "Decision Making in Autocratic Regimes: A Poliheuristic Perspective." *International Studies Perspectives* 6: 114–128.

Kinsella, David. 1998. "Arms Transfer Dependence and Foreign Policy Conflict." *Journal of Peace Research* 35(1): 7–23.

Klein, Gary A. 1989. "Recognition-Primed Decisions." In *Advances in Man-Machine System Research*, ed. William B. Rouse. Greenwich, CT: JAI Press.

Krasner, Stephen. 1972. "Are Bureaucracies Important? (Or Allison Wonderland)." *Foreign Policy* 7: 159–179.

Krause, Keith. 1991. "Military Statecraft: Power and Influence in Soviet and American Arms Transfer Relationships." *International Studies Quarterly* 35: 313–336.

Kropatcheva, Elena. 2006. "Russian Foreign Policy towards Ukraine: A Case of New Imperialism?" Paper presented at the International Young Researchers Conference, Hayighurst Center, Miami University, Oxford, OH, October 27–29.

Kruglanski, Arie W. and Isaac Ajzen. 1983. "Bias and Error in Human Judgment." *European Journal of Social Psychology* 13: 1–44.

Kuklinski, James, Robert Luskin, and John Bolland. 1991. "Where is Schema? Going Beyond the 'S' Word in Political Psychology." *American Political Science Review* 85(4): 1341–1356.

Lau, Richard. 2003. "Models of Decision-Making." In *Oxford Handbook of Political Psychology*, ed. David Sears, Leonie Huddy, and Robert, Jervis. New York: Oxford University Press.

Lau, Richard and Jack Levy. 1998. "Contributions of Behavioral Decision Theory to Research in Political Science." *Applied Psychology* 47(1): 29–44.

Leites, Nathan. 1953. *A Study of Bolshevism*. Glencoe, IL: The Free Press.

Levitin, Michael. 1986. "The Law of Force and the Force of Law: Grenada, the Falklands, and Humanitarian Intervention." *Harvard International Law Journal* 27: 621–657.

Levy, Jack. 1975. "Alliance Formation and War Behavior: An Analysis of the Great Powers, 1495–1975." *Journal of Conflict Resolution* 25(4): 581–613.

Levy, Jack. 1989a. "The Causes of War: A Review of Theories and Evidence." In *Behavior, Society, and Nuclear War*, vol. 1, ed. Philip E. Tetlock, Jo L. Husbands, Robert Jervis, Paul C. Stern, and Charles Tilly. New York: Oxford University Press.

Levy, Jack. 1989b. "The Diversionary Theory of War: A Critique." In *Handbook of War Studies*, ed. Manus Midlarsky. Boston: Unwin Hyman.

Levy, Jack. 1992. "An Introduction to Prospect Theory." *Political Psychology* 13(2): 171–186.

Levy, Jack. 1994. "Learning and Foreign Policy: Sweeping a Conceptual Minefield." *International Organization* 48: 279–312.

Levy, Jack. 2000. "Loss Aversion, Framing Effects, and International Conflict: Perspectives on Prospect Theory." In *Handbook of War Studies II*, ed. Manus Midlarsky. Ann Arbor, MI: University of Michigan Press.

Levy, Jack. 2001. "Economic Interdependence, Opportunity Costs, and War." Unpublished manuscript, Rutgers University.

Levy, Jack. 2003. "Political Psychology and Foreign Policy." In *Oxford Handbook of Political Psychology*." ed. David O. Sears, Leonie Huddy, and Robert Jervis. New York: Oxford University Press.

Levy, Jack and Lily Vakili. 1992. "Diversionary Action by Authoritarian Regimes: Argentina in the Falklands/Malvinas Case." In *The Internationalization of Communal Strife*, ed. Manus Midlarsky. London: Routledge.

Livingston, Steven. 1997. "Clarifying the CNN Effect: An Examination of Media Effects According to Type of Military Intervention." Unpublished manuscript, Joan Shorenstein Center on the Press, Politics and Public Policy, John F. Kennedy School of Government, Harvard University.

Livingston, Steven and Todd Eachus. 1995. "Humanitarian Crises and U.S. Foreign Policy: Somalia and the CNN Effect Reconsidered." *Political Communication* 12(4): 413–429.

MacDonald, Paul. 2003. "Useful Fiction or Miracle Maker: The Competing Epistemological Foundations of Rational Choice Theory." *American Political Science Review* 97(4): 551–565.

Maiese, Michelle. "Emotions." In *Beyond Intractability: A Free Knowledge Base on More Constructive Approaches to Destructive Conflict*, ed. Guy Burgess and Heidi Burgess. Conflict Research Consortium, University of Colorado, Boulder. Posted July 2005. http://www.beyondintractability.org/essay/emotion/ (accessed Sept. 3, 2009).

Mandel, Robert. 1986. "Psychological Approaches to International Relations." In *Political Psychology*, ed. Margaret Hermann. San Francisco: Jossey-Bass.

Maoz, Zeev. 1990a. "Framing the National Interest: The Manipulation of Foreign Policy Decision in Group Settings." *World Politics* 43(Oct.): 77–110.

Maoz, Zeev. 1990b. *National Choices and International Processes*. Cambridge: Cambridge University Press.

Maoz, Zeev and Bruce Russett. 1993. "Normative and Structural Causes of Democratic Peace, 1946–1986." *American Political Science Review* 87(3): 624–639.

March, James G. and Johan P. Olsen. 1996. "Institutional Perspectives on Political Institutions." *Governance* 9(3): 247–264.

Markman, Keith and Philip Tetlock. 2000. " 'I Couldn't Have Known': Accountability, Foreseeability, and Counterfactual Denials of Responsibility." *British Journal of Social Psychology* 39(3): 313–325.

Marra, Robin, Charles Ostrom, and Dennis Simon. 1990. "Foreign Policy and Presidential Popularity." *Journal of Conflict Resolution* 34: 588–623.

Martinsons, Maris G. 2001. "Comparing the Decision Styles of American, Chinese and Japanese Business Leaders." Best Paper Proceedings of Academy of Management Meetings, Washington, DC, August.

Maule, A. John and Isabel Andrade. 1997. "The Effects of Time Pressure On Decision Making: How Harassed Managers Cope." IEEE Colloquium on Decision Making and Problem Solving, Digest No. 1997/366: 4/1–4/6.

Mayer, Kenneth. 1991. *The Political Economy of Defense Contracting*. New Haven, CT: Yale University Press.

McCrae, Robert and Paul Costa Jr. 2006. *Personality in Adulthood: A Five-Factor Theory Perspective*, 2nd ed. New York: The Guilford Press.

McDermott, Rose. 1992. "Prospect Theory in International Relations: The Iranian Hostage Rescue." *Political Psychology* 13: 237–263.

McDermott, Rose. 2004a. *Political Psychology in International Relations*. Ann Arbor, MI: University of Michigan Press.

McDermott, Rose. 2004b. "The Feeling of Rationality: The Meaning of Neuroscientific Advances for Political Science." *Perspectives on Politics* 2(4): 691–706.

McDermott, Rose, Jonathan Cowden, and Stephen Rosen. (Forthcoming). "The Role of Hostile Communication in a Simulated Crisis Game." *Journal of Peace and Conflict*.

McDermott, Rose, Dominic Johnson, Jonathan Cowden, and Stephen Rosen. 2007. "Testosterone and Aggression in a Simulated Crisis Game." *Annals of the American Academy of Political and Social Science* 614(1): 15–33.

Mearsheimer, John. 1995. "The False Promise of International Institutions." *International Security* 19(3): 5–49.

Mingst, Karen. 2002. *Essentials of International Relations*, 2nd ed. New York: W. W. Norton.

Mintz, A. 1988. *The Politics of Resource Allocation in the U.S. Department of Defense*. Boulder, CO: Westview.

Mintz, Alex. 1993. "The Decision to Attack Iraq: A Non-Compensatory Theory of Decision Making." *Journal of Conflict Resolution* 37: 595–618.

Mintz, Alex. 1995. "The Noncompensatory Principle of Coalition Formation." *Journal of Theoretical Politics* 7(3): 335–349.

Mintz, Alex ed. 2003. *Integrating Cognitive and Rational Theories of Foreign Policy Decision Making*. New York: Palgrave Macmillan.

Mintz, Alex. 2004a. "How Do Leaders Make Decisions? A Poliheuristic Perspective." *Journal of Conflict Resolution* 48: 3–13.

Mintz, Alex. 2004b. "Foreign Policy Decision Making in Familiar and Unfamiliar Settings." *Journal of Conflict Resolution* 48: 91–104.

Mintz, Alex. 2005. "Behavioral International Relations." Presented at the annual meeting of the International Studies Association, Honolulu, HI.

Mintz, Alex. 2006. "How Leaders Make Decisions?" Unpublished manuscript, United Nations Studies, Yale University.

Mintz, Alex. 2007a. "Why Behavioral IR?" *International Studies Review* 9(1): 157–162.

Mintz, Alex. 2007b. "Decision Making of Leaders of Terrorist Organizations." Paper presented at the 7th Annual Herzliya Conference, January 21–24, 2007, Herzliya, Israel.

Mintz, Alex and Allison Astorino-Courtois. 2001. "Simulating Decision Processes: Expanding the Poliheuristic Theory to Model N-Person Strategic Interactions in International Relations." Paper presented at the annual meeting of the International Studies Association, February, Chicago.

Mintz, Alex and Nehemia Geva. 1993. "Why Don't Democracies Fight Each Other? An Experimental Study." *Journal of Conflict Resolution* 37: 484–503.

Mintz, Alex and Nehemia Geva. 1997. "Marketing Peace in the Middle East." Discussion Paper, Program in Foreign Policy Decision Making, Texas A&M University.

Mintz, Alex, Nehemia Geva, and Karl DeRouen Jr. 1993. "Mathematical Models of Foreign Policy Decision Making: Compensatory vs. Noncompensatory." *Synthese* 100(3): 441–460.

Mintz, Alex, Nehemia Geva, Steven B. Redd, and Amy Carnes. 1997. "The Effect of Dynamic and Static Choice Sets on Political Decision Making: An Analysis Using the Decision Board Platform." *American Political Science Review* 91: 553–566.

Mintz, Alex, Nehemia Geva, Edward Vogelpohl, and Christopher Hanson. 1995. "Democratic War." Paper presented at the annual meeting of the American Political Science Association, August–September.

Mintz, Alex, Shaul Mishal, and Nadav Morag. 2005. "Victims of Polythink? The Israeli Delegation to Camp David 2000." Unpublished manuscript.

Mintz, Alex and Steven Redd. 2003. "Framing Effects in International Relations." *Synthese* 135: 193–213.

Mintz, Alex and Steven Redd, ed. (Forthcoming). *Advances in Foreign Policy Analysis.*

Mintz, Alex and Bruce Russett. 1992. "The Dual Economy and Arab-Israeli Use of Force: A Transnational System?" In *Defense, Welfare and Growth*, ed. Steve Chan and Alex Mintz. London: Routledge.

Mintz, Alex, John Tyson Chatagnier, and David Brule 2006. "Being Bin Laden: Applying Applied Decision Analysis to Analyzing Terrorist's Decisions." In *Root Causes of Suicide Terrorism*, ed. Ami Pedhazur. London: Taylor and Francis.

Mintz, Alex and Yi Yang. (Forthcoming). "The Contributions of the Experimental Methodology to International Relations." In *Advances in Foreign Policy Analysis*, ed. Alex Mintz and Steven Redd.

Monroe, Kristen R. and Kristen Hill Maher. 1995. "Psychology and Rational Actor Theory." *Political Psychology* 16(1): 1–21.

Morgan, T. Clifton. 2004. "Rational Choice and Game Theoretic Approaches: Introduction." In *Multiple Paths to Knowledge in International Relations*, ed. Zeev Maoz, Alex Mintz, T. Clifton Morgan, Glenn Palmer, and Richard J. Stoll. Lanham, MD: Lexington Books.

Morgan, T. Clifton and Kenneth N. Bickers. 1992. "Domestic Discontent and the External Use of Force." *Journal of Conflict Resolution* 36(1): 25–52.

Morgan, T. Clifton and Glenn Palmer. 2000. "A Model of Foreign Policy Substitutability: Selecting the Right Tools for the Job(s)." *Journal of Conflict Resolution* 44(1): 11–32.

Morgan, T. Clifton and Glenn Palmer. 2003. "To Protect and To Serve: Alliances and Foreign Policy Portfolios." *Journal of Conflict Resolution* 47(2): 180–203.

Morrow, James. 1997. "A Rational Choice Approach to International Conflict." In *Decision Making on War and Peace: The Cognitive-Rational Debate*, ed. Nehemia Geva and Alex Mintz. Boulder, CO: Lynne Rienner.

Moss, J. Jennings and Paul M. Rodriguez. 1991. "Leader on Hill Praise Bush's Handling of War." *Washington Times*, February 28.

Most, Benjamin and Harvey Starr. 1989. *Inquiry, Logic, and International Politics*. Columbia, SC: University of South Carolina Press.

Motley, James. 1983–1984. "Grenada: Low-intensity Conflict and the Use of U.S. Military Power." *World Affairs* 146: 221–238.

Neustadt, Richard. 1960. *Presidential Power*. New York: Wiley.

Neustadt, Richard and Ernest May. 1986. *Thinking in Time: The Uses of History for Decision Makers*. New York: The Free Press.

Norris, Pippa, Montague Kern, and Marion Just. 2003. *Framing Terrorism: The News Media, The Government and The Public*. New York: Routledge.

Nye, Joseph S. Jr. 2004. "The Decline of America's Soft Power." *Foreign Affairs* 83(3) (May/June): 16–20.

Oneal, John, Bruce Russett, and Michael Berbaum. 2003. "Causes of Peace: Democracy, Interdependence and International Organizations, 1885–1992." *International Studies Quarterly* 47(3): 371–393.

Ostrom, Charles and Brian Job. 1986. "The President and the Political Use of Force." *American Political Science Review* 80(2): 541–566.

Ostrom, Charles and Dennis Simon. 1984. "Managing Popular Support: The Presidential Dilemma." *Policy Studies Journal* 12: 677–690.

Ostrom, Charles and Dennis Simon. 1985. "Promise and Performance: A Dynamic Model of Presidential Popularity." *American Political Science Review* 79: 334–358.

Page, Benjamin and Robert Shapiro. 1989. "Educating and Manipulating the Public. In *Manipulating Public Opinion*. ed. Michael Margolis and Gary Mauser. Pacific Grove, CA: Brooks/Cole Publishing Company.

Palmer, Glenn, Patrick Regan, and Tamar London. 2004. "What's Stopping You? The Sources of Political Constraints on International Conflict Behavior in Parliamentary Democracies." *International Interactions* 30: 1–24

Payne, John. 1976. "Task Complexity and Contingent Processing in Decision Making: An Information Search and Protocol Analysis." *Organizational Behavior and Human Performance* 16: 366–387.

Payne, John, James Bettman, and Eric Johnson. 1988. "Adaptive Strategy Selection in Decision Making." *Journal of Experimental Psychology* 14: 534–552.

Payne, John W., James R. Bettman, and Eric Johnson. 1993. *The Adaptive Decision Maker*. Cambridge: Cambridge University Press.

Pillar, Paul. 1983. *Negotiating Peace: War Termination as a Bargaining Process*. Princeton, NJ: Princeton University Press.

Peña, Monica. 2003. "News Media and the Foreign Policy Decision-Making Process, CNN or Washington?" *Razon y Palabra* 32. http://www.razonypalabra.org.mx/anteriores/n32/mpena.htm (accessed Sept. 3, 2009).

Post, Jerrold, ed. 2003. *The Psychological Assessment of Political Leaders*. Ann Arbor, MI: University of Michigan Press.

Post, Jerrold. 2007. *The Mind of the Terrorist: The Psychology of Terrorism from the IRA to al-Qaeda*. New York: Palgrave MacMillan.

Powell, Robert. 1987. "Crisis Bargaining, Escalation, and MAD." *American Political Science Review* 81(3): 717–735.

Preston, Thomas. 2001. *The President and His Inner Circle: Leadership Style and the Advisory Process in Foreign Affairs*. New York: Columbia University Press.

Preston, Thomas and Paul 't Hart. 1999. "Understanding and Evaluating Bureaucratic Politics: The Nexus between Political Leaders and Advisory Systems." *Political Psychology* 20: 49–98.

Prins, Brandon and Christopher Sprecher. 1999. "Institutional Constraints, Political Opposition, and Interstate Dispute Escalation: Evidence from Parliamentary Systems, 1946–1990." *Journal of Peace Research* 36: 271–287.

Pugh, Michael. 1989. *The ANZUS Crisis, Nuclear Visiting and Deterrence*. Cambridge: Cambridge University Press.

Pundak, Ron. 2001. "From Oslo to Taba: What Went Wrong?" *Survival* 43(3): 31–45.

Putnam, Robert. 1999. "Diplomacy and Domestic Politics: The Logic of Two-Level Games." In *Theory and Structure in International Political Economy*, ed. Charles Lipson and Benjamin J. Cohen. Cambridge, MA: MIT Press.

Quattrone, George A. and Amos Tversky. 1988. "Contrasting Rational and Psychological Analyses of Political Choice." *American Political Science Review* 82: 719–736.

Randle, Robert R. 1973. *The Origins of Peace: A Study of Peacemaking and the Structure of Peace Settlements*. New York: Free Press.

Ratner, Michael and Michael Smith. 1997. *Che Guevara and the FBI: The U.S. Political Police Dossier on the Latin American Revolutionary*. Melbourne, Australia: Ocean Press.

Redd, Steven. 2002. "The Influence of Advisers on Foreign Policy Decision-Making." *Journal of Conflict Resolution* 46(3): 335–364.

Regan, Patrick. 2000. "Substituting Policies During U.S. Interventions in Internal Conflicts: A Little of This, a Little of That." *Journal of Conflict Resolution* 44(1): 90–106.

Renshon, Jonathan and Stanley Renshon. 2008. "The Theory and Practice of Foreign Policy Decision Making." *Political Psychology* 29(4): 509–536.

Richards, Diane, T. Clifton Morgan, R. K. Wilson, V. L. Schwebach, and G. D. Young. 1993. "Good Times, Bad Times and the Diversionary Use of Force: A Tale of Some Not-So-Free Agents." *Journal of Conflict Resolution* 37: 504–535.

Richardson, Neil and Charles Kegley. 1980. "Trade Dependence and Foreign Policy Compliance: A Longitudinal Analysis." *International Studies Quarterly* 29: 191–216.

Riker, William. 1995. "The Political Psychology of Rational Choice Theory." *Political Psychology* 16(1): 23–44.

Robinson, James A. and Richard C. Snyder. 1965. "Decision-Making in International Politics." In *International Behavior: A Social-Psychological Analysis*, ed. Herbert C. Kelman. New York: Holt, Rienehart, and Winston.

Robinson, Piers. 1999. "The CNN Effect: Can the News Media Drive Foreign Policy?" *Review of International Studies* 25(2): 301–309.

Rosati, Jerel. 1981. "Developing a Systematic Decision-Making Framework: Bureaucratic Politics in Perspective." *World Politics* 33(2): 234–252.

Rosati, Jerel. 1993. *The Politics of United States Foreign Policy*. Orlando, FL: Harcourt Brace Jovanovich.

Rosati, Jerel. 2004. *The Politics of United States Foreign Policy*, 3rd ed. Belmont, CA: Wadsworth.

Rosato, Sebastian. 2003. "The Flawed Logic of the Democratic Peace." *American Political Science Review* 97(4): 585–602.

Ross, Lee. 2008. "Barriers to Dispute Resolution – and How to Overcome Them." Paper presented at the MA Seminar at the Lauder School of Government, IDC-Herzliya.

Rubner, Michael. 1985–1986. "The Reagan Administration, the 1973 War Powers Resolution, and the Invasion of Grenada." *Political Science Quarterly* 100: 627–647.

Russett, Bruce. 1963. "The Calculus of Deterrence." *Journal of Conflict Resolution* 7(2): 97–109.

Russett, Bruce. 1990. *Controlling the Sword: The Democratic Governance of National Security.* Cambridge, MA: Harvard University Press.

Russett, Bruce and Gad Barzilai. 1992. "The Political Economy of Military Actions: Israel and the United States." In *Political Economy of Military Spending in the United States,* ed. Alex Mintz. London: Routledge.

Ryan, Henry Butterfield. 1998. *The Fall of Che Guevara.* New York: Oxford University Press.

Sage, Andrew, ed. 1990. *Concise Encyclopedia of Information Processing in Systems and Organizations.* New York: Pergamon Press.

Sandaña, Rodolfo. 2001. *Fertile Ground: Che Guevara and Bolivia.* New York: Pathfinder.

Sathasivam, Kanishkan. 2003. "'No Other Choice': Pakistan's Decision to Test the Bomb." In *Integrating Cognitive and Rational Theories of Foreign Policy Decision Making,* ed. Alex Mintz. New York: Palgrave Macmillan.

Schafer, Mark and Stephen Walker. 2006. *Beliefs and Leadership in World Politics: Methods and Applications of Operational Code Analysis.* New York: Palgrave Macmillan.

Schelling, Thomas with Morton Halperin. 1961. *Strategy and Arms Control.* New York: The Twentieth Century Fund.

Schultz, Kenneth. 2001. *Democracy and Coercive Diplomacy.* Cambridge: Cambridge University Press.

Schwartz, Barry. 2004. "The Tyranny of Choice." *Scientific American* 290(4): 70–75.

Schwartz, Barry. 2005. "The Sunk-Cost Fallacy: Bush Falls Victim to a Bad New Argument for the Iraq War." *Slate,* Sept. 9, http://www.slate.com/id/2125910/ (accessed Sept. 3, 2009).

Schwarzkopf, Norman. 1993. *It Doesn't Take a Hero: The Autobiography of General Norman H. Schwarzkopf.* New York: Bantam.

Sciolino, Elaine and Patrick Tyler. 2001. "A Nation Challenged: Saddam Hussein." *New York Times,* October 12.

Shapiro, Walter et al. 1983. "Testing Time: 'Reagan was Reagan.'" *Newsweek,* November 7.

Sher, Gilad. 2001. *Just Beyond Reach: The Israeli-Palestinian Peace Negotiations 1999–2001.* Tel Aviv: Yedioth Ahronot and Hemed Books.

Shultz, George. 1983. "Shultz's Opening Statement at News Session on Mideast." *New York Times,* September 1, p. 8, http://www.nytimes.com/1983/09/01/world/shultz-s-opening-statement-at-news-session-on-mideast.html?scp=3&sq=&st=nyt.

Shultz, George. 1993. *Turmoil and Triumph: My Years as Secretary of State.* New York: Scribner.

Shweder, Richard A., Martha Minow, and Hazel Rose Markus, eds. 2002. *Engaging Cultural Differences: The Multicultural Challenge in Liberal Democracies*. New York: Russell Sage Foundation.

Simmel, Georg. 1898. "The Persistence of Social Groups." *American Journal of Sociology* 4: 662–698, 829–836.

Simon, Herbert. 1957. "A Behavioral Model of Rational Choice." In *Models of Man: Social and Rational*, ed. Herbert Simon. New York: John Wiley and Sons.

Simon, Herbert. 1959. "Theories of Decision-Making in Economics and Behavioral Science." *American Economic Review* 49: 253–283.

Simon, Herbert. 1960. *The New Science of Management Decision Making*. New York: Evanston.

Simon, Herbert. 1969. *Sciences of the Artificial*. Cambridge, MA: MIT Press.

Simon, Herbert. 1978. Information-Processing Theory of Human Problem Solving. In *Handbook of Learning and Cognitive Processes*, ed. William K. Estes. Hillsdale, NJ: Lawrence Erlbaum and Associates.

Simon, Herbert. 1985. "Human Nature in Politics: The Dialogue of Psychology with Political Science." *American Political Science Review* 79: 293–304.

Siverson, Randolph and Joel King. 1979. "Alliances and the Expansion of War." In *To Augur Well: Early Warning Indicators in World Politics*, ed. David Singer and Michael Wallace. Beverly Hills: Sage.

Smith, Alistair. 1996. "Diversionary Foreign Policy in Democratic Systems." *International Studies Quarterly* 40: 133–153.

Snyder, Richard, H. W. Bruck, and Burton Sapin. 1954. *Decision-Making as an Approach to the Study of International Politics*. Foreign Policy Analysis Project Series 3. Princeton, NJ: Princeton University Press.

Snyder, Richard, H. W. Bruck, and Burton Sapin, eds. 1962. *Foreign Policy Decision-Making: An Approach to the Study of International Politics*. New York: The Free Press of Glencoe.

Staudenmaier, William. 1987. "Conflict Termination in the Nuclear Era." In *Conflict Termination and Military Strategy*, ed. Stephen Cimbala and Keith Dunn. Boulder: Westview Press.

Stein, Janice. 1975. "War Termination and Conflict Reduction or, How Wars Should End." *Jerusalem Journal of Conflict Resolution* 37(3): 544–568.

Stein, Janice. 1991. "Deterrence and Reassurance." In *Behavior, Society and Nuclear War*, vol. 2, ed. Philip Tetlock, Jo Husbands, Robert Jervis, Paul Stern, and Charles Tilly. NewYork: Oxford University Press.

Steinbruner, John. 1974. *The Cybernetic Theory of Decision*. Princeton, NJ: Princeton University Press.

Steinbruner, John. 2002. *The Cybernetic Theory of Decision: New Dimensions of Political Analysis*, 2nd ed. Princeton, NJ: Princeton University Press.

Steiner, Miriam. 1983. "The Search for Order in a Disorderly World: Worldviews and Prescriptive Decision Paradigms." *International Organization* 37: 373–413.

Stern, Eric. 1997. "Probing the Probability of Newgroup Syndrome: Kennedy and the Bay of Pigs." In *Beyond Groupthink: Political Group Dynamics and Foreign Policy-making*, ed. Paul 't Hart, Eric Stern, and Bengt Sundelius. Ann Arbor, MI: University of Michigan Press.

Strong, Robert A. 1992. *Decisions and Dilemmas: Case Studies in Presidential Foreign Policy Making*. Englewood Cliffs, NJ: Prentice Hall.

Tannen, Deborah. 1990. *You Just Don't Understand: Women and Men in Conversation*. New York: HarperCollins.

Tarr, David. 1981. "The Employment of Force: Political Constraints and Limitations." In *U.S. Policy and Low-Intensity Conflict*, ed. Sam Sarkesian and William Scully. New Brunswick, CT: Transaction Books.

't Hart, Paul, Eric Stern, and Bengt Sundelius. 1997a. *Beyond Groupthink: Political Group Dynamics and Foreign Policy-making*. Ann Arbor, MI: University of Michigan Press.

't Hart, Paul, Eric Stern, and Bengt Sundelius. 1997b. "Foreign Policy-making at the Top: Political Groups Dynamics." In *Beyond Groupthink: Political Group Dynamics and Foreign Policy-making*, ed. Paul 't Hart, Eric Stern, and Bengt Sundelius. Ann Arbor, MI: University of Michigan Press.

Thorndike, Tony. 1989. "Grenada." In *Intervention in the 1980s: U.S. Foreign Policy in the Third World*, ed. Peter Schraeder. Boulder: Lynne Rienner.

Treverton, Gregory F. 1987. "Ending Major Coalition Wars." In *Conflict Termination and Military Strategy*, ed. Stephen J. Cimbala and Keith A. Dunn. Colorado: Westview Press.

Tsebelis, George. 1999. "Veto Players and Law Production in Parliamentary Democracies. An Empirical Analysis." *American Political Science Review* 93: 591–698.

Tversky, Amos. 1972a. "Elimination by Aspects: A Theory of Choice." *Psychological Review* 79: 281–299.

Tversky, Amos. 1972b. "Choice by Elimination." *Journal of Mathematical Psychology* 9: 341–367.

Tversky, Amos and Daniel Kahneman. 1981. "The Framing of Decisions and the Psychology of Choice." *Science* 211(4481): 453–458.

UNICEF. 1996. *The State of the World's Children*. http://www.unicef.org/sowc96/ (accessed Dec. 17, 2007).

United States Congress. *Committee on Armed Services*. 1990. *U.S. Low-Intensity Conflicts 1899–1990*. 101st Cong., 2d sess. Committee Print no. 13.

Van Belle, Douglas. 2003. "Bureaucratic Responsiveness to the News Media: Comparing the Influences of the *New York Times* and Network Television News Coverage on U.S. Foreign Aid." *Political Communication* 20(3): 263–285.

Van Wagner, Kendra. 2008. "What Is Cognitive Psychology?" About.com, http://psychology.about.com/od/cognitivepsychology/f/cogpsych.htm (accessed Sept. 3, 2009).

Verter, Yossi. 2007. "How We Missed Annapolis." *Haaretz*, November 22.

Vertzberger, Yaacov. 1990. *The World in their Minds: Information Processing, Cognition, and Perception in Foreign Policy Decisionmaking*. Stanford, CA: Stanford University Press.

von Neumann, John and Oskar Morgenstern. 1947. *Theory of Games and Economic Behavior*. Princeton, NJ: Princeton University Press.

Voss, James and Ellen Dorsey. 1992. "Perception and International Relations: An Overview." In *Political Psychology and Foreign Policy*, ed. Eric Singer and Valerie Hudson. Boulder, CO: Westview Press.

Walker, Stephen. 1977. "The Interface Between Beliefs and Behavior: Henry A. Kissinger's Operational Code and the Vietnam War." *Journal of Conflict Resolution* 21: 129–168.

Walker, Stephen. 1983. "The Motivational Foundations of Political Belief Systems." *International Studies Quarterly* 27: 179–201.

Walker, Stephen 1991. "Game Theory and Foreign Policy Decisions: Solution Strategies and Restructuring Strategies in the Vietnam Conflict." Paper presented at the annual meeting of the American Political Science Association, Washington DC.

Walker, Stephen and Mark Schafer. 2000a. "The Political Universe of Lyndon B. Johnson and His Advisors: Diagnostic and Strategic Propensities in Their Operational Codes." *Political Psychology* 21: 529–543.

Walker, Stephen and Mark Schafer. 2000b. "The Operational Codes of Bill Clinton and Tony Blair: Beliefs Systems or Schemata?" Paper presented at the annual meeting of the American Political Science Association, Washington, DC, August 31–September 3.

Walker, Stephen and Mark Schafer. 2004. "Dueling with Dictators: Explaining Strategic Interaction Patterns between the United States and Rogue Leaders." Paper presented at the annual meeting of the American Political Science Association, Chicago. September 2–5.

Walker, Stephen and Mark Schafer. (Forthcoming). "Operational Code Analysis and Foreign Policy Decision-Making." In *Advances in Foreign Policy Analysis*, ed. Alex Mintz and Steven B. Redd.

Wallace, Michael. 1979. "Arms Races, Escalation, and War: Some New Evidence." *Journal of Conflict Resolution* 23(March): 3–16.

Wallace, Michael. 1982. "Armaments and Escalation: Two Competing Hypotheses." *International Studies Quarterly* 26(March): 37–56.

Waltz, Kenneth 1979. *A Theory of International Politics.* New York: McGraw Hill.

Weber, Cynthia. 2001. *International Relations Theory: A Critical Introduction.* New York: Routledge.

Weyland, Kurt. 1996. "Risk Taking in Latin American Economic Restructuring: Lessons from Prospect Theory." *International Studies Quarterly* 40: 185–208.

Wikipedia. "Chicken Game." http://en.wikipedia.org/wiki/Chicken_game (accessed Sept. 3, 2009).

Winograd Interim Report 2007. http://www.haaretz.com/hasen/spages/854051.html (accessed Sept. 3, 2009).

Winter, David. 2003. "Personality and Political Behavior." In *Oxford Handbook of Political Psychology*, ed. David Sears, Leonie Huddy, and Robert Jervis. New York: Oxford University Press.

Wittman, Donald. 1979. "How A War Ends: A Rational Model Approach." *Journal of Conflict Resolution* 23(4): 743–763.

Wolfsfeld, Gadi. 2004. *Media and the Path to Peace.* Cambridge: Cambridge University Press.

Woodward, Bob. 1991. *The Commanders.* New York: Simon and Schuster.

Woodward, Bob. 2004. *Plan of Attack.* New York: Simon and Schuster.

Yang, Yi, 2004. "Cross-cultural Differences in Information Processing in Foreign Policy Decision-making: An Experimental Inquiry." Paper presented at the International Studies Association Annual Conference, March 17–20, Montreal.

Yang, Yi, Nehemia Geva, and Jiu Chang. 2003. "A Comparative Evaluation of the Prospect Theory in Foreign Policy Decision-making: The U.S. and China Case." Paper presented at the 61st annual meeting of the Midwest Political Science Association, Chicago, April 3–6.

Yetiv, Steve. 2004. *Explaining Foreign Policy: U.S. Decision Making and the Persian Gulf War.* Baltimore, MD: Johns Hopkins University Press.

Zagare, Frank C. 1983. "A Game-Theoretic Evaluation of the Cease-Fire Alert Decision of 1973." *Journal of Peace Research* 5(1S): 73–86.

Index